THE MODERN ART OF CROSS-EXAMINATION

Robert E. Goldman

THE MODERN ART OF

CROSS-EXAMINATION

Robert E. Goldman

PRENTICE HALL LAW & BUSINESS

Permissions, Prentice Hall Law & Business
270 Sylvan Avenue, Englewood Cliffs, NJ 07632

Printed in the United States of America.
ISBN 013-109182-4

Dedication

This book is dedicated with the highest respect to

Frank S. Hogan

Rightly known as "Mr. District Attorney," Frank Hogan embodied the finest ideals of the administration of justice. He gave his assistants the greatest of responsibilities and held them accountable if they did not meet it. While vigorously enforcing the law, he did not shy away from a dismissal. His two often repeated rules were "if you're not convinced yourself, don't try to convince a jury" and "never play politics with peoples' lives."

Joseph E. Brill

Universally respected, Joseph Brill was the consummate trial lawyer. Nothing, not even an unending string of personal tragedies, deterred him from giving each client a full measure of dedication or caused him to cross the line to questionable practice. His enemies lasted only for the duration of the current trial, his friends lasted forever.

Contents

Dedication v

Foreword xv

CHAPTER 1: INTRODUCTION 1

CHAPTER 2: THE THEATER AND THE PLAYERS . . . 13

§2.1 Overview 13
§2.2 Judges 14
§2.3 Jurors 14
§2.4 Lawyers 16
§2.5 Courts 18
§2.6 Testimony 18

CHAPTER 3: EMERGING CAUSES OF ACTIONS 21

§3.1 Issues in Litigation 21
§3.2 Environmental Issues 21
§3.3 Product Liability Issues 22
§3.4 Medical Issues 22
§3.5 Financial and Accounting Issues 23
§3.6 Intellectual Property Issues 23
§3.7 Criminal Law Issues 23

§3.8 Development of Cross-Examination Techniques ... 24

CHAPTER 4: THE RULES OF EVIDENCE 25

§4.1 Enactment of Federal Rules of Evidence 25
§4.2 Inclusionary Nature of Rules 26
§4.3 Relevance 26
§4.4 Expert Witnesses 28
§4.5 Impeachment of Witnesses 29
§4.6 Prior Inconsistent Statements 29
§4.7 Hearsay 30
§4.8 Discovery 32

CHAPTER 5: PREPARATION 35

§5.1 Life Preparation 35
§5.2 What's the Punch Line 37
§5.3 Environment 38
§5.4 The Human Factor 39
§5.5 Accepting the Penalty 42
§5.6 The Particular Case 42
§5.7 Cross-examination and Summation 43
§5.8 Sequence 43
§5.9 Internal and External Logic 44
§5.10 Establishment of Objectives 44
§5.11 Counterpoint 45
§5.12 Wording of Questions 46
§5.13 Know the Documents 48
§5.14 Prepare Cross-examination by Areas 50

CHAPTER 6: INVESTIGATION 53

§6.1 Introduction 53
§6.2 Analysis of Habits and Personality 55
§6.3 Tenacity 55
§6.4 U.S. v. Miller and Adolf 56

CHAPTER 7: THE THEME 91

§7.1 Introduction 91
§7.2 Marcos and Helmsley Cases 92
§7.3 Tyson Case 94
§7.4 Trying Two Different Cases 97

CHAPTER 8: CONTROL 99

§8.1 Introduction 99
§8.2 Intimidation 99
§8.3 Action and Reaction 100
§8.4 The Duel 100
§8.5 Misdirection of Attention of Witness 103

CHAPTER 9: CONTROL BY LEADING QUESTIONS .. 107

§9.1 Introduction 107
§9.2 Provide an Easy Way Out 108
§9.3 Building in the Answer 108
§9.4 The St. Johns' Athletes 109
§9.5 Controlling the Most Difficult Witness 119

CHAPTER 10: CONTROL: STRIPPING AWAY THE MYSTIQUE 125

§10.1 Introduction 125
§10.2 Being More Knowledgeable 128
a. An Every Day Conversation 128
b. In the Courtroom 130
§10.3 Extending the Answer to Its Logical Conclusion 132
a. An Every Day Conversation 132
b. In the Courtroom 133
§10.4 Isolating the Issue 135
a. An Every Day Conversation 135
b. In the Courtroom 136
§10.5 Suggesting Access to Information 138
a. An Every Day Conversation 138

	b. In the Courtroom	139
§10.6	Duress Dictates the Testimony	140
	a. An Every Day Conversation	140
	b. In the Courtroom	141
§10.7	Aggressiveness	142
	a. An Every Day Conversation	143
	b. In the Courtroom	143
CHAPTER 11: CONTROL BY HUMOR		147
§11.1	Introduction	147
§11.2	Circumstances; Examples	147
CHAPTER 12: CLOSING THE ESCAPE HATCH		151
§12.1	Introduction	151
§12.2	Learning the Hard Way	151
§12.3	Which Evidence to Protect	155
§12.4	Certification of Accuracy of Testimony	156
CHAPTER 13: PACE AND TEMPO		159
§13.1	Significant Questions	159
§13.2	Increasing the Tempo	159
§13.3	Slowing Down the Tempo	162
CHAPTER 14: SETTING UP THE WITNESS		165
§14.1	Time to Set Up Control of Witness	165
§14.2	Techniques	165
§14.3	The Skirmish	166
§14.4	"Yes" or "No" Answers	168
§14.5	The Oath	169
§14.6	Duty or Obligation	172
§14.7	Partisanship	174
§14.8	Bias	174
CHAPTER 15: LEADING TO SUMMATION		177
§15.1	Introduction	177

§15.2 Take Nothing for Granted 178
§15.3 The Explanation is Better Coming From You 183
§15.4 A Matter of Instinct 186
§15.5 Plowshares Into Swords 186
§15.6 Inconsistency and the Passage of Time 188
§15.7 The Testimony of the Missing Witness 191

CHAPTER 16: EXPERT TESTIMONY 193

§16.1 Introduction 193
§16.2 Scope of Expert Testimony 193
§16.3 Discovery 195
§16.4 Don't Cross-examine on Examinations Before Trial . . . Except 196
§16.5 Financing Expert Testimony 196
§16.6 Mastering the Subject Matter 198
§16.7 Keep Your Own Case and Cross-examination Simple 199
§16.8 Know the Answer 201
§16.9 Aiming Beyond Total Destruction 202
§16.10 Advantage–Cross-examiner 203

CHAPTER 17: SCIENTIFIC TESTIMONY 205

§17.1 Introduction 205
§17.2 Opening the Door 209
§17.3 Frye and Cross-examination 210
§17.4 Process 211
§17.5 Lack of First Hand Knowledge 213
§17.6 What is Left Out 213
§17.7 Leaping to Conclusions 214
§17.8 Exploit the Variables 215
§17.9 The Scientific Open End 216
§17.10 The Jury Insists on Patterns and Orderly Sequence . . 217
§17.11 Impressions 222

CHAPTER 18: STATISTICS 225

§18.1 Introduction 225

§18.2 Confirmation of Statistics 225
§18.3 Toxic Tort Cases 226
§18.4 Antitrust Cases 227

CHAPTER 19: THE COLLATERAL ATTACK 231

§19.1 Killing the Messenger 231
§19.2 Overall Impression 231
§19.3 Qualifications 232
§19.4 Bias 234
§19.5 Assumptions 237
§19.6 Charts and Diagrams in Reverse 240
§19.7 Garbage In—Garbage Out 240
§19.8 Conflict Among Experts 241
§19.9 Expert Trump 242
§19.10 Prior Inconsistent Statements 242

CHAPTER 20: CROSS-EXAMINATION OF THE MEDICAL EXPERT 245

§20.1 Theories and Assumptions 245
§20.2 Collateral Attack 246
§20.3 Application of Methodology 257

CHAPTER 21: THE EXPERT IN CRIMINAL PROSECUTIONS 259

§21.1 Preparation and Execution 259
§21.2 U.S. v. Young 260
§21.3 Basis for Opinion 263
§21.4 The Badge of Virtue 264
§21.5 Limited Discovery 264
§21.6 Opinion Not Fact 265
§21.7 Bias 265
§21.8 Opinion Contains Internal Inconsistencies 270
§21.9 Transference 274

CHAPTER 22: THE ELECTRONIC WITNESS 277

§22.1 Introduction 277
§22.2 Video 277
§22.3 Audio 278
§22.4 Chain of Custody 279
§22.5 Process 281
§22.6 Converting Cases to Cross-examination 284
§22.7 Tampering 285
§22.8 Content to Purpose Mismatch 291

CHAPTER 23: GOVERNMENT WITNESSES 299

§23.1 Who is Government Witness 299
§23.2 Plea Bargaining 299

CHAPTER 24: ANATOMY OF CROSS-EXAMINATION OF AN EXPERT WITNESS 303

§24.1 Introduction 303
§24.2 The Opinion Testimony 304
§24.3 Early Skirmish and Demonstration of Preparation Asserting Control 304
§24.4 Development of the Theme 306
§24.5 Garbage In—Garbage Out 307
§24.6 Development of the Theme (2) 311
§24.7 Development of the Theme (3) 312
§24.8 Development of the Theme (4) 314
§24.9 More Garbage In—Garbage Out 316
§24.10 Control and Knowledge Negating an Element of the Defense 317
§24.11 When the Witness Gets Away 319
§24.12 Overview 321

CHAPTER 25: THE EMPEROR'S NEW CLOTHES 327

§25.1 Conde and Santangelo 327

§25.2 Freddie Mac 333
§25.3 The Mortgage Bank 335
§25.4 The Genesis of the ''Fraudulent'' Rent Roll 336
§25.5 The ''Special'' Agent 353
§25.6 The Case Built on Quicksand 357

Foreword

As long as human beings exist, the subject of cross-examination will never be exhausted. Despite the innumerable additions of technical subject matters or new frontiers to which the mind and imagination can be taken, it still remains the dissection of the human organism that reveal weaknesses and the frailties of human nature that are the essence of effective cross-examination. The fascination derives from the same motivations that lead people to be intrigued by prize fights, fencing matches, hockey games or any other direct confrontation in which one or the other of the participants could be hurt. Just as there are endless advances in all technologies and disciplines, there are ever increasing ways in which witnesses can be wounded in the course of cross-examination. Within the rules, it is the trial lawyer's job to inflict that wound on the adverse witness.

There is no concomitant requirement that the wound must be inflicted in a surly or disrespectful manner. It may be accomplished in phrases utilizing the utmost courtesy or confined within an appealing Trojan Horse and, on some occasions, with as much cold bloodedness and aggression as the system permits.

Litigation today means that diplomacy has failed and war has been declared. In previous times, there was lip service, if not actual subservience, paid to maintaining the eagle's perspective in unfailingly acting in a courteous manner. Lawyers were ever aware of their image and devoutly desired to be regarded as courtly practitioners. However, today the court system is a system in crisis; the only certainties are that everything is uncertain. The assignment of judges who have varying viewpoints and who are so overburdened so that, whatever their viewpoint, it may not be able to be brought to bear. The frequent judicial emergencies, the varying of decisions based upon new interpretations or even political concerns all contribute to the uncertainty which one can be sure will attend almost every significant trial.

A recent phenomenon is the pressure placed upon juries by an awareness of what effect their verdict will have upon thousands of people outside the courtroom. Everyone is aware of the military buildup that virtually took place surrounding the Rodney King case in California and the recent trial in Florida. The rioting that followed the acquittal of the accused in the Crown Heights case attests to the ever-increasing frequency that events outside the courtroom have a direct and material impact on the proceedings taking place within the courtroom. Juries, judges and lawyers are under pressures never before experienced, but which dramatically govern their conduct.

The focal point of these phenomena is cross-examination since that is where the conflict is most clearly defined. When all is said and done, the greatest impact upon any particular case will be the human element. How to approach the finder of fact who is distracted by intense matters that are surrounding him in everyday life is much more complex than in simpler times. The human dimension is far more convoluted today and lawyers are required to understand themselves and the environment in which they function far more than was previously the case. It is no longer practical to advocate a position which, while technically precise and unassailably correct, does not have a certain simplistic appeal to the trier of the fact, the court itself and, as is often the case, the media.

The system today does not permit the long nurturing process that so often formed trial lawyers in past years. When I began my legal career, trial lawyers all knew that, if possible, they should serve an internship in the office of a prosecutor, the Legal Aid Society or an insurance company where they would have a substantial work load and responsibility immediately handed to them wherein they would be on trial frequently and learn their craft the hard way by making mistakes and taking some very hard hits in the process. They were forced to endure a salary which never came close to meeting their expenses in recognition of the fact that the experience that they were being given and the responsibilities with which they were being entrusted were worth more than dollars at the present moment.

Following this apprenticeship, there was a period of residency with a seasoned practitioner. The practitioner rarely took time to sit down and explain anything and, more often than not, would simply bark instructions since he was under pressure. The young associate was left to fend for himself as to the best manner of accomplishing the task. I recall my first job after the District Attorney's Office of Frank Hogan with the then premier trial lawyer in New York City, Joseph E. Brill, who would frequently say "make believe you just hung out a shingle and I wasn't here, as I grappled with a particular case."

Most of the learning was done simply by watching him rather than as the result of patient guidance. I don't think Joe could have explained most things if he wanted to since, by that time in his career, it was a question of absorbing the facts and letting instincts that he had come to trust take over.

More often than not, the greatest education came at 2:00 a.m. when Brill was fatigued and an impossible situation was being presented which had to be resolved by the next day. It was in watching his reactions, and the methods by which he went about attacking the problems, that were the most enlightening. Over the years, I found myself, when faced with an impossible problem, asking, "what would Joe do now." After a while, the process gives birth to your own instinct.

Law books are available to all, and there is no shortage of pundits who are willing to explain the words contained in those books. However, there is no one who can adequately explain what your reactions ought to be when your client is absolutely guilty or has the weaker side of the case, or how to conduct yourself and still present a substantial position for your client when the money simply is not there, the time is short, the spirit is weak, the witness uncooperative, and you have a family or other personal matters competing for your time. It is only in watching somebody live through it that you begin to get a glimmer that not only can it be done, but how it can be done.

This is the number one disadvantage suffered by many of the lawyers entering the profession in recent years. In large firms, it is rare that the young associates ever get a chance to see the leading litigators of the firm with "their pants down." Yet, it is at those moments when the meaning of fortitude and steadfastness, imagination and resourcefulness, is often learned.

Those are also the moments when the greatest skill of all is developed, turning a weakness into the strongest point for your case. In other words, it is the observation of all of the things which are never recorded but which develop insights into the human condition, both with regard to the problem and as to the lawyer who must deal with it.

This book is not designed to recite interesting anecdotes or to necessarily provide cross-examinations which have no application other than to the case in which they were developed. Rather, each of the cross-examinations have been selected because they are interchangeable, regardless of the nature of the case or the technical aspects of the evidence. In essence, they are templates.

A great deal of time must be spent in evaluating the environment in which the trial will occur and some of the myriad human conditions that will be brought to bear.

I hope that this book will assist in the development of instinct that will permit the attorney to get the most out of his case and obtain the best result for the client. That is why cross-examinations can be templates. Properly honed instincts, some ability level and preparation are all things that can be consistent in an otherwise uncertain system.

To the extent that the United States has become a fast food society, some of the cross-examinations must be likened to fast food as compared to a gourmet meal that one would prefer to enjoy, provided time and money were available.

On any given day, obtaining a critical ruling in court is unreliable. The lawyer must continue notwithstanding. It is for that reason that many of the cross-examinations are selected or conducted in court on an almost simplistic basis, tagged to one of the few rules that are unassailable. Dependency on a sophisticated ruling by a judge supposedly concentrating completely on the case at hand is often an overly optimistic illusion.

Everyday experience provide excellent training for developing skills in cross-examination since it provides the most available repetition and response through which instinct is developed. A cross-examination which makes sense only to other lawyers or to an Appellate Court is not an effective cross-examination. It must be something which appeals to, and evokes a response from, people in all walks of life, many of whom might not even have a high regard for lawyers.

Today, the subjects are so varied that the active trial lawyer finds himself in situations so endless that there needs to be developed some sort of common skeleton that will serve in most cases upon which the flesh of a particular trial can be hung. Hopefully, that is what this book will accomplish; and, as indicated before, the cross-examinations are really templates which can be customized or varied to fit most any case. The object will always be the same, has the witness lied or made a mistake, said too much, said too little or failed to do what reasonably is expected of him.

Cross-examination today plays a far greater role than ever before. Given the fact that the courts are a system in crisis, cross-examination is relied upon as "the magic bullet," or the safeguard against all the foibles, fictions and hypocrisies built into today's trials. It is presumed that, if any mistakes are made, ignored or overlooked, the lawyer will straighten it all out and set it right upon cross-examination.

Another aspect of the learning process that was learned in earlier years was to become hardened and to expect every form of personal attack that the opponent could muster. This did not mean yelling or screaming or even using coarse language but rather, if a weakness was perceived, the lawyer could anticipate that the opponent would attempt to exploit it. Thus, a lawyer with a few strands of gray hair could anticipate being regarded as geriatric by a younger opponent; and, vice versa, the younger opponent could anticipate that the older practitioner would frequently make reference to the impetuousness of youth and inexperience. Every politically incorrect comment would be made in the testing of an opponent; and, if any reaction were divined, it was exploited, albeit in the most elegant and refined of terms. Should an attorney show that vulgarity offended him and broke his concentration, he could expect to be confronted with language that would make Eddie Murphy blush in every non-recorded conversation. It was in this environment that the young trial lawyer learned to respond to such ad hominem statements by smiling and simply stating, "flattery will get you nowhere."

In a significant trial a number of years ago, I was approached by the prosecutor who asked me if I had had any experience in the particular subject of the instant trial. I indicated that I had not, whereupon my opponent informed me that I was destined to fail since it was a highly sophisticated subject, little understood by persons who had worked in the field for many years, and that there was no way that I could master the idiosyncracies and technicalities of such a matter. I do not suggest that such jousting is to be desired or even that it is commendable; but it exists and the trial lawyer must learn to deal with it without taking offense and without regarding it as anything personal and without being intimidated. The opposing lawyer offered me his patronizing sympathy for the situation in which I was soon to be embarrassed. My only answer was to smile and recall that my grandmother used to say that she would "rather hear Rachmaninoff play a piano piece for the first time than to listen to a hack who had practiced it for thirty years." In other words, the situation had to be dealt with without taking offense and without regarding it as personal. The client was acquitted to the obvious delight of my long deceased grandmother who had never heard of Rachmaninoff.

It is not to suggest that such jousting or schoolyard tactics are to be admired. They simply exist and will always exist in matters of human confrontation. There is no place to become offended and to permit the distraction to throw the lawyer off stride, which it is designed to do. Of course, this is something that is always learned by watching a seasoned practitioner, followed by taking a few direct blows and learning that it is all part of the equation.

There are probably few shortcuts; but, if there are any, they are in addressing the human element instead of the technicalities of cross-examination, which is attempted to be accomplished here. By way of analogy, I have a friend who is extremely adept at any sport in which he chooses to engage. At the outset, he retains as good a coach as he can find and undertakes a series of lessons. However, he is in no hurry to get to the actual playing field. When taking ski lessons, rather than pressing to get to the slopes, he insists on talking to the ski instructor for innumerable hours prior to even putting on skis. In those hours, he questions the ski instructor as to the variety of terrain and snow textures. After all the questions, he simply speaks to the instructor trying to get a feel for the instructor's mentality.

The same is true with regard to cross-examination. The mountain will never be the same, the snow conditions will vary endlessly depending on minute changes in the weather and even the skier will vary from time to time depending on how he feels. However, by following this course, when my friend finally took to the slopes, he started quickly and, in a variety of conditions, became an expert skier, while others, years later, were struggling to remember to keep their knees bent, their hands in front of them, their body facing downhill, which ski to put the weight on and the principles of angulation.

The reason was that he understood what he was doing and what he was trying to accomplish. He also had a sense of how he should feel and how he was doing particular maneuvers and sensed along the way as to whether or not they were working. At the moment when all the different questions and instructions came together under the umbrella of understanding and instinct that became automatic or second nature, he was an expert.

It has often been said that only experience will develop a good trial lawyer or a good cross-examiner. While that is generally true, it does not go far enough. It is at the moment when experience turns to instinct that a good trial lawyer or cross-examiner is developed. And when that instinct is developed it must be one which can function in a variety of ever changing conditions and dealing with an endless number of persons or situations, each one different than the last.

Introduction 1

"All planning, particularly strategic planning, must pay attention to the character of contemporary warfare."

Karl Von Clausewitz, "*On War*," 1832.

Cross-examination is the blood sport of the legal profession. It has been the subject of intrigue and interest, both legal and otherwise, throughout history. It has survived ongoing revisions in the Rules of Evidence and evolving interpretations of what constitutes fair play. It has often been referred to as an art; at the very least, it is a craft.

Writings on cross-examination have set out interesting interrogations of defendants for their interest in the idiosyncrasies of a particular case. It is left to the reader to dig out principles which could be applied to any given case, regardless of its nature, the issues involved and the characters playing principal parts. While many of the principles of cross-examination remain unchanged, the methods necessary for effective results have changed dramatically. The courts, the lawyers, the rules and the very nature of litigation have changed so extensively that today's trial lawyer must go far beyond the techniques that existed a short generation ago.

It has often been said that the adversarial system of litigation is a confrontation from which the truth emerges. That is not entirely accurate. It is the process from which the perception of truth emerges.

It may often occur that perception and truth are one and the same, but not always. When they are not, perception will prevail.

Today, the practitioner who spends his career in courtrooms falls into two categories: the trial lawyer and the litigator. While a trial lawyer is always a litigator, a litigator is not always a trial lawyer. A litigator may ply his trade in the vineyards of motions, examinations before trial, document production or appellate matters. A trial lawyer functions in a courtroom arguing, pleading or begging for a decision from a trier of fact. The principles and craft of cross-examination apply to those litigators who are trial lawyers.

The trial lawyer is substantially similar to a lighting designer who knows that the positioning and intensity of the lights will often determine the effect that they will have upon the viewer. Consequently, where a trial lawyer places the "lights" and the intensity with which they illuminate will often determine the context and perception of the facts under review.

Perception can make the entirely truthful witness appear to be lying or at least disingenuous and the honest error perceived to be a deliberate misstatement. It is through cross-examination that such perception often develops.

Throughout our legal history, the often repeated ethical question that is posed to a criminal defense attorney is how he can represent and seek to have acquitted a person whom he knows to be guilty of a crime. The usual response is in terms of the system and dedication to the principles of justice which espouse that a person is presumed to be innocent until proven guilty and, if not proven guilty, he should go unpunished.

Subsumed in that great ethical debate is the one question that is never asked. How a lawyer can ethically make a witness known to be telling the truth appear to be lying, mistaken or disingenuous, or a superb technician into a bumbler. It is not only the lying witness who is successfully cross-examined but also any adverse witness, even one espousing ultimate truth.

Since cross-examination is depended on to resolve the injustices and errors inherent in our legal system, the question is avoided, there being no satisfactory answer. While the requirements of our Constitution and form of law require defending guilty persons, there is no overt obligation built in that, on a particular cross-examination truth should be made to appear as something less. Yet, that is the requirement imposed upon the lawyer solely by virtue of his oath and dedication to the interests of his client. However, cross-examination perseveres since there is no known substitute for testing a witness under oath. It is the civilized equivalent of ordeal by fire.

Cross-examination requires the greatest degree of craft by the trial attorney. Just as the witness may not be prepared for the questions posed by the cross-examiner, the lawyer may not be prepared for the answers given or the manner in which they are given. The lawyer is often required to shift gears to incorporate a particular response into the examination in order to get it back on course and regain control. The lawyer may be required to instantaneously abandon a prepared cross-examination if it is fruitless or ill conceived.

More difficult may be the requirement upon the lawyer to seize upon an unexpected answer, regard it as an opportunity and launch an entirely different attack than the one prepared. Suffice it to say, it is the only aspect of the trial that relies upon direct confrontation in which every question and answer is tested in the immediate crucible of that confrontation.

The cross-examiner must always keep in mind the entire testimony rendered to that point so that no shift in direction is permitted by the witness or an inconsistency allowed to escape notice. The lawyer must, when a witness recites a fact or an act, swiftly calculate the next logical fact or event that human experience suggests would follow. When the next logical step or act does not follow, the lawyer must be aware that he has an opportunity for effective cross-examination.

A trial lawyer must be a chameleon. He must, within acceptable limits, mold not only the facts of the case to the most compelling common denominator presentation but also his own personality. When cross-examining a sympathetic witness, he must show concern and consideration while asking difficult questions. In the face of arrogance, he must project humility; and, in the face of a handicap, he must not appear too strong. On other occasions, he must be belligerent and aggressive, mercilessly "closing in for the kill" on a wounded witness. It will depend upon a lawyer's experience and understanding of human frailty as to which part he must play.

There is no finer reference treatise on cross-examination than the classic manual on military operations written by Karl Von Clausewitz entitled *On War*, first published in 1832. The book is remarkable not only for its analysis of the essentials of successful military strategies but also upon the psychological aspects that must be considered when waging war. In many ways, a trial resembles war except that the weapons are different and certain imposed rules of civilization sometimes make the analogy mistakenly rejected. However, there should be no mistake; trials of significant matters are often a matter of life and death, either physical or financial.

Many of the concepts advanced by Von Clausewitz have direct application to the courtroom, particularly with regard to cross-examination. As with the military principles espoused in "*On War*," the secret to successful trial management is strategy and tactics.

Strategy is the overall plan, and tactics are the methods by which the plan is executed. Every part of the trial, especially cross-examination, has to be consistent with the plan. Cross-examination is the foremost method by which the plan may be implemented since it can have the greatest effect upon the opponent and also the greatest likelihood of interfering with and inhibiting his case, thus permitting your client to prevail.

It is manifest that trial preparation and planning, particularly in determining cross-examination, must pay attention to the character of the contemporary judicial scene. It is this awareness that permits a courtroom presentation to be effectively incorporated into that environment and, in so doing, maintain credibility.

In a complex society, the key is simplicity and comforting coordination of all the elements. As Von Clausewitz states:

> A prince or a general can best demonstrate his genius by managing a campaign exactly to suit his objectives and his resources, doing neither too much nor too little. But the effects of genius show not so much in novel forms of action as in the ultimate success of the whole. What we should admire is the accurate fulfillment of the unspoken assumptions, the smooth harmony of the whole activity, which only become evident in final success.

* * *

> The student who cannot discover this harmony in actions that lead up to a final success may be tempted to look for genius in places where it does not and cannot exist.
>
> * * *
>
> In fact the means and forms that the strategist employs are so very simple, so familiar from constant repetition, that it seems ridiculous in the light of common sense when critics discuss them, as they do so often, with ponderous solemnity.

The ultimate truth embodied in the above principles was further reiterated:

> Everything in strategy is very simple, but that does not mean that everything is very easy. Once it has been determined, from the political conditions, what a war is meant to achieve and what it can achieve, it is easy to chart the course.

It is axiomatic that simplistic will prevail over complex or detailed. A simplistic approach is easily absorbed and, if it does not offend common sense, is eagerly grasped by a jury. Complex explanations, even if accurate with computer-like precision, are often too difficult to follow or require too much concentration to absorb. It is these considerations that the cross-examiner must focus upon and rarely forget.

This is the guiding principle of this writing; it is more a manual than a text or treatise. As pertains to trial and, particularly, cross-examination, once an effective strategy is determined, the methods by which such a strategy is executed are relatively simple. Once all of the conditions are analyzed and the objectives determined, the questions will really suggest themselves and can, with some factual modification, be used in case after case.

The difficulty is always in the proper assessment of conditions and strategies, as well as in carefully evaluating both your own and your client's strengths and weaknesses.

As with all matters of simplicity, true genius is in the selection of approaches and questions from among various available options. The test is not whether it appears brilliant upon its face but how well it works within the totality of accomplishing the objective.

It is difficult to create or even recreate in a book "cross-examinations" which are, on their face, brilliant. A truly brilliant cross-examination may extend over a period of hours, if not days, gradually chipping away at various linchpins which were established over hundreds of pages of earlier testimony to make a single point that may be obscure until summation. An appreciation of the questioning can only occur if preceded by a lengthy explanation of the point to be made and the use to which it is ultimately put. Rarely can cross-examination be crystallized into a few short questions so that the whole point is apparent or reveals the effort or the ability that went into it. However, the fungible methods of cross-examination can.

Virtually everything that occurs in a trial should build toward summation; and so, many times, the most successful cross-examinations are not apparent until one reads the summation and sees how the point extracted from the witness was utilized in weaving the tapestry that comprises the summation.

In attempting to explain the principles of cross-examination, it is impossible to avoid certain concepts or considerations which, standing alone, seem obvious and repetitious. However, successful cross-examination may depend on exploiting what is obvious since that can strike the greatest responsive chord in a jury. It is much like Edgar Allan Poe's "purloined letter" which was hidden because it was in plain sight.

An example is the trite phrase "tried and true." Yet it is well known that most people accept that common phrase as an accurate assessment of reality. Lawyers are hired because they have good track records, often over far more intellectually gifted lawyers who simply lack experience or the "name." In dealing with the most complex scientific testimony, if cross-examination can show that a device was tested on ten occasions and failed on three, the decision of the jury may well reflect that, although the device was tried, it was untrue.

As with all lethal weapons, cross-examination should never be undertaken if a lawyer is not prepared to exploit its full potential which may necessitate belligerency or aggressiveness. He cannot avoid seeking to control and often demolishing the witness personally as a means of negating his testimony if the opportunity arises. Fear and respect are the epithets that he seeks, rather than love.

A trial, and the facts elicited during its course, is merely the tip of the iceberg. Applicable to cross-examination, that often means that style and impression will prevail over content; this applies to the lawyer as well as the witness. An absolutely truthful witness who avoids eye contact may give the impression of lying or being evasive. An absolute liar who delivers testimony in a confident and apparently detailed manner while making a nice appearance may be regarded as a singular purveyor of the "whole truth and nothing but the truth."

Recently, I represented a client who was accused of fraud based upon the testimony of accountants who were testifying at length that certain financial statements issued by my client were false and inaccurate.

What accountants often forget, coupled with a public generally unaware, is that financial statements are dependent on evaluations, allocations and many projections in determining the financial status of a particular enterprise or individual. They treat their opinions as facts because they lead to a specific finite number. Many of the entries contained in a financial statement are allocations or projections, accruals based upon an accountant's theory or paper profits and losses that have virtually nothing to do with the ongoing operations of the business or the amount of money available for working capital on a cash flow basis. These subjective assessments can give a picture of an individual's or an entity's financial status that is inconsistent with reality.

The accountants called by the opposing party believed themselves to be absolutely truthful. Were one hundred accountants to be similarly examined, there would be no question but that ninety-eight, following generally accepted accounting principles, would arrive at exactly the same conclusions of financial status or offer the same testimony as the instant witnesses.

Upon examination, I selected every entry which involved a subjective opinion, allocation, appraisal or accrual. In a series of questions, it was pointed out that, as to each entry the accountant had the option of making a number of decisions rather than the single one chosen. By the time that cross-examination was finished, it appeared that the accountant had ignored an infinite number of possibilities and had stubbornly selected only those consistent with his preconceived hypothesis of fraud.

When the accountant recognized how he was made to appear, he rigorously defended his honor, thereby becoming even more stubborn in the face of suggested options or alternatives. As he continued to do so, it appeared to the jury that he was no longer interested in impartiality or fairness but only in defending the choices that he had made which were all consistent with his innate determination of establishing fraud.

The harder he tried, the more rigid he became and the worse it got. It was not long before it appeared that the mere suggestion of options, even if only superficially reasonable, highlighted his continual insistence upon rejecting any opposition by refusing to acknowledge an alternative regardless of its significance. The witness appeared absolutely unreasonable. Since his testimony was the heart of the prosecution's case, the jury did not linger long in rendering a verdict of acquittal.

Shortly after his testimony, I met the accountant outside the courtroom. He continued to be distraught and yelled at me, "You made me out to be a crook and you know I'm not."

I asked him if there was any item of evidence which I had contrived or fabricated. He responded there was none. I asked him if he was precluded from reviewing any documents which he believed might have influenced his testimony. Again, he acknowledged that such was not the case. I asked him if the options that I had proposed to him were, in fact, actual and recognized options, while agreeing that some of them had less significance than others he had chosen. He agreed.

I then told him that, since I had played by the fair rules of cross-examination and the end result of asking such questions made him appear to be blindly prejudiced at the expense of truth or gave rise to such an inference, my job was done and my client was entitled to no less.

Cross-examination is the one thing in the course of a trial that is absolutely unique. If an attorney is good at cross-examination, he essentially is good at trial since the rest is easily dealt with. Openings and summations are similar to the delivery of any other speech in any other forum. Presentation of direct witnesses, again, is based upon preparation prior to trial wherein the choice of words is carefully selected to present the best possible position and in all likelihood, rehearsed.

Cross-examination is the only moment in the trial where there is a direct confrontation. On all other occasions, the presentation is being made in tandem in that one side goes first and the other side responds and vice versa. It is only in cross-examination that a statement is tested at the moment of utterance.

It is also the moment in the trial at which things can change most dramatically and suddenly. A single answer can cause an attorney to abandon all preparation and be forced to pursue on the spur of the moment an entirely different line of questioning than anticipated. A witness may seize control of the examination and the attorney must then, by a series of questions, reassert his control. Conversely, a witness dropping a bombshell can cast the die of the entire trial regardless of whatever else takes place or is presented.

It is only after the conclusion of a cross-examination that the question is formulated as to whether "the witness was hurt" or "did the witness survive intact."

Commercial attorneys, whether they draw contracts, wills or structure a particular business transaction are consumed with details in an attempt to shield against future storms or possible difficulties. The visions of ghosts lurking in every potential closet cause documents to become lengthy, well meaning, but often superfluous.

Once a trial commences, the problems are real and immediate and instinct counts for more than thoughtful reflection. This is not to suggest that details are to be ignored. In fact, they are critical, but not at the expense of the big picture and a feel for what is going on. To a trial lawyer, details are critical but they must be dealt with before the trial starts. A jury may well lose sight of a tree, but rarely of a forest. While the trial lawyer must be familiar with all the details, he must recognize that too many details may only serve to confuse a jury and dilute the essential presentation or divert attention and focus from an issue which is critical.

It is for that reason that trial lawyers are more consumed by impressions and what impression is conveyed by the aggregate of the selected details that are being elicited, rather than bogging down on any particular one.

The trial lawyer can be faulted for his version or interpretation of what happened yesterday if it does not conform to common sense, human experience and the known facts of what occurred. If a trial lawyer gets mired in details in his presentation, he is regarded as quibbling and insensitive. A trial lawyer is limited by what has already happened and must bring to bear all sorts of effort to change the interpretation or impression of the event being viewed. If a commercial lawyer protects against things that never happen and imagines scenarios far beyond any common sense, he may be highly regarded since the future does not provide a litmus test of the lawyer's present reasoning and efforts. The more scenarios that he can contrive, the more thorough and careful he may appear.

By contrast, were a trial lawyer to contrive scenarios and try to impose interpretations that did not conform to common sense or what is actually known, he is not regarded seriously and his cross-examinations will have little or no effect. Unlike the commercial lawyer who can never be wrong in predicting or anticipating the future at the moment the prediction is made, a trial lawyer is locked into history and instantly judged.

Commercial lawyers deal with legal matters when everything is in evolution. Even in an adversarial negotiation regarding the structure of a business transaction, there is an incomplete process that is going on by which the parties may ultimately agree and some compromise reached by parties working together.

The trial lawyer is in a different situation. He plies his trade against a declared adversary when something has already gone wrong and all of the means by which problems are resolved have failed.

Were a commercial lawyer to make an error, in the vast majority of circumstances the error will go unnoticed, even to the extent of failing to recognize that an error has been committed since a situation may never arise that highlights the error. Quite often, it is a case of "no harm, no foul." Even if the error should some day surface, there may be no damage to the extent that the subsequent events have overtaken the error and rendered it negligible.

Not so in the case of the trial lawyer. There, diplomacy has failed and war has been declared. If he makes an error, his client's cause may be lost or, at the very least, compromised seriously.

All of the above is heightened when it comes to cross-examination. In all other aspects of trial, there is a certain time tolerance which permits recovery or further explanation. Thus, an additional witness can be produced, new evidence offered, even subsequent explanations can mitigate the damage done. There are little or no fireworks which must be resolved within ten seconds in the course of any other aspect of the trial. With regard to summation, one may have days or weeks to prepare it and think about it, even as the evidence evolves. Strategy and planning, while critical, are not done under circumstances of sudden death. But, with regard to cross-examination, things occur in an instant from which there may be no recovery.

An active trial lawyer must consider everything which includes not only the case, the personality of his client, his own character traits and even, as we shall subsequently see, the weather.

The Theater and the Players 2

§2.1 OVERVIEW

If today's judicial system were put under a microscope, there would be basic similarities; but, in all refinements, the view would reveal a wholly different organism than existed a generation ago. The court, judges, jurors, causes of action and the rules of evidence have undergone such massive changes, evolutionary, practical and statutory, that a trial lawyer who ceased active practice in 1970 would hardly recognize what goes on in today's courtroom and the rules by which the judicial system is administered.

Courtrooms are no longer placid repositories of dignity given crowded calendars as a result of proliferating civil litigation and escalating crime. The courtroom resembles a bazaar, forced to utilize the practices of the bazaar.

New concepts have sprung up such as the "blockbuster parts" whose sole function is to reduce calendar congestion by resolving cases expeditiously. In criminal cases, historically, there was a question of the punishment fitting the crime. Today, it is more likely a question of what plea of guilty will be acceptable, leading either to a negotiated sentence in state court or one which fits into a particular niche in the Federal sentencing guidelines. In civil cases, it is not so much the right decision but, invariably, how much will a plaintiff accept and how much will a defendant pay, the costs of litigation dramatically influencing both decisions. This is the case throughout the country not only the large urban centers.

Obtaining a trial in the first instance has become positively Darwinian. Given the crowded courtrooms and the necessities of thinning out the mass of litigation, a trial has become a necessary evil in the methods of dispute resolutions.

Cross-examination has to take into account those realities of the environment as well as the others that must be considered.

§2.2 JUDGES

The previous image of a judge as a Solomon-like dispenser of wisdom is often a hope shattered by experience. While not suggesting that there are not many such judges currently sitting, the likelihood is that today's judge is harassed and harried by a calendar that defies human effort while prodded by an equally harried court administrator monitoring open cases on the judge's calendar. Shrinking budgets often restrict needed assistance. It is not uncommon for a judge in an urban area to greet each day with a calendar exceeding 150 cases. While in other jurisdictions the number may vary, the number is usually greater than will permit thorough dealing with each case. As a result, quality must suffer and the potential for error increases.

Both State and Federal criminal courts are driven by the speedy trial rules under the United States Constitution. As a result, criminal cases choke the calendars to the extent that, from time to time, there are declared "judicial emergencies" which result in no civil cases getting to trial at all during an extended period.

Commercial courts have their own converse version of the speedy trial rule. Advising a judge that a forthcoming trial may consume more than two or three days almost always results in the case becoming the modern embodiment of the "Flying Dutchman." Should a case successfully navigate the calendar's clogged waters, the admonition to the lawyers and parties will be repeatedly heard, "let's move along, counselor."

§2.3 JURORS

Today's jurors, and judges when they act as finders of the fact, are vastly different than those of the 1930's and the 1950's. Television has had a dramatic effect on all people. The contemporary juror has recently been the possessor of a box seat to a war taking place on the other side of the world, has been an eyewitness to the most dramatic of tragedies and the most vicious of crimes. He has witnessed and been privy to the most exotic and complex of financial schemes resulting in the displacement of hundreds of millions of dollars. He has seen soldiers, spacemen, politicians and even his neighbors in the most intimate and revealing of circumstances. He is no longer cloistered and protected from any aspect of human nature.

He has also been privy to the most artless form of cross-examination such as occurs at the press conference or media interview. There, the public is constantly afforded the opportunity to watch and hear the lethally loaded question that jolts the person to whom it is put, which question would never be permitted in a courtroom. He is all too familiar with the ambush form of questioning and finds it interesting and exciting.

Such questions have no imposed restriction of fairness and can be harassing or constitute an unanswerable speech in the form of a question. The "question" may be premised on facts which are unsubstantiated or have never been established as a valid predicate for the questions. There is no one present to make the objection that will cause the question to be overruled or withdrawn. Such questions would normally be excluded in the courtroom because they are irrelevant or too remote as to time or place to have any probative value in the matter on trial or are based on facts that have not been established. They may be complex or multifaceted so as to be objectionable as a matter of form.

They are designed to be inflammatory and attention getting, far overshadowing their validity or relevance. If the person questioned refuses to answer, it is not the question that is condemned but, rather, the refusal to answer.

The juror has become attuned to this "knockout punch" form of questioning thereby developing a shortened attention span for the well-crafted cross-examination which develops through a series of questions and the evolution of a concept. In reality, the well-developed cross-examination is far more dramatic to a juror inasmuch as he is a partner in the examination. The jury watches it develop, tracks its evolution and, on occasion, is treated to being able to anticipate its outcome before the witness does. A juror may sense the trap to which the witness is slowly proceeding and eagerly await its springing. He forms the questions in his own mind which he hopes will be asked. Unfortunately, the heightened expectations brought by a Mike Wallace, a Geraldo Rivera or a Phil Donahue have heightened jurors' expectations to an unreasonable degree, so that engaging and holding their attention is infinitely more difficult.

This higher threshold of impact cannot be ignored by those seeking to conduct successful cross-examinations. Clearly, it is harder to hold the juror's interest or attention and convince him that a minor bloodless fact holds vast significance if such juror has gone through adulthood upon a regular diet of disaster, multiple killings, complex financial crimes and $100 million lottery prizes.

§2.4 LAWYERS

Lawyers, too, have undergone evolutionary changes, not all of them for the better. Historically, lawyers were regarded with respect and dignity; and, a trial lawyer was regarded as the lonely bulwark against injustice. It was the lawyer who was the defender of the oppressed and the pursuer of justice. The greatest name recognition with positive reactions among the general public were those of trial lawyers.

It is recognized that the most significant social advances in this country were brought about in trial and appellate courts by trial lawyers pursuing a particular case on behalf of a client. Developments and advances in reducing racial, sexual or age discrimination had their birthplace in noted court cases. Quality in education took its greatest strides in a case brought by Thurgood Marshall. Protection of the aged, making medical care more responsible and making the government more responsive to its citizens in various social programs all had the common breeding ground of the trial court.

Conversely, the modern image of the trial lawyer could not be more negative. While still regarded as a hired gun, he is no longer the marshal brought in to clean up the town but, rather, the gunfighter brought by the venal cattle baron to run off the settlers. A vice-presidential candidate campaigned by assessing many of the evils of modern society upon "the trial lawyers." A recent appointee for the office of Attorney General, the nation's foremost lawyer, concurred in the opinion that trial lawyers should be muzzled.

Modern legal procedures have also brought about changes required of trial lawyers. The advent of discovery and its explosion has had a material effect not only upon the lawyers but upon the trial itself and erosion of the skills of cross-examination.

Discovery has been liberalized to the extent that, in a civil matter, virtually anything is discoverable and any question is askable. Criminal cases are not far behind concerning documents but have yet to encompass the full examination before trial. It is in this environment that "litigators" have evolved. Litigators are not necessarily trial lawyers and may go an entire career conducting depositions, requesting documents and, on occasion, fashioning motions addressed to furthering discovery. Documents are requested simply because they exist and questions asked simply because the mind is capable of conjuring the question.

Discovery takes on a life of its own and all too often becomes the complete battlefield upon which the case is litigated. One side or the other may try to drown the opponent in discovery and, thus, bring the case to a conclusion on that basis. Discovery is the singular most responsible event for the escalation of legal fees in litigation since there are few limitations on discovery and it can continue to fill any vacuum that may exist financially.

Pertaining to the development of the lawyer, the questions often posed in discovery lack focus so that the lawyer does not hone his skills in wording questions appropriately or asking them in sequences which provide the maximum effect. There is no immediate test as to whether or not the question is valid, objectionable or seeks relevant information. No mistake is dramatic since the case may never reach trial or, if it does, the question may not be admitted. At the very least, there is ample opportunity to prepare to minimize its effect or any surprises.

In the more focused atmosphere of the courtroom, questions are immediately tested in the crucible of objections and rulings. They are tested by the development of a relevant, carefully crafted presentation. Finally, the questions are tested by the verdict that is ultimately rendered which indicates that the questioning has successfully brought forth certain points or was ineffective to accomplish that purpose.

In another sense, the trial lawyer has to be more versatile. Many years ago, each trial could be shaped to meet the style and methods of the attorney. The style and manner of a Clarence Darrow or a Lloyd Paul Stryker would vary little from trial to trial. The entity known as the trial would be molded by their style and personality. Today, the lawyer has to vary his approach from trial to trial. This ability cannot be developed in discovery or motion practice. It is an attribute that is honed only in the courtroom and only after giving and receiving many wounds.

§2.5 COURTS

Because of the clogging of calendars and the volume of litigation pending in the courts, the considered judgment has given way to soundbytes and quick dispositions, whether upon trial or by way of settlement. The search for the truth has given way to the perception of truth and is more likely determined by impressions rather than facts.

Previously, cross-examination started with the *voir dire* or jury selection. An experienced lawyer could virtually try an entire case while questioning the panel and elicit certain responses. Defects in the case could be explained away and promises extracted that virtually elicited a commitment from the juror to vote in the lawyer's favor. At the least, sound questioning could probe for adverse bias without offending the panel.

Presently, the pressures of time have virtually eliminated the lawyer conducting the questioning upon jury selection in Federal courts and state courts are rapidly adopting the practice. While the lawyer for each side presents questions that he wishes the judge to ask, the judge does not necessarily have to adopt or ask such questions. Such questions are asked by the numbers, such as "are there any jurors who have relatives in law enforcement. If so, raise your hand," thus eliminating probing below the surface to unearth deep seated bias or other disqualifying traits.

§2.6 TESTIMONY

Another change to which a lawyer must be attuned is the constant change in patterns of testimony that will occur from time to time upon a certain issue. Recognizing such changes alerts the lawyer to the testimony that will be forthcoming and allows him to prepare effective cross-examination.

A graphic example of universal applicability is demonstrated in this following story. In the late 1950's, when I first became a prosecutor, the general rule was that evidence illegally seized could be admitted into evidence. At that time, young assistant district attorneys in Manhattan were given their initial trial training by being assigned to "gambler's court." Gambling was then considered a crime and legions of people were prosecuted each year for what now is a staple of existence.

The greatest number of prosecutions involved the "numbers game." There, people selected a three digit number, wrote it on a slip of paper and gave it to a collector who was known as a "numbers" runner. In the course of a day, the numbers runner had large numbers of slips of paper in their pocket which they later turned in to the game's operator or the numbers "bank." The number for the day was determined either by the last three digits of the dollar amount wagered in parimutuel betting throughout New York State or the dollar volume of transactions on the New York Stock Exchange. The odds were 600 to 1.

The police testimony following the arrest of a numbers runner was invariably the same. Both sides knew that an illegal search would not preclude evidence from being admitted into evidence against the accused. The police routinely stopped the numbers runner, reached into his pocket and obtained the betting slips that were evidence of guilt. The runners, knowing this, on every occasion when they saw the police coming would throw the slips away so that they would not be found on their person. The defense would then contend that the slips offered in evidence were picked up from the ground from among all sorts of litter and so could not be identified with the defendant.

The police would recover the slips from the ground, but the testimony would invariably state that they had been removed from the defendant's pocket, clearly demonstrating that the defendant had possession of the slips and was conclusively guilty.

In 1960, the United States Supreme Court decided *Mapp v. Ohio* which held that illegally seized evidence could no longer be admitted into evidence against a criminal defendant. Within three days, the testimony in gambling cases dramatically changed. Now, each numbers runner knew that a policeman could not go into his pocket without a search warrant and so the approach of a law enforcement officer did not occasion the throwing away of the numbers slips since the safest place for the accused to have them was in his pocket.

The police testimony universally shifted so that it routinely became that, upon approach, the defendant abandoned the evidence by throwing it to the ground. Consequently, cross-examination was exclusively directed to the fact that the slips were improperly seized from the defendant's pocket and should be suppressed.

In other words, initially the facts were that the evidence was abandoned and police testimony invariably stated it was removed from the defendant's pocket. Upon a significant legal ruling, the facts were that the slips were removed from the defendant's pocket and the police testimony universally became that the slips were abandoned.

The same holds true in a wide range of criminal and civil cases. Shortly following an appellate decision establishing a principle, the testimony presented in similar cases will mold itself to that principle. Defendants will no longer testify in breach of contract actions that they did not read the contract before signing it, and plaintiffs will testify avoiding a position that an appellate court ruled was insufficient or constituted a waiver.

To the cross-examiner, an awareness of the above phenomenon is critical. Knowing the recent decisions permits a cross-examiner to anticipate testimony that is likely to be faced, thus focusing preparation on the testimony likely to be given. By analyzing the facts against the holding, a highly successful cross-examination can be accomplished.

Emerging Causes of Actions 3

§3.1 ISSUES IN LITIGATION

A dramatic difference has taken place in the very nature of the causes of action that currently constitute the bulk of significant litigation. Even when a cause of action itself may not be materially different, the issues which will arise in the course of the litigation and the method by which they are proven are significantly different.

It cannot be said that the issues did not exist prior to a generation ago but they were not the stuff of which lawsuits were made. The Rules of Evidence then in existence basically excluded the testimony and the documents by which such causes of action are currently established. There is no area of litigation that has escaped material revision, both as to the nature of the game and as to the rules by which the game is played.

With each advance, cross-examination changed. Formerly, the Rules of Evidence were primarily exclusionary so that the cross-examiner knew that there were limitations on the kinds of problems that would be faced. Today, the Rules of Evidence are inclusionary and the problems that a cross-examiner will face are without limit.

§3.2 ENVIRONMENTAL ISSUES

While environmental concerns have been expressed throughout the history of this country, they did not really mature into common litigation until well into the 1960's. Today, environmental litigation such as the toxic tort is one of the dramatic examples of exploding litigation. Cases proven through the testimony of experts who previously would not have been qualified or whose testimony would have been regarded as too problematical or speculative are now commonplace.

The occurrence or damage is usually a given fact while the cause is strenuously disputed. The testimony, more often than not, is from legions of experts, be they toxologists, immunologists, medical doctors, as well as psychiatrists and psychologists who attest to the trauma or emotional harm brought about by the toxic element. Oftentimes, the cause and effect of such testimony is established statistically which requires the testimony of another kind of expert.

§3.3 PRODUCT LIABILITY ISSUES

Product liability has mushroomed since the days of Ralph Nader's demonstrating that the Chevrolet Corvair was improperly designed and, therefore, unsafe at any speed. Historically, product liability concerned itself with instances where a single purchased product did not work causing damage to a particular plaintiff.

Today, both environmental and product liability litigations are, more often than not, class actions with plaintiffs ultimately numbering in the thousands. The results of a particular case can affect thousands of lives, as well as cause the restructuring or decline of entire industries and national policy. Companies are forced into bankruptcy or financial decline by virtue of the existing number of lawsuits pending against them. A graphic example is the Johns-Manville Company which was forced to seek protection of the Bankruptcy Court by virtue of pending asbestos claims.

The thalidomide cases, benedictin and claims involving contraceptive devices all illustrated how a single design or manufacturing flaw can dramatically affect a company or an entire industry.

§3.4 MEDICAL ISSUES

In the medical field, new techniques for identifying and diagnosing illness, as well as advances in surgical procedures, have caused an explosion in malpractice claims. Absent these devices and techniques, a valid claim usually existed if the damage claimed occurred within a short time after the alleged precipitating event. However, with these new techniques, cause can be traced back over a generation so that there is virtually no time limitation, provided the chain can be established.

§3.5 FINANCIAL AND ACCOUNTING ISSUES

In the financial and accounting fields, the nature of the testimony has similarly changed so that instead of relying upon the opinion of a certified public accountant, a forensic accountant or the isolated opinion of a financial expert, information is now computed which can uncover, reconcile and distinguish masses of figures and financial histories that would have been beyond the ability of any expert as recently as 20 years ago. Computers cannot only unravel history and absorb every fact that previously existed but they can also project financial figures and offer assessments and appraisals that were previously beyond the credible capability of any witness. Absent the use of the computer, no witness could ever have been permitted to speculate as to the projections which are accepted as a matter of course from the computer.

§3.6 INTELLECTUAL PROPERTY ISSUES

Intellectual properties always required expert testimony of a scientific, technical and intellectual nature. Today, however, significant cases in intellectual properties more often than not involve computer software and whether or not there has been a patent or copyright infringement in that area. A whole new language, technology and concepts involving source codes and other computer technology, both as to hardware and software, are recent arrivals upon the litigation scene. Patents and rights to discoveries in genetic engineering are subjects that twenty years ago were regarded as science fiction. As in the other areas, they require the development of new cross-examination techniques and a far greater expertise on the part of the cross-examiner.

§3.7 CRIMINAL LAW ISSUES

The criminal field is not without its modern day advances that require changes in the nature of cross-examination. Fingerprint identification seems always to have been with us but, today, more often than not, it will be DNA fingerprinting which requires different and more complex testimony and cross-examination. Everyone is able to understand matching swirls but to understand the basic elements of DNA or other genetic fingerprinting is a different matter altogether. Changes in method and technique have occurred in ballistics and document identification, not to mention the common use of radar and certain breatholyzer tests in driving while intoxicated cases.

The criminal field has been entirely overtaken by the electronic era in that a vast number of major cases will include audio and visual surveillance that generates tape recordings and video film creating entirely new and different problems for cross-examination. In earlier times, a prosecutor would more often than not open to the jury by admitting that "we do not have a picture to show you." Today, the converse is more likely to be the case; and, the prosecutor asks the jury to rely on their eyes and ears rather than their intellect.

§3.8 DEVELOPMENT OF CROSS-EXAMINATION TECHNIQUES

The above list is by no means exhaustive, but it demonstrates the dramatic changes that have taken place in litigation and, consequently, cross-examination. When one recognizes the nature of the testimony by which such cases are presented and defended, as well as the exhibits offered in support of such testimony, the differences are dramatic.

Understanding the problem is the first step to solving it. In cross-examination, the first step to the solution is to develop techniques that realize that less and simpler is more. The subject matter today is too complex and diverse and dependent on opinions rather than facts which are part of the common experience of judges and juries.

It is for the trial lawyer to feed the emerging causes of action, the complex issues and the wide diversity of opinions into the funnel to emerge in a form that can be absorbed by a modern jury given its current traits and foibles.

Cross-examination is the most effective method to accomplish that task as that is the moment when the judge's or jury's attention is most attracted.

The Rules of Evidence 4

§4.1 ENACTMENT OF FEDERAL RULES OF EVIDENCE

Keeping pace with the changes in causes of action or, more likely, being responsible for the evolution of such causes and the method by which they are established or defeated, are material changes in the Rules of Evidence.

Historically, the Rules evolved generally by sequential interpretations, which were subsequently followed in other jurisdictions. However, in 1975, the comprehensive Federal Rules of Evidence made its appearance; and, the course of litigation changed forever. It was not only that the Rules provided the latitude by which new causes of action could be developed but they also generated new kinds of witnesses testifying about matters and possessing qualifications that previously would not have been recognized or summarily excluded.

Given the new Rules, it was the rare case which would exclude expert testimony, even going so far as to permit opinions by experts as to the reliability of other witnesses in the case. The subject matter of such testimony now has virtually no limitation. The result required development of universal cross-examination techniques which could be customized on a case-by-case basis since the fact patterns and issues of each particular case that a lawyer might be required to face would not permit the wheel to be reinvented in each case.

The Federal Rules of Evidence codified much of the evolution which had taken place over a period of years prior to their promulgation. In numerous other instances, they blazed new trails both as to admissible testimony and acceptable witnesses.

Subsequent to their enactment, given their comprehensive nature and the forces of inertia, many local jurisdictions simply fell into line and adopted their version of specific Federal Rules, if not the Rule itself. While the drift toward the Federal Rules may not yet be complete, it continues on a regular basis. It is becoming increasingly rare that a state court will make an evidentiary ruling which is diametrically opposed to the principles upon which the Federal Rules are based.

§4.2 INCLUSIONARY NATURE OF RULES

Previously, the Rules of Evidence were of an exclusionary nature. The focus of the Rules was generally to state that which could not be admitted into evidence and questions and areas which could not be pursued on cross-examination. Anything which survived a specifically stated exclusion was admitted.

The Federal Rules and their progeny are basically inclusionary in nature in that they take great pains to specify what can be admitted and what can be pursued upon cross-examination.

The changes are both specific and generic. A review of the changes graphically demonstrates the ways in which cross-examination has also had to evolve lest it become only an inconvenient and annoying sideshow that has little effect on the outcome of a case.

§4.3 RELEVANCE

Overall, relevance was the litmus test that defined the size of the tip of the iceberg that constituted admissible testimony in a trial. Decisions concerning relevance and evidence which fit under that umbrella usually evolved around common usage and understanding.

> Webster's New Universal Unabridged Dictionary (1979), Second Edition, defines "relevant" as:

> Bearing upon or relating to the matter at hand; to the point; pertinent; applicable; as, the testimony is relevant to the case; the argument is relevant to the question: . . .

The Federal Rules of Evidence, Moore's Federal Practice, Second Edition, 1992, **Rule 401**, defines relevant evidence as:

> Relevant evidence means evidence having any tendency to make the existence of any fact that is of consequence to the determination of the action more probable or less probable than it would be without the evidence.

The two definitions are hardly on speaking terms with each other, let alone acquainted. Previously, relevance was determined by the nexus to the issue which was required to be somewhat, although imperfectly, direct. The current Rule is open ended and goes to proving or disproving a given fact or circumstance by the law of probability, itself an elusive concept.

The significance to cross-examination is that questions may be put from a greater variety of possibilities than heretofore existed.

Thus, while possession of a fishing license would historically never have been admitted in an effort to establish that a person was fishing upon a particular day, today cross-examination as to the existence of such license could make it more probable that the person was fishing on the day in question.

A generation ago, relevant evidence was virtually never excluded. Through case law development, some exclusion was possible if it were believed that the probative value of the proffered evidence was overshadowed by its inflammatory nature. Today, relevant evidence can be excluded if it is believed to create unfair prejudice, confusion, is misleading or deemed a waste of time.

This creates particular problems for cross-examination. All cross-examination is designed to create prejudice, while unfair is a subjective concept. The prejudice is either by undermining testimony which has been given or substituting in its place information which is adverse to the interests of the opposing party.

While misleading is never to be advocated, confusion is another matter. Converting certitude into uncertainty upon cross-examination and clarity into lack of clarity is a valid effort. The foregoing can generate confusion; and, where one party has the burden of proof either by civil or criminal standards, confusion serves to defeat that burden of proof. It is an effort owed to a client.

Ironically, it is difficult for a court which is not privy to all of the aspects of a case to determine if an area of examination is a waste of time. Relevancy is a concept that applies not only to the presentation of a case in chief but also to cross-examination and wider latitude should be accorded in that area. While it is true that unduly restricting cross-examination is a valid ground for appeal, nevertheless, a cross-examiner faces the possibility of a restriction based upon the criteria for permissibly excluding relevant evidence.

§4.4 EXPERT WITNESSES

While the subject of expert witnesses is dealt with more fully subsequently, a brief reference is appropriate at the outset. Formerly, experts to be accepted as such had to possess certain clearly defined qualifications and offer testimony upon a subject that was similarly identified in a limited number of areas as applicable to be rendered by experts, thus permitting an opinion to be offered.

Today, while there is still a requirement of skill, knowledge, training, experience or education, those attributes are required only in the conjunctive. Many of the foregoing give no assurance of expertise, particularly when the requirements are not cumulative.

Rule 702 of the Federal Rules of Evidence requires that to be qualified as an expert only requires the possession of some scientific, technical or "specialized knowledge;" the latter phrase wholly incapable of precise definition. Clearly, cross-examination of such "experts" requires a universal approach requiring only modifications to the instant case.

This is particularly true since once accepted as an expert, such expert can, pursuant to **Rule 704**, render an opinion as to the ultimate issue. Formerly, the offering of such opinion was regarded as invading the province of the jury or the finder of fact. Today, the opposite is true and to make such an objection is to seriously date oneself.

§4.5 IMPEACHMENT OF WITNESSES

One modification of the Rules of Evidence that favors the cross-examiner is the expanded ability to impeach one's own witness. The old maxim was that a party was bound by its own witnesses and such witnesses could not be impeached unless they first demonstrated hostility, which an intelligent witness could avoid.

Consequently, it was only after a witness called by a party was determined to be hostile that the questioning could then proceed by way of leading questions or, in other words, cross-examination. A change brought about by the current Rules is to institutionalize a cross-examining technique to be used frequently.

Rule 607 of the Federal Rules provides that a party can be impeached by any party calling that witness and removes the necessity of demonstrating that witness' hostility. It need only be shown that the witness is somehow identified with the opposition, a circumstance which is usually self-evident. In such an event, the questioner can proceed directly to cross-examination without first eliciting hostility.

This has led to the device on cross-examination of calling the opposing party or his witnesses to the stand on the direct case and cross-examining them directly.

The benefits are virtually unlimited. Initially, it permits a party to present its case making use of damaging admissions or impressions extracted from the opposing side. This is then followed by exploiting the negative impressions or damaging admissions when subsequently presenting your witnesses. The reaction of the jury and their initial view of the case can be dramatically altered in your favor.

Secondly, it materially weakens the opponent's case in that he does not get to present his position in the orderly and coherent manner that was carefully prepared.

When this is coupled with the modern treatment of the prior inconsistent statements, the method of establishing a case by cross-examination can produce dramatic results.

§4.6 PRIOR INCONSISTENT STATEMENTS

Previously, a prior inconsistent statement, the staple of cross-examination, could only serve to minimize or negate testimony rendered by an opposing party or one of its witnesses. However, in modern practice, pursuant to **Rule 801**, *et seq.*, a prior inconsistent statement can now serve to affirmatively establish the factual content of such statement.

It is now possible to call an opposing party or any of his witnesses on your direct case. Proceeding by way of cross-examination, you may then inquire and bring out the position or statement which is favorable to your side, which, if he acknowledges, substantially advances the meeting of your evidentiary burden. Failing the witnesses' cooperation, the witness can be confronted with the prior inconsistent statement and, that being admitted, can serve to establish the point that you are making while damaging the credibility of the witness and, ultimately, the opposition's position.

It should not be lost that proceeding in this manner also serves to disorient and inhibit the presentation of your opponent.

§4.7 HEARSAY

Hearsay was previously excluded from being offered in evidence subject only to a few mild exceptions to that rule. Generally, if the hearsay utterance could be made part of the *res gestae*, i.e., incorporated within and part of the actual events, it was admissible.

The classic basis for excluding hearsay is that the person making the original statement was not present and, therefore, not available for cross-examination. Under the circumstances, the truth or falsity of the statement could not be fairly tested.

Even when admitted into evidence, the statement could not be offered for the truth or falsity of its contents but, rather, only to establish that the statement was made. Today, the statement may be given qualitative weight since it can serve to establish probability pursuant to **Rule 401** or the exceptions enumerated in **Rule 803.**

Rule 803 of the Federal Rules of Evidence sets forth an almost unending list of exceptions. *Res gestae* is retained as an exception although more elegantly stated as a "present sense impression" or "excited utterance." The concept is expanded when, without necessarily being contemporaneous with an event, it evidences an "existing mental, emotional or physical condition."

The Rule goes on to create exceptions for statements made for the purpose of medical diagnosis or treatment on the assumption that people do not lie to doctors from whom they need medical assistance. Of course, the concept is invalid in cases where there is an existing or contemplated lawsuit in which exaggerated symptoms and conditions may be the rule, rather than the exception.

Recorded recollections are now acceptable but under much more lenient circumstances than previously was the case when a witness had to first lay the foundation by stating a particular failure of recollection, coupled with a recollection that at some time in the past his knowledge found its way into print or tape.

The absence of an entry also is admitted under the hearsay exception even though the absence of an entry can have a dual meaning. On one hand, the absence of an entry can serve to establish that an event, transaction or conversation did not actually take place in the face of numerous other entries which record similar events although that requirement is not clearly stated. Conversely, the absence of an entry of the kind routinely made could just as easily establish that the event did occur but was wrongfully withheld or obliterated by the witness or party. While the exception is dubious, it creates serious difficulties for a cross-examiner which may be compensated by other advantages depending on the skill of the cross-examiner for accurate interpretation.

Learned treatises and general history are also now recognized as exceptions to the hearsay rule, although how to rebut a general history is a significant problem on cross-examination. A general history can be composed of myths, gossip, legend or perpetuated error, thereby contributing little or nothing to the ascertainment of truth.

Two of the latter subdivisions of the Rule insure that all but the most flagrant hearsay will somehow find its way into evidence and pose a problem upon cross-examination. Thus, hearsay which is "more probative than any other evidence that can be procured by reasonable efforts" is an exception. Even though hearsay, it suggests that, if there is a failure to secure more trustworthy evidence, hearsay can be introduced to fill the gap on some undefined showing that reasonable efforts have failed to secure such other trustworthy evidence. This does not eliminate the problem that such evidence suffers by not being directly available to attack upon cross-examination. Nor does it address the former conclusion. If more trustworthy evidence was not produced, it did not exist and the standard for divining truth would not be lowered.

For good measure, anything which does not fit under the stated exceptions can still be introduced into evidence based upon "the general purposes and interests of justice." This catchall, incapable of definition on any structured basis, makes the admission of hearsay an *ad hoc* adventure on a trial by trial basis.

The Rules were not unmindful of some of the problems that were being created with regard to the protection afforded by cross-examination as **Rule 806** so indicates. In substance, the Rule specifically authorizes an attack upon the credibility of the declarant of a hearsay statement. However, since the credibility of any witness was always subject to attack, whether testifying to hearsay or otherwise, the Rule does not seem to deal with the special problems created by the expansion of the hearsay exceptions.

By analogy, while the opponent has been permitted to progress in its weaponry, the cross-examiner is still restricted to the use of the bow and arrow, which he always had available.

The hearsay exceptions also permit hearsay within hearsay. Now it is possible to be presented with testimony by witness "X" stating that witness "Y" heard "Z" make such statement. It is another example where cross-examination must focus upon killing the messenger since the message is virtually indecipherable.

The Rules of Evidence were previously a coat of armor which kept the playing field of the trial within narrow and defined limits. In such a circumstance, the introduction into evidence was restricted while cross-examination was accorded wider latitude recognizing the disabilities that the cross-examiner possessed. Today, the situation is precisely the reverse. The cross-examiner in many ways must remain in place while the evidence against which he must do battle has been granted ever widening latitude.

The above is not to suggest that the recitation of changes is complete but, rather, to show that the most significant areas affecting cross-examination have been materially changed. There are new causes of action with broad latitude in the presentation of such matters of which a cross-examiner must be aware and deal with accordingly.

§4.8 DISCOVERY

Perhaps the contemplated antidote to the expanding frontiers of admissible evidence is the unlimited expansion of discovery.

Second to instinct and experience, discovery is the greatest single weapon in the cross-examiner's arsenal. In civil matters, discovery is virtually unlimited; and, therefore, the search for grist for the cross-examiner's mill knows no bounds. It is here where all kinds of contradictory evidence can be uncovered, as well as pinning parties and witnesses down to stories from which they have great difficulty in escaping in the course of a trial. Questions can be asked simply because they can be conjured and documents can be requested simply because they exist. Patterns can be established which can be crystallized upon cross-examination during trial with significant effect.

Although not as expansive as in civil cases, discovery in criminal cases has also been greatly enlarged. The information that can be sought by a Bill of Particulars has been accorded greater flexibility. Statements of witnesses in state court under *People v. Rosario* and its progeny, and in the Federal Courts pursuant to the Jencks Act, **Rule 3500**, are now available. Of course, the time at which such material is obtained is critical; and, it is yet a development of the future where a prosecutor is obliged to reveal such statements prior to the time that a witness concludes his testimony during trial.

It is only within the current generation of trial lawyers that the furnishing of exculpatory evidence defined in *U.S. v. Brady* has become the rule which is vigorously enforced, such material being any evidence in the possession of the prosecutor indicating a lack of culpability on the part of the accused. A plethora of hearings have sprung up which include not only the suppression of evidence but also a required revelation by the prosecutor of any intention to use any statements deemed to be admissions or confessions, prior criminal records and even identification of the accused. Tape recordings, both audio and visual, must similarly be furnished, together with transcripts, in advance and fair opportunity given to challenge them. However, there is not yet examination before trial except that which can be extracted in preliminary hearings on closely restricted issues.

It is not an unblemished advantage in that the defense must participate in reciprocal discovery and, therefore, admit to the prosecution certain insights as to the defense. However, reciprocal discovery is a more recent phenomenon and has not fully caught up to the disclosures required of the prosecution prior to trial.

As with all discovery, the better financed party has a built in advantage in extracting the full benefit of discovery, both in terms of obtaining the information in the first instance and exploiting the leads which may be developed from such disclosure. The advantages of discovery may well depend on the size of a party's pocketbook.

As with cross-examination itself, the benefits to be derived from discovery vary from lawyer to lawyer. The most damaging facts can be presented dully or lacking in significance, while others can truly make a mountain out of a mole hill.

Discovery can provide the tools for effective cross-examination. The craft with which those tools are used will vary from lawyer to lawyer.

Preparation 5

The essentials to a good cross-examination are preparation and controlling the witness so that the preparation bears fruit. Preparation includes marshalling the facts, evaluating the case, organizing the examination into themes and conducting such investigation as may uncover facts or documents with which to confront the witness to damage his testimony. These are the technical aspects of preparation.

§5.1 LIFE PREPARATION

Overall preparation begins the moment you decide to become a lawyer and specialize in trial work. Almost everything you see and hear sharpens your instinct and develops your senses to succeed in the instantaneous give and take of the courtroom and the impressions needed to be created there. Should a problem arise, there is no one with whom you can confer nor is there any time to conduct research. Reactions must be instantaneous and instinctive. Your instincts will develop on a day-to-day, year-by-year, basis. To that extent, a trial lawyer is analogous to a cartoonist whose forte is caricatures. A few squiggly lines or an accentuated trait identifies the entire subject in the manner the cartoonist wishes.

Without any particular case in mind, trial lawyers must notice how people react to different situations. What are the telltale gestures that suggest evasiveness, whether in or out of the courtroom? To what temptations do most people respond, especially the most righteous?

What approach has been the most effective in confrontations, such as debates, business negotiations or routine arguments?

The trial lawyer must always be sensitive, not only to what he is saying, but also to the effect that he is having on the person to whom he is speaking. It is often recognized that litigators can be nasty and abrasive while at other times utterly charming. This is simply because in different circumstances the trial lawyer is seeking to achieve a different effect and is conscious of that effect.

Trial lawyers are, by necessity, calculating and instinctively manipulative, but in the best sense. A trial lawyer who does not plead guilty to that charge is simply not being candid. A trial lawyer in large measure takes responsibility for the life and often the fortune and the future of every client whom he represents. He may get ten seconds to one minute to make the most critical of decisions which can affect that client for the rest of his life. It is unrealistic to expect that any caring lawyer undertaking such a responsibility would take anything for granted, such as uttering a statement without knowing what effect it would have on the listener or failing to recognize the signs that a critical adverse witness might be lying or trying to hide something which may have the most dire consequences for his client. Under such circumstances, a trial lawyer cannot shy away from manipulation and calculation if in the interest of a client it would serve to break through smugness, righteousness or deceit.

The necessary instincts are developed over a lifetime. Something is gained every day by a lawyer who keeps his eyes peeled for such insights and by being a constant observer of the passing parade. It is often a case that if something works well in general conversation or debate we find that it works well in the courtroom.

There is a program on television called "The Family Feud." Without question, the producers of that show could, with training, become great cross-examiners. The essence of the show is that they ask one hundred people a certain question and assess a point for each response. The Master of Ceremonies asks the questions of the contestants and calls for the top five responses that were received from the hundred persons questioned. A typical example would be that a group of contestants would be asked that, of one hundred people questioned, what were those one hundred people most likely to forget when leaving the house in the morning? The top five answers, please.

If fifty-three persons questioned said keys, the contestant who said keys would get fifty-three points. If the top five answers were guessed by the contestants they would win the game.

The show has been on the air for over 15 years; and, in the course of that time, thousands and thousands of questions have been propounded and thousands of people have been asked for their responses. Quite clearly, if the producers of that show were to ask any of the questions that they previously asked and tested, they would have an excellent idea of what the response would be. They would have a tremendous advantage over the millions of people who had never engaged in such exercise, who would have little or no idea of the responses. Witness the number of contestants who fail to guess the correct answer on the show.

Trial lawyers do not have the luxury of conducting endless surveys and questions of people in order to determine responses and reactions. They have to conduct their own surveys by analogizing and reconciling responses and reactions from a variety of events over extensive periods of time. The trial lawyer must understand the foibles of human nature and be an absolute pack rat in filing away bits and pieces of significance.

If a lawyer fails to engage in this kind of preparation, then the maximum will not be extracted from whatever information is marshalled and whatever contrary facts are developed for trial. Technical preparation may tell you that a piece of information in your possession is important. A lifetime of experiences will tell you the significance of that information, when and how to use it or forget it and how to enhance its effect to the best advantage of your client.

§5.2 WHAT'S THE PUNCH LINE

To be successful in pursuing cross-examination, a lawyer must know what is acceptable or unacceptable to most people. To pursue a line of questioning that develops facts which are technically accurate but unacceptable to a jury is counterproductive. In other words, you have to have a sense of what people are thinking, what it is that they really care about and what are their likely reactions when confronted in different ways. The best technical presentation in which every separate element is unimpeachable but which leads to a draconian result will be rejected.

The point was well demonstrated when New York promulgated penal laws which provided long-term mandatory jail sentences for narcotics possession. When that became the appropriate sentence for an eighteen-year old first offender for possession of a small amount of marijuana, juries simply would not convict. The public rejection of the result led to a *de facto* rewriting of the law in which a first offender of narcotics possession is barely prosecuted or almost automatically receives probation.

A state may have the death penalty; but, if a jury feels, after a perfectly presented case, that death is too harsh a penalty given the facts of that case, they will not convict on the count for which the death penalty can be imposed.

The same is true of cross-examination. If an excellent cross, perfectly and even interestingly executed leads to an unacceptable position, it will be ignored.

§5.3 ENVIRONMENT

When trying a case outside of New York City, I make it a point to arrive at the location of the trial a day or two early. The first day is to scour all the local news. I want to know what the people from whom the jury will be selected are reading that morning at breakfast, what the local columnists are writing about, what the issues are that seem to concern that locality and what positions are being taken and discussed. That, plus walking in the streets and eating at local establishments for a day or two, begins to give a sense or feel for the attitudes of the local citizens from which a jury will be drawn.

Another device is to identify all of the local officials elected in the last election and the platforms on which they ran. In addition, it serves to adjust my tempo to the tempo of the location. In a trial in New Orleans, Louisiana, while other lawyers were holding news conferences on the steps of the courthouse, I sat in my rented car parked in front of the courthouse with the window open listening to Dixieland music, eating a sandwich.

Anticipating that the initial reaction of the jury and the various witnesses is to regard me as a smart aleck lawyer from the "big city," I make a point early on, even in the *voir dire* of the jury, to make remarks indicating familiarity with matters of local interest with which

I became familiar. Whether because the jury is flattered that I took the time and trouble to familiarize myself with local affairs or because they believe that I had a genuine interest, I never knew. I only know that within a day or two after the trial started I was just another lawyer.

§5.4 THE HUMAN FACTOR

The studying of human nature and developing an accurate eye is invaluable in cross-examination.

A number of years ago I tried a case in Duluth, Minnesota. The essential facts were that a New York executive had contacted a Minnesota corporation that produced mylar and offered to effect sales for that company in exchange for a ten percent commission. The Minnesota company agreed. The New York executive made two phone calls to a previous contact and arranged for $6 million in sales which occurred over the next two years.

The Minnesota company paid the executive $50,000 while refusing to pay the balance of $550,000 claiming that $50,000 was enough for two phone calls. Upon its persistent refusal to pay, my client commenced suit in the United States District Court for the Southern District of New York.

The Minnesota company retained prestigious New York counsel who immediately made a motion for a change of venue to Duluth, Minnesota. The court granted the motion upon the grounds that most of the witnesses and records were in that location. As we left the New York courtroom, my opponent remarked to me that I could consider the case dead. When I asked him why, he responded that two "New York people" going out to Minnesota to appear before a jury where the average annual income was then $16,000 claiming that my client should get $600,000 simply for making two phone calls which took him less than half a day were on a fool's errand. He chuckled when he envisioned the effort by two New York City residents to get such money from a Minnesota jury on those grounds.

The case was placed on the trial calendar in Duluth on 48-hours notice. To make matters more interesting, we got a phone call to appear for trial while Minnesota was experiencing the worst blizzard in 42 years with a wind chill factor which caused the temperature to be -53°. I was never sure whether or not the call was deliberately made because of those conditions since, when I suggested that the case should be postponed awhile to permit the weather conditions to improve, my request was denied. For years, I referred to the Minnesota Federal District Court's "Local Blizzard Rule" for out-of-state litigants.

We made it to Minnesota only to learn that my opponent was the President of the Minnesota State Bar Association and the sitting judge was his former law partner. If I had not thought so before, I was now beginning to believe that my New York opponent's evaluation of the case was prophetic.

The only solution seemed to be to correctly gauge the character of the location that we were in and present a very simple case directly to that perceived character. Certainly, no effective presentation could be made about my client's efforts or that $50,000 was not an appreciable amount of money.

Duluth, Minnesota has a strong Scandinavian and Germanic culture and very deep-seated traditional values. The trial also had to be kept extremely simple since everybody was consumed with the weather and the damage that it was causing, possibly to their homes, while they were sitting in the courtroom.

The defendant, the president of the Minnesota corporation, testified that he had, in fact, had a conversation with my client in which he did indicate that he would be prepared to pay ten percent for any sales which the plaintiff directed to his company. Two short letters seemed to confirm some sort of understanding. However, he indicated that he had no idea of the magnitude of the sales that would be generated. Consequently, he felt somewhat bamboozled by the fact that he believed that my client knew of his ability to effect those sales easily prior to the time that he entered into the commission discussion with the plaintiff. The witness stated that it should have been disclosed. The defendant concluded by stating that, under the circumstances, he felt that $50,000 was enough payment for two phone calls.

The cross-examination was extremely short. The defendant was asked:

Q: Did you ever lead my client to believe that you would pay the plaintiff ten percent for any sales which he effected?
A: Yes.
Q: Did you really care how he got you those sales as long as he got them legally?

A: Well, I . . .
Q: The truth now.
A: I never thought about it.
Q: The truth now.
A: I guess not.
Q: Did you pay him ten percent for the sales which he effected?
A: No.
Q: In other words, you did not keep your word?
A: Well, I—
Q: Did you honor your commitment to pay ten percent on the sales which he effected?
A: But, I—
Q: Its a matter of honor and fairness. Did you honor your commitment?
A: Well, the way you put it, I didn't pay ten percent.
Q: You thought the plaintiff made enough by getting $50,000 for two phone calls?
A: Yes.
Q: Did you place any limits on the amount of profit that you would make as being enough?
A: That's silly.
Q: In other words, as much as you could make that would be perfectly acceptable and proper, would it not?
A: That's why we're in business.
Q: But that doesn't apply to my client, isn't that what you're saying? No further questions.

The stature of my opponent, a judge who turned out to be scrupulously fair, location and out-of-town plaintiffs and lawyers notwithstanding, the jury deliberated less than two hours and came back and gave the plaintiff every penny that he requested plus interest.

Parenthetically, it is interesting to note that, when the defendant appealed to the Eighth Circuit Court of Appeals, the lead point in his brief was that I inflamed the passions of the jury by focusing on nothing but fairness and honor in my entire presentation, particularly in cross-examination. Given the fact that it was a commission case about a common product, I took that as a high compliment. I also thought I earned high marks from the jury simply by making it to the courthouse every day without making a big deal about the weather, especially coming from New York.

The point is that the preparation for that cross-examination, as well as the entire trial, took place over a lifetime to that point. I could have argued my client's outstanding credentials and that two phone calls from him was worth more than a year long effort of a farmer, which would have been ruinous. I could have attempted to wrap him in some sort of virtue and try to make some economic argument regarding value of services which, again, would have been ineffective. But, in addressing the character of the people in that location, I apparently hit a chord to which the jury responded.

§5.5 ACCEPTING THE PENALTY

Unfortunately, the trial lawyer falls victim to this life-long preparation. Since he constantly focuses on the response to his every comment, it unfortunately carries over into everyday life. All too often a trial lawyer is reminded by his friends and family, "you're not talking to a jury now" or "save it for the courtroom." To anyone less than a friend, he is simply a manipulative control freak. It is just another price to pay for choosing to practice in that area of the legal profession and seeking to be proficient at cross-examination.

However, the ability to instantaneously marshal facts and spit them out in some sort of coherent statement leads many people to conclude that every word out of a trial lawyer's mouth is either posturing or contrived. It is neither. The all-consuming mistress of the courtroom and the ever-present responsibility for the well being of another causes the professional and private person to blend so that a single instinct is developed. Unfortunately, when you teach a dog a trick, the dog doesn't only do it when you want it to. Its just part of the preparation.

§5.6 THE PARTICULAR CASE

Having considered the non-specific preparation which provides the crucible in which the trial lawyer is developed, the preparation for a particular case is no less three dimensional.

Obviously, at the outset of a particular case, it is necessary to review the pleadings and documents as well as speak to all of the witnesses to whom there is access. It is essential to get a feel for what story emerges or what impression is conveyed before any refinements are made or the process of reorganization begins. It may well be that that first impression is the best possible approach to take and the tactics of the trial are simply to deflect and repel all efforts to tamper with it. Always to be remembered is that a first impression is all that a jury gets since they only hear it once.

§5.7 CROSS-EXAMINATION AND SUMMATION

The next step before proceeding is to attempt to write and fashion the summation. When all the evidence is in, witnesses questioned and the charge to the jury delivered by the judge, what would you like to be able to say as the last word.

Backtracking over the documents and information at your disposal, it is necessary to recognize the gaps in your case that detract from the ability to give such a summation. Aside from obtaining additional documents or witnesses which might not be available, the primary method of filling in the blanks and obtaining the missing pieces is through cross-examination. Thus begins the preparation for cross-examination within the context of a particular case.

§5.8 SEQUENCE

It is clear that the first cousin to establishing a context and theme in which the questions are asked is to prepare a sequence in which the questions or areas of questions will be asked. It is such sequence that will heighten the effect of the points that are sought to be made or dilute a point needed to be explained away. The object of the cross-examination is to create a perspective.

Perspective is the means by which most things are measured and from which reactions are obtained. A baseball is large next to a marble; but, in relation to a basketball, the baseball itself would be regarded as small. Thus, if the object were to create in the minds of a jury that a baseball is large, the preceding questions should concern themselves with marbles or, conversely, if the object was to suggest that a baseball is small ask about basketballs.

Earlier in this chapter, I refered to a case in Duluth, Minnesota in which a company paid $50,000 to a plaintiff who had made two phone calls. Measured against the average annual income of the jury, it was a vast sum. Measured against the total potential commission of $600,000, it took on much more modest attributes and, compared to the profits made by the company on the sales generated by the plaintiff, it was an absolutely paltry sum paid by someone who appeared to be breaking his word to avoid payment of a just obligation.

§5.9 INTERNAL AND EXTERNAL LOGIC

The story line, context and sequence all have to have an external and internal logic. External logic exists by relating the testimony to all known surrounding circumstances. Questions designed to elicit answers confirming the existence of a spaceship in the year 1910 would demonstrate the witness' lack of credibility. Given the external circumstances that exist in the year 1993, such a proposition could easily be accepted as credible.

Internal logic is tested within the cross-examination itself. To put it simplistically, picnics do not take place on rainy days; and, testimony involving sunbathing in a blizzard would not be internally logical.

A likely application of that principal surfaces on cross-examination wherein a person whose testimony established that he had a history of being intelligent, thorough and generally in control of his circumstances were to suddenly testify that a certain act was the result of stupidity, inadvertence or lack of understanding. Cross-examination would immediately seize upon the discrepancy or lack of internal logic to show that the excuse given is without merit. Internal and external logic is necessary not only as a basis of attacking the opponent's testimony but also to advance the story line's being advanced in cross-examination.

§5.10 ESTABLISHMENT OF OBJECTIVES

It is vital to assess what you are able to get on cross-examination. Equally important is to determine what you need on cross-examination. Do not try to get more than you need and settle for what you realistically can get. It is in overreaching for more than you need that a cross-examiner is most likely to fail. Since it is reaching for something that is not essential, it is an improvident risk to try.

If all you need is a "maybe," don't fight to try to get the witness to say "no." Quite often, an effective cross-examination need only move a witness slightly from a hard position to an equivocation; and, the summation can exploit the distinction.

It is not always necessary to get an expert to admit that he is wrong, a herculean task. Rather, it would suffice merely to have the expert agree that what appears to be a fact is, in whole or in part, an assumption or that further study needs to be done. Were that to occur, it then becomes possible on summation to substitute other assumptions or what additional study might conclude, thereby invalidating the testimony of the witness altogether. Getting a witness to admit that, while his opinion remains unchanged, other qualified people may have conflicting opinions may be enough. Of course, getting the witness to agree with you that what you suggest is "possible" is a time-honored example of this approach.

Persons familiar with professional football have often heard victorious quarterbacks in post-game interviews make the statement, "I took what they gave me." The reference is that, if the defense was playing deep, the quarterback marched his team up the field with short passes. Conversely, if the defense was playing close in, then long passes became the order of the day. So, too, it is the case with the cross-examiner since, in many cases, the cross-examiner has to take what the other side gives him and exploit it.

§5.11 COUNTERPOINT

If a witness is arrogant and stubborn, cross-examination should seek to bring out and enhance the arrogance and stubbornness while conducting the examination in a humbler manner to highlight the arrogance. If a witness gives a broad picture with little detail, then cross-examination would try to bring out all of the details which were possibly ignored or trivialized. If the testimony of the witness is laced with detail, cross-examination should seek to demonstrate an ignorance of the big picture or hypertechnicality without sensitivity.

As a young prosecutor, I quickly learned what all experienced advocates come to know. There is no case that you cannot argue both sides nor is there any position which a witness takes that cannot be characterized in equally dual fashion. Thus, if a witness testified in logical sequences complete with credible detail in a fluent and coherent manner, it would be argued to the jury that such testimony and the manner in which it was given is a clear indication of truth, since "truth has its own ring and you can see from the clarity of the testimony that this witness is telling the truth."

Conversely, another witness gets on the stand and stumbles, has serious gaps in recollection and generally gives faltering testimony. About such a witness it was often argued that the witness was obviously truthful since, if the witness were lying, he could have made a better job of it.

The opposition argues that the straight story is "too good" and, thus, a lie, while the garbled testimony is false as evidenced by the fact that the witness could not keep the story straight.

Cross-examination can achieve the same effect.

§5.12 WORDING OF QUESTIONS

The wording of questions on cross-examination is critical. After a few trials, it becomes apparent that witnesses answer the adjective that is included in the question or the characterization or implication of the question rather than the question itself. Thus, if someone would be asked whether John Doe was a major supplier of drugs, the witness will respond to the word major and answer "no" if the amount of drugs sold was something less than the witness considered major.

This phenomenon was recently seen in the last presidential election. Opponents of President Clinton circulated stories that he was a major anti-war organizer while a student in England. The responses were rapidly forthcoming aimed at refuting the adjective "major" or the implication of high-powered revolutionary conduct. Later, it was brought out that, on an occasion, the candidate had actually participated in a student anti-war demonstration and possibly might have even played some part, however nominal, in organizing that isolated event. The media and the public seized upon the fact of anti-war effort, quickly forgot that the initial reaction was to deny the word "major" and concluded that there had been a lack of candor. Would there have been any reaction to an initial story about an isolated minor student rally?

This is what happens in the courtroom every day on cross-examination. Ask the question, and the witness will almost invariably respond to either the adjective or the characterization contained in the question; and then, subsequently, when confronted with the actual fact which has a different objective weight, the witness appears either to have lied or to have been less than candid. It was not a valid exercise in the search for truth as pertains to President Clinton; but, as the example demonstrated, it works and, thus, has found its place in often repeated cross-examination techniques.

The choice of words not only permits the cross-examiner to control the witness but generates occasions which completely turn a trial around. A number of years ago I defended a public figure against charges of tax evasion and, as part of the defense, produced several character witnesses. I was informed that one of the character witnesses who had agreed to appear for the defendant was the real life hero of the book "A Bell for Adano." Being interested in keeping the jury awake and providing interesting aspects wherever possible, I wanted to find a way to bring this to the jury's attention although it was not completely appropriate. I realized at the moment that I got into the subject the prosecutor would object and the matter would be left hanging. I, therefore, attempted to fashion a single question which would incorporate everything that I wanted to ask and convey to the jury the background of this exemplary individual and the humaneness of the achievement of this character witness.

Shortly after the witness identified himself, I asked him the single question:

> Are you the military commander about whom John Hersey wrote a Pulitzer prize winning novel from which a movie was made concerning your exploits with the Bell of Adano?

Having built everything into a single question I quickly moved on to the substance of the anticipated character testimony after the witness answered "yes."

Apparently, the prosecutor was the only person in the courtroom who had not read "A Bell for Adano" or seen the movie. He jumped to his feet in cross-examination to ask who was the "Belle of Adano." The witness looked at him quizzically and said, "I can tell you what, I can't tell you who.'' The prosecutor, realizing he might have stepped into murky waters, quickly dropped the subject.

However, he had committed the greatest fear of all cross-examiners, which is to open the door to subject matter which might otherwise be inadmissible. I, of course, took advantage of the situation and asked the witness if he would tell us ''what'' was the ''bell of Adano.'' There, in the courtroom in the midst of a tax evasion trial, the witness then told the story of the bell.

He told how, having been appointed military commander of the town of Adano shortly after the Allied victory in World War II, he approached the elders of the town. In an attempt to gain support and foster goodwill for the American occupation, he asked the elders what their town needed most, anticipating that they would answer either food or shelter or some basic need of that order. Instead, he was told that the thing that was needed most was their church bell which had been taken away by the Germans during their occupation.

The witness continued and told how, ''with God's help,'' he scoured Europe and found where the church bell had been taken and, moving heaven and earth and ''with God's help,'' had it brought back to the town. In a voice that no movie could duplicate or book really recreate, he told how he waited to install the bell during the night when the entire town was asleep. The following morning as the town awoke and began the day, the church bell pealed. The witness described how the people in the street stood transfixed and tears began to run down their cheeks. He described the scene of people running from their homes to the church and the tears and elation that followed.

Neither the judge nor prosecutor dared to interrupt that story and, before the witness was finished, the jury itself was in tears.

After such an experience, a conviction was out of the question. The jury returned within two hours with a verdict of acquittal. It all turned on a word.

§5.13 KNOW THE DOCUMENTS

This is not to suggest that details are not overwhelmingly important in preparation for cross-examination. The only point here is that details follow, rather than precede, theme, sequence, logic and semantics. If done in this sequence, all of the details can be used to the best advantage so that they will be credibly inserted into the entire presentation to serve the purpose desired.

Knowing of and assimilating all the contents of any documents is absolutely vital when it comes to cross-examination. In the first instance, a document may be a deterrent against a runaway witness. A prior inconsistency can tear away the credibility of the entire testimony. Getting the witness to acknowledge its existence can lay the foundation of the introduction into evidence of the document and establish an affirmative point that is vital to your client.

The benefit may be twofold. In federal courts, a prior inconsistent statement may not only destroy a witness' credibility but can also be offered to establish the truth of its contents. It is essential to know every document and their contents.

All known documents and their contents have to be reviewed. First, they lead to other documents or information. It is never known what documents will be important at a particular moment when a witness gives a specific answer. A document thought to be not terribly significant may take on critical meaning in refreshing the recollection of a witness who is suddenly forced to change his testimony in the face of such document. A wholly insignificant document may otherwise serve to catch a witness in error about dates, times or even the general subject matter. Confronting a witness with a document that contradicts testimony even on a minor point is significant.

In the first instance, documents serve as the safeguard that may serve to control the witness and mandate that the witness function within certain confines or go in a certain direction. No witness can say that he did not reach an agreement if there is a document with his signature on it or that he wasn't at a particular location if there is a signed credit card voucher.

The documents in their entirety will also permit the cross-examiner to evaluate if the entire story told by the witness is consistent with the aggregate of the documents. In those instances, when the story told by the witness either conflicts with certain documents or excludes from consideration their existence, then the witness is ripe for successful cross-examination.

An equally compelling reason to know every document and its contents is to insure that, upon cross-examination, you are similarly not confronted with a document of which you are unaware and which can completely negate the effect of your cross-examination.

Equally important in preparation when it comes to documents is the handling of such exhibits. No cross-examination can be effective if there is a fumbling of documents if for no other reason than the witness gets time to think and prepare the answer with regard to a document of which he has now been apprised. Needless to say, the specter of an attorney fumbling with documents does not make a good impression on the jury as to the importance of the point being made or the competence of the lawyer.

While not a devotee of rehearsing precise questions on cross-examination, it is essential to handle every document that is to be used on cross-examination and line them up in the sequence in which it is hoped they will get into evidence. It is also good practice to prepare a second set of documents for your own reference with particular portions of the document highlighted which you intend to stress upon cross-examination. Thus, a glance at the highlighted copy immediately directs your attention to the portion upon which you intend to focus and from which the questions will flow.

In attempting to ascertain the existence of documents, it is not enough to simply ask for them on discovery and take your chances that the person answering the question will make a full disclosure. It is necessary to evaluate the entire person and determine for yourself what sort of documents such a person is liable to generate as a matter of normal routine. Thus, accountants generate not only financial statements but worksheets which themselves should contain certain data. Businessmen generate checkbooks, inventory sheets, order forms and a whole raft of similar documents which make their world go round. The bureaucracy of every day life requires people in virtually all walks of life to generate and maintain records as a normal course.

Were a witness to take the stand and admit to an absence of those records, however modest, the witness' credibility is seriously impaired and a jury concludes that the person is hiding something. Therefore, in cross-examination, it is essential not only to get the documents that somebody provides but also to measure that production against what you believe should exist given the particular situation of the witness or the party upon trial.

§5.14 PREPARE CROSS-EXAMINATION BY AREAS

As indicated before, it is not the best practice to prepare precise questions for cross-examination, even if those questions are aligned as to context, sequence or theme. The difficulty in preparing specific questions is that the lawyer gets married to those questions and almost tries to memorize them. However, witnesses do not cooperate and often change the subject or negate the question before it is asked.

Most experienced trial lawyers prepare areas of cross-examination and develop a good idea of what questions they wish to ask within that area and what documents, if any, they hope to utilize in conducting such questioning. Thus, in a criminal case, a lawyer's notes with regard to questioning the witness about prior convictions will not develop a list of questions but a simple note which states:

> "1. Prior convictions—1987—larceny."

Similarly, in a civil case involving a lease dispute, the note might read:

> "1. Lease—1990—clause 23(a)(1)—non-disturbance."

With regard to such a note in this case, it would be followed by "7" to indicate that you want document number 7 from the stack of documents that you tagged for easy handling as you proceed with the questioning of the witness.

If the areas are aligned by sequence but are self-contained the lawyer can respond immediately should the witness jump sequence and effective cross-examination can continue without loss of momentum. To use a military analogy, a commander may ascertain that the fight is first to consist of rifle fire, followed by mortars, followed by heavy artillery and, ultimately, tanks. However, depending on how the engagement develops, the commander, knowing that he has heavy artillery available, may use that first as it may be the most effective at that moment when a particular weakness of the opponent suddenly becomes apparent.

In other words, know what you have, know the areas that you wish to develop and be prepared to jump right to it if the necessity arises and keep weaving that area into the overall theme.

Investigation 6

§6.1 INTRODUCTION

The cross-examination was superb. The witness demonstrated that he was a liar or, at the very least, exaggerated so much that any credibility was lacking. Brought home was that the witness had repeatedly withheld material facts, both about the incident which was the subject of the trial and about his own background which further demolished his credibility. The witness appeared to be without confidence and was reduced to giving even the poorest of answers in a subdued and mumbling tone. The court had to repeatedly admonish the witness to "keep your voice up," as if a soft-spoken, mumbled response presented something less of a profile to smack up against the wall of disbelief which had been erected.

The cross-examining attorney is admired for his destruction of the witness. It is recognized that he has prepared his interrogation well. However, what is little recognized is how the attorney assembled the raw material from which he crafted the cross-examination.

It would be a mistake to assume that the facts and information were provided by the client or even from witnesses supplied by the client. Clients will invariably filter the information that they provide to their lawyer for a number of reasons, none of which need be deliberate or in bad faith. Clients and witnesses suffer from the malady of all persons, faulty recollection or recall that has been colored by repression or wishful thinking.

While most clients know that they should tell their attorney the complete truth, they are selective to gain their attorney's good opinion in the belief that it will make him fight harder. Clients simply do not understand that a professional trial lawyer's presentation of the case does not depend upon the personal opinion of the attorney regarding the client.

For the sake of the client, the trial lawyer should always assume that the client has related less than the full story.

Equally axiomatic is that the trial lawyer will develop his own belief in the cause if only because he is waging it. The reasons for developing this sincere belief in the justice or worthiness of the cause are personal to the attorney and may rest upon facts or circumstances that are not considered significant by the client.

At times, I have looked favorably on a client's case because the client excused himself repeatedly during the course of preparation to bring food to his mother at a hospital. I remarkably concluded that such a person could not be guilty of the charge which he faced. More often than not, it is the lawyer's own fantasies or the weight that he ascribes to the facts that will lead to his belief in the case. Rarely, if ever, does that feeling come because the client says it is a good case or even that he is innocent. Rather, it comes as the facts are developed in the course of investigation.

Interrogating one's own client is a talent unto itself. The lawyer must form a judgment at some point on how deeply he is prepared to rely on something that the client relates. All too often, lawyers have become sadder but wiser when documents provided by their client turn out to be forged, altered or non-existent, and events turn out to be materially different than as related by the client.

A client may minimize a case or the amount of detail which will go into its composition in order to induce the lawyer to accept a more modest fee or because they do not know more detail. Conversely, a client may maximize and add detail when trying to convince an attorney that the chances of success are so overwhelming that the lawyer should agree to a contingency. Somewhere in between lies the truth. A lawyer must insure finding the precise point at which a perception, which does not offend truth, exists.

The only way to accomplish that is to begin by forming no judgment of what your client says until you have gathered the facts from every possible source other than the client. The process is known as investigation. Preparation is only as good as the investigation which precedes it.

There are no rules as to how to conduct the right investigation for a particular case. They cannot be set out as a checklist of things to do which, having been done, insures that all of the necessary facts that can be marshalled in your client's favor have been gathered. Rather, it depends on the imagination and initiative of the trial attorney to analyze the leads in a particular situation.

§6.2 ANALYSIS OF HABITS AND PERSONALITY

By analyzing a client's habits and personality, there begins to develop a feel as to whether or not such an individual's *modus operandi* can be reconciled with the circumstances of the case, whether plaintiff or defendant, civil or criminal. Does he normally congregate with the kinds of persons or entities that are involved in the case? Are they the kinds of incidents which, with the exception of accident cases, the client is not remote? Simplistically, a couch potato is an unlikely candidate to be guilty of sophisticated insider trading and a person living in Rhode Island is unlikely to hold up a gas station in Texas.

The information supplied by the client should initially be regarded as leads to be confirmed wherever possible and to be expanded upon through further investigation if there is a likelihood that any favorable information can be developed. Investigation requires an infinite number of phone calls and the expenditure of a great deal of shoe leather and, most often, must be done by the attorney himself unless he is fortunate to have the services of a good investigator. The reason for having such a good investigator—which may be the attorney himself—is that, if a material fact is come upon, the investigator will know it when he sees it or have the insight to follow it to the next step, if there is one.

§6.3 TENACITY

Tenacity is another virtue in investigation. It is not often known what will lay at the end of the road of exploration. The only thing that the attorney must know is that he must get to the end of the road. It is a certainty that no one will be completely cooperative, either deliberately, or because they simply do not understand what you are looking for, or because it is not a priority on their agenda and they cannot be bothered. More often than not, the basis for the most effective cross-examinations is created by the kind of investigation in which nothing is taken for granted, every possibility is explored and every source is pushed beyond their convenience level.

One of the most devastating sources of material for cross-examination is to gather every statement or utterance that a prospective witness has made in order to determine if there are any statements previously made which are inconsistent, suffer from critical omissions or even strike a different tone than the anticipated testimony. The uncovering of such statements, or the lack thereof in some instances, is an investigation all of its own.

§6.4 *U.S. V. MILLER AND ADOLF*

The effectiveness of cross-examination preceded by tenacious investigation that accounts for its success is illustrated in the recent trial of Mel Miller and Jay Adolf.

Virtually all of the questions put to the witness upon cross-examination in the portion recounted here were not within the knowledge of either Mr. Miller nor Mr. Adolf so they could not have related them to their attorneys. Similarly, Gerald Lefcourt, Mr. Miller's attorney, could have no basis for knowing the information used in his cross-examination, which was uncovered simply because Lefcourt covered all bases and spread a far reaching net in which to ensnare any statements made by the witness against Messrs. Miller and Adolf, i.e., Aviezer (''Avi'') Cohen.

Mel Miller was the Speaker of the New York State Assembly who, ironically, was also Chairman of the Assembly Codes Committee which handled criminal justice legislation. He was the second highest ranking elected Democratic official in New York State and enjoyed an excellent reputation. Mr. Miller practiced law together with his partner, Jay Adolf, under the firm name of Adolf & Miller.

During the 1980s, the United States Attorney's Office in Brooklyn began an investigation into the activities of Mr. Miller. This investigation dealt with his duties as a member of the Assembly or were in connection with his political life; but this investigation was fruitless. No charges have ever been suggested or leveled with regard to that. Curiously, the government then turned its attention to Mr. Miller's activities as a private attorney.

One of the significant legal matters that had been handled by Messrs. Miller and Adolf was the representation of tenants in the Philip Howard Apartments, an apartment complex in Brooklyn consisting of over six hundred apartments. Miller represented the tenants in the usual vigorous negotiations with the sponsor in order to get the best deal for the tenants in the buying of their apartments if the sponsor was successful in converting the buildings from rental to cooperative or condominium ownership.

During a portion of the period when Miller represented the tenants, the building manager at the Philip Howard Apartments was Aviezer Cohen. Cohen's wife was a real estate agent in Brooklyn and between them they were deeply steeped in the real estate business. Miller met Cohen during the course of his representation of the tenants of the apartment complex.

As in the case of all conversions, the sponsor sought to sell as many apartments as possible which included both vacant and occupied apartments. A sponsor's fondest dream is to sell off all the apartments which he owns and leave the scene with the maximum amount of funds. However, given the size of the Philip Howard complex, the sponsor was left with in excess of 200 apartments over and above the apartments for which existing tenants signed subscription agreements after Messrs. Miller and Adolf hammered out the terms of purchase for them.

Cohen advised a friend, Meyer Rosenbaum, known to be an investor in occupied apartments in the hopes that Rosenbaum would be interested in making a substantial purchase of a number of apartments in the complex. Cohen had arranged to receive commissions to be paid by the sponsor if he could introduce purchasers. Rosenbaum, consistent with his usual business practice, was interested in the situation and inquired of Cohen for the name of the attorney who represented the tenants. It was Rosenbaum's belief that this attorney was already educated in the matter and had obviously earned the respect of the sponsor so that he could save a great deal in legal fees and obtain the most effective representation by not having an attorney who had to learn the entire situation from ground zero.

Cohen approached Mr. Miller and advised him of Rosenbaum's interest in the apartments as well as his interest in retaining the services of Mr. Miller. After discussion, Rosenbaum retained Miller under an arrangement wherein Rosenbaum agreed to pay a certain price for the shares in the cooperative apartments and Mr. Miller's commission would be whatever lesser figure Miller could obtain the shares for.

Rosenbaum had put together an investor group from whom he obtained a commission agreement as a result of his promotional activities. Once all the pieces were in place, the financial arrangements were a byzantine puzzle, albeit legal and not uncommon.

Cohen had negotiated with the sponsor for a commission in the event he produced any purchasers. He arranged with Rosenbaum to share his commission for putting together the investor group and arranged with Miller for a portion of the savings that Miller was able to effect below the price that Rosenbaum had agreed to pay for the apartments.

Miller negotiated with the sponsor; and, after such negotiations, the sponsor agreed to sell 122 apartments of which 90 were occupied and 32 were vacant, for a purchase price in excess of $2 million.

Rosenbaum advised Miller to deal with his partner, Cohen, with regard to the transaction. Cohen at one point designated eight of the 122 apartments for his private investment and invited Miller to participate. Miller agreed in the belief that anything coming from Cohen had been cleared with Rosenbaum; and, as Rosenbaum later acknowledged, the private investment in eight of the available apartments by Miller was perfectly acceptable to him and did not conflict with any understanding which he had with Miller.

The government contacted Cohen in the early part of 1989 and advised him that they were conducting an investigation into the role of Messrs. Miller and Adolf with regard to the transactions involving the Philip Howard Apartments. Mr. Cohen was advised that he was only a witness and that there were no indications that he had any personal vulnerability. At first, the government queried Mr. Cohen as to whether Messrs. Miller and Adolf had defrauded the tenants in failing to represent them properly. When that proved fruitless, Cohen was then interrogated as to whether or not there had been "inside information" with regard to the representation or subsequent transactions. Failing that, they focused on the possibility that the sponsor had been defrauded and ultimately whether or not Meyer Rosenbaum had been somehow defrauded.

The government had simultaneously contacted Meyer Rosenbaum, also as a potential witness and, by virtue of the fact that the attorney representing Cohen had represented Rosenbaum's brother a number of years earlier and obtained for him an acquittal after trial of charges involving nursing home administration, coincidentally retained the same attorney as Cohen. The dual representation continued while both men were being assured they were merely witnesses and there was no apparent conflict existing.

However, in the spring of 1990, Cohen was informed that he, together with Mr. Miller, was now a potential target as a result of unspecified acts. To the astonishment of the attorney representing both men and who was aware of the relationship between them and their statements made regarding Miller, the government advised Cohen that he was a target of an investigation for acting in concert with Mr. Miller to defraud Mr. Rosenbaum. Despite the astonishment regarding the government's ill-defined theory, the attorney was obliged to withdraw from the men's representation as there now existed a conflict.

In December of 1990, Mel Miller and Jay Adolf were indicted on conspiracy to commit mail fraud and a number of substantive violations of the mail fraud statute. In essence, the indictment charged that Messrs. Miller and Adolf, acting with Aviezer Cohen, defrauded Meyer Rosenbaum when they purchased eight apartments for their own benefit without obtaining the specific advance consent of Rosenbaum.

Mel Miller was represented by Gerald Lefcourt, a highly skilled defense attorney, from the outset of the investigation.

In the course of preparation for the trial, Lefcourt, touching all bases in order to secure any statements made by Cohen which might prove inconsistent with statements to be made at the forthcoming trial or which would impair his credibility so that his testimony would be discounted, sent out a number of subpoenas. Among other things, the subpoenas sought notes or documents reflecting any statement made by Cohen to the government. Subpoenas were served upon Cohen's then current attorneys, as well as upon the prior attorney who had represented both Cohen and Rosenbaum prior to withdrawal because of the conflict.

What was anticipated were notes made during the course of any interviews which would reflect the statements made by Cohen to investigators or to the United States Attorney. However, because the request made was broad enough to encompass "any statement," the subpoena struck oil in that there were statements contained in the prior attorney's file which constituted statements to the government but which were separate and distinct from notes of interviews.

The attorney was obliged to respond to the subpoena accurately and, thus, advised Lefcourt that there were documents in his file which might be covered by the subpoena but which could not be released or their contents revealed to Lefcourt absent a court order. The attorney also alerted the current attorneys for Mr. Cohen, now a Washington and a New York firm, who took the position that no documents should be furnished to Mr. Lefcourt.

It soon developed that the documents were not privileged in that they involved statements made to the government and, in fact, had actually been "furnished" to the government. Notwithstanding, the attorney still took the position that, in view of the posture taken by Mr. Cohen's then attorneys, a court order would be necessary to obtain the documents. As it turned out the statements made to the government were amended tax returns that were filed after the investigation started.

Lefcourt made an application for the court order and the court ultimately directed that the documents be furnished to Mr. Lefcourt. The day after the court issued its decision, the government delivered to Lefcourt several cartons of documents which they claimed they recently received from Cohen and which included documents that were in the prior attorney's files and which were given to Lefcourt in compliance with the order of the court.

The initial investigation which sought statements made to the government without limiting the context, coupled with the tenacity to overcome vigorous objection and obtaining court orders, resulted in the following cross-examination, in significant part, of Aviezer Cohen:

Q: Good morning. Mr. Cohen, my name is Gerald Lefcourt. Have you ever met me?
A: No, never.
Q: You have refused to meet me, correct?
A: I have refused, correct.
Q: You have refused to talk to me, correct?
A: Correct.

Q: Yesterday you told the ladies and gentlemen of the jury that you have lied on numerous occasions, correct?
A: Correct.
Q: As a matter of fact, you lied every year from 1983 to 1989 on your tax returns, correct?
A: Correct.
Q: And you lied to your business partners, correct?
A: I lied to my business partners, Mr. Rosenbaum and his investors, correct.
Q: You lied to your employer, Isaac Rikowsky?
A: Correct.
Q: And you forged documents?
A: Correct.
Q: Now, would you lie to stay out of jail?
A: Would I lie to stay out of jail?
Q: Yes.
A: No, I would not lie.
Q: You wouldn't. Would you lie to save money?
A: Would I lie to save money? I wouldn't lie to save money.
Q: Didn't you lie every year on your tax returns to save money?
THE COURT: People can't hear you, Mr. Cohen. Please keep your voice up.
A: I lied on my tax returns.
Q: To save money?
A: Yes, to save money.
Q: You said that you would not lie to save money and that was a lie?
A: It wasn't a lie. I didn't understand your question properly.
Q: Didn't understand? Mr. Cohen, in August of 1989, is it true that you learned that the United States Government was investigating Mel Miller?
A: Yes, I did.
Q: And did you learn that from friends such as Evelyn Kligman or a business partner such as Meyer Rosenbaum?
A: I don't know who I heard it from, but I heard it.
Q: Didn't you hear that the Government had gone to some of these people that you knew in connection with the Philip Howard apartments asking questions about Mel Miller?

A: Yes, sure.

Q: And you knew from the beginning they were interested in Mel Miller, correct?

A: Did I know that they were interested in Mel Miller?

Q: That is the Government, yes.

A: The Government was interested in Mel Miller? That is correct.

THE COURT: I'm afraid, Mr. Cohen, you will have to do better with that voice of yours. We had a good period yesterday where we could hear you. Speak up.

A: That is correct.

Q: And in August of '89, Mel Miller was the Speaker of the Assembly of the New York State Legislature?

A: That is correct.

Q: Now, when you heard that this investigation was underway, isn't it a fact that in August of '89 the first thing you did was to get an attorney, or maybe it was in July.

A: It was—I don't remember the exact month. It was some time in '89, correct.

Q: And is it true that the next thing you did, before you ever spoke to the Government, was to file an amended tax return for the year 1985?

A: That is correct.

Q: And isn't it true, you did that because you were frightened, that you knew that you had committed serious crimes on your 1985 tax return?

A: That is correct.

Q: And so you amended the return approximately August 18 or so, 1989, correct?

A: That is correct.

Q: You wanted to sort of cover your tracks a little bit, correct?

A: That is correct.

Q: And in this amended tax return, you picked up an additional $190,000 of income, right?

A: Right.

Q: You figured that if you did that would be enough to satisfy them, right?

A: That was my hope.

Q: But you knew that was a total lie, you had much, much more income; is that right?

A: That's right.
Q: But you only gave them in August of '89, on this amended tax return, that which you thought you could give them and get away with it, correct?
A: That is correct.
Q: And that was a knowing and intentional perjury when you signed that August 1989 tax return, right?
A: That's right.
Q: Did you feel bad?
A: I don't understand the question, did I feel bad.
Q: Did you feel bad that you were lying?
A: Did I feel bad that I was lying, sure. Sure I felt bad I was lying.
Q: You felt bad that you were lying in August of '89 when you filed that tax return, right?
A: Anytime I lie I feel bad.
Q: But you lie often, so you feel bad often, right?
A: As far as my taxes are concerned I lied, you are absolutely right.
Q: But you felt bad about doing it, right?
A: I felt bad, sure. I perjured myself on my taxes, I felt very bad.
Q: But you did it anyway, although it made you feel bad?
A: That's right, I did it.
Q: That is because you didn't want to part with money, right?
A: If I could have gotten away with it, I was hoping that I could get way with it.
Q: In any event after you filed this perjurious tax return, you heard more. The Government approached you with your lawyer, correct?
A: That is correct.
Q: And they wanted to talk to you, right?
A: The Government wanted to talk to me, that is correct.
Q: And in December of 1989, you met with the Government, didn't you?
A: December of 1989? I think I met with them in May of 1990, I'm not sure.
Q: Excuse me. I want to show you what has been previously marked as 3500-14C. These are some notes. They are in handwriting. And there is a typewritten transcription. I show

you these and I ask you if these refresh your recollection that you met representatives of the Government on December 7, 1989.

[Document shown to witness]

A: Some of these things I'm a little confused. What does DN stand for?
THE COURT: The question is whether or not looking at that document refreshes your recollection as to whether or not you first met with the Government in December of '89?
A: Yes, I did.
Q: The meeting took place in your attorney's office in Mineola, correct?
A: That is correct.
Q: And you met with representatives of the Government, correct?
A: That is correct.
Q: Including Mr. Valenti?
A: That is correct.
Q: And, again, you were asked questions at that time concerning Mr. Miller and Philip Howard, correct?
A: I think that is correct.
Q: And you gave answers, correct?
A: I gave answers.
Q: During the course of that meeting, is it fair to say that you had an understanding with the Government about this conversation, to the extent that whatever you said wasn't going to be used against you, anything like that?
A: I don't think I had that understanding at all.
Q: Were you told in sum and substance that they were not interested in you, that you were only a witness, that you weren't a subject, that you weren't a target of any investigation?
A: Yeah, I think that was told to me.
Q: So you knew at that point, December 7, 1989, that the Government only looked at you as a witness, right? You were told that?
A: I wasn't told as a witness, no.
Q: You were told that they were not looking to charge you, you were not a target of their investigation, right?

A: I was told that they wanted to know any business relationships that I had with Mel Miller and Jay Adolf.
Q: Is it true that what you discussed a moment ago with me, that you were not a target of the investigation?
A: Yes, I was told that.
Q: And you gave them answers to their questions?
A: What I was asked I answered.
Q: At that point after that meeting, is it fair to say that you came away feeling well, it's going to blow over, right?
A: I wouldn't say that at all.
Q: You had filed this return a few months earlier, that picked up $190,000 in income. You now met with the Government. You were told that you weren't the target and you gave answers, right?
A: I gave answers, sure.
Q: Nobody said we don't believe you, right, at that meeting?
A: Right.
Q: So you thought you had gotten away with it so far, right?
A: To that point, maybe I got away, but I didn't know eventually that I would get away with it.
Q: Now, there came a time, just a few months later, is it true, in the spring, early spring, maybe March of 1985, excuse me 1990, where your status changed in what you were told now that you were being looked at, not that you were not a target, but that they were looking at you, correct?
A: That is correct.
Q: Is it fair to say that you were very frightened?
A: Sure was.
Q: Did they tell you what it was that you had done wrong that they were looking at?
A: I remember getting a document that just said that I was under criminal investigation.
Q: But you didn't know what it was for, right. Didn't say what it was for, did it?
A: The specifics, no, didn't say.
Q: Is it fair to say that you panicked?
A: Frightened, very frightened, sure.
Q: Well, this was in March of 1985, excuse me, I keep making that mistake, March of '90?

A: March of—
Q: '90?
A: '90.
Q: Let's establish the date. I'm going to show you a document and ask you whether 3500-14G refreshes your recollection as to whether it was March 5, 1990?
A: This is dated March 5, 1990, right.
Q: That was the day, was it not, or thereabouts, that your status, in your own mind, changed, because the Government told you that you were under criminal investigation, correct?
A: That is correct.
Q: And you were afraid because you knew, did you not, that you had committed many, many different crimes, correct?
A: That is correct.
Q: And that fear, you were afraid of going to jail, number one, correct?
A: Correct.
Q: You were also afraid, were you not, of losing all of your money, correct?
A: That's also correct.
Q: And at that time, would it be fair to say that you had a net worth of about $12 million?
A: How much?
Q: $12 million?
A: That is news to me.
Q: News to you?
A: I don't think. I mean that's—I don't know.
Q: You don't think.
A: I don't remember that. That I don't remember.
Q: Let me see if I can show you something to refresh your recollection. I show you what I have marked as Defendant's Exhibit 016.

[Document shown to witness]

"I ask you whether in or about March of 1990, you weren't worth about $12 million?"

A: Assets?

Q: Assets, that's what I mean.

* * *

A: Yes.
Q: Isn't it a fact that it says your net worth is $12 million?
A: Would you show me where it says net worth. It says assets, doesn't it?
Q: What does it show as your net worth?
A: $12,388,090.
Q: That is a document that you signed, correct, on the front page?
A: Yes, I did.
Q: And that was prepared by accountants that represented you, correct?
A: Excuse me, what?
Q: This document was prepared by your accountants?
A: Yes, it was.
Q: By the way, these are the same accountants that prepared most of your tax returns, correct?
A: Correct.
Q: And this document showing net worth was submitted to a bank in order to borrow money, correct?
A: I don't know which bank it was submitted to.
Q: I didn't ask you which bank. I asked was it submitted to a bank to borrow money?
A: I don't remember.
Q: You don't know. In any event, in March of '89—
THE COURT: Excuse me, it was prepared for some purpose?
A: It's possible what Mr. Lefcourt said is true, it was possibly prepared to obtain a loan from a bank. I don't remember which loan it would have referred to, which bank.
Q: But you tell us you remember the conversation, details of the conversation in 1983, '84 and '85, right?
A: Yeah, sure.
Q: When you prepared a $12 million net worth to borrow money, you don't remember when that was used; is that right?
A: I didn't say that. I said I don't know which particular loan you are referring to, which particular bank you are referring to.

Q: Do you remember any bank that you submitted your $12 million net worth to?
A: Could be if we purchased some buildings in that year this was submitted to get some bank for a mortgage.
Q: Do you remember?
A: Which particular building, I don't remember.
Q: Do you remember any building that year that you submitted a net worth statement showing $12 million for?
A: In the year of '89?
Q: We're only talking about two years ago, now?
A: Right. If I remember I'll gladly tell you, no problem.
Q: Mr. Cohen, you have testified that you remember accurately conversations that occurred in 1983, '84 and '85, correct?
A: That is correct.
Q: In any event, in March of 1990, when you are told, Mr. Cohen, we're looking at you and you are under criminal investigation, you already told us that you are afraid of going to jail. And now you are telling us that you are afraid of losing your wealth?
A: Correct.
Q: You knew that if all of your crimes unfolded that they could take all of your money, right?
A: That is correct, could be. Very possible.
Q: You had a serious problem, all this wealth that you accumulated, and fear of jail was playing on your mind in March of 1990, right?
A: That's right.
Q: Now, on April 2, 1990, you do something, correct, to try to keep them away from you. You file another tax return, right?
A: Correct.
Q: And this time you pick up $643,000 more income again, just for the year 1985, right?
A: That is correct.
Q: And did you do that because you were worried about this criminal investigation of you?
A: Yes, I was.
Q: And you thought that this would be a good thing to do, right?
A: Yes, I did.

Q: Give a little more. You had given 190 in August, but you figured that wasn't enough, so you would give a little more in April of '90, right.
A: I wanted to come totally clean on my '85 taxes.
Q: Totally clean? We'll get to that later. You also do something else, you change lawyers at about that time, right?
A: That is correct.
Q: And you hired two law firms, correct?
A: That is correct.
Q: One New York law firm and one Washington, D.C. law firm?
A: That is correct.
Q: Now, at that time, in April and May of 1990, you realized in order to save your money, and save you from going to jail, that one way to do it was to try to help the Government in what they wanted, correct?
A: To try to help the Government in what they wanted? Could you rephrase that question? What do you mean to help the Government?
Q: Isn't it a fact that you wanted to stay out of jail and save your money?
A: Sure.
Q: And isn't it a fact that you knew now for more than seven or eights months that what the Government wanted was Mel Miller, the Speaker of the Assembly, correct?
A: I don't know if the Government really wanted him. I know the Government was investigating him. I didn't know if the Government really wanted him.
Q: Didn't you know that they were asking questions of many people that you knew?
A: That is correct.
Q: Now, did the Government, in April and May of 1990, want you to plead guilty to a crime?
A: Did the Government ask me when?
Q: April, May, 1990. Didn't they want you to plead guilty to a crime?
A: I don't recall that.
Q: No?
A: I don't recall if they did. It's possible that they did.

Q: Needless to say, you didn't want to plead guilty to any crime, did you?
A: That is correct, I didn't.
Q: What you wanted was to have immunity, correct?
A: That is correct.
Q: You wanted to stay out of jail and keep all that wealth, right?
A: That is correct.
Q: Now, in order to get what you wanted, did you have certain sessions with the Government, proffer sessions, meetings, in May of 1990?
A: Yes, I did.
Q: And these sessions with the Government were with you and your two law firms, correct, and members of the Government?
A: Some of them were with me and my lawyers and many of them, I think, were between my lawyers and the U.S. Government.
Q: Your lawyers would meet with the Government privately?
A: Yes, they did.
Q: And then there were times that you met with your lawyers and the Government, right?
A: Correct.
Q: And you were hoping that you could get immunity?
A: That is correct.
Q: You remember the first meeting in May of 1990, when you had a session with the Government for this purpose, to try to get you immunity? In May of 1990 we're talking about.
A: I don't know if the first session was about immunity. I really don't recall that.
Q: Weren't they all about getting you immunity until you actually got it, on June 11, 1990?
A: I think that the Government was interested to the best of my knowledge—
Q: Excuse me, the question was, wasn't the meeting about you getting immunity, having a proffer session in order to see that you were going to get immunity, until the time that you got it?
A: The answer to that is simple. I was never a party of any discussion about immunity. Maybe my attorneys and the Government discussed it. I personally was not a part of any discussion that had to do with immunity?

Q: Weren't you present, for instance, on May 16, 1990, in the presence of your lawyers, when that was discussed, immunity? Do you remember that?
A: I don't recall that.

* * *

Q: I ask you to look at the first page of that document and ask you whether that refreshes your recollection that you were present when discussions about immunity were going on between your lawyers and the Government?
A: This is a transcript of the handwritten one, that is what it is?
Q: Yes.
A: I would like to read this first. You don't mind if I read it, do you?
Q: Look at the first page. I think the information on the first page either will or won't refresh your recollection.
A: This document—
THE COURT: Mr. Cohen, listen to me, this is liable to reoccur. You are asked a simple question, and that is whether looking at the document refreshes your recollection. If you look at that document, if you don't have anymore recollection then before the document was shown to you, say so.
THE WITNESS: May I have the questions again?
Q: Yes. Looking at 3500-14E, does that help you refresh your recollection as to whether or not in the presence of your attorneys and the Government, a discussion was had on May 16, 1990 about immunity to you?
A: And if I was present at that meeting?
Q: Yes.
A: This does not refresh my recollection that I was present at that meeting.
Q: Do you recall a conversation, whether it was on May 16 or some other meeting, in the Spring of '90, where it was discussed that you wanted assurance that nothing that you said during the session would count against you in not getting immunity?
A: I was told that the first three sessions—
Q: Did you hear the question?

* * *

A: That means anything that I said would not be used against me, is that what you mean?
Q: Yes.
A: Yes.
Q: To clarify that, you wanted to have an understanding with the Government that if you said something bad that you did, they wouldn't use that against you in not giving you what you wanted, which was immunity, right?
A: My understanding was if I said bad, that they could not use it against me.
Q: That is what you wanted, right?
A: That was my understanding, that they couldn't use it against me.
Q: Isn't it a fact they said no, we're not giving you a precondition. We'll listen to what you have to say. We're not going to tell you up front that if you admit to something terrible we're not going to use that in our calculation as to whether you get immunity?
A: I was never told. They may have told it to my attorneys, again, but I don't remember that being told to me.
Q: Again, I show you what is before you, 3500-14E, and I ask you if that refreshes your recollection that they were not giving you a precondition, and that what you said could be used in their calculation as to whether to give you immunity?
A: I don't understand the line of questioning.
THE COURT: Your question, please.
Q: Let me give you an example. You are sitting with the Government, you are trying to get immunity. If you tell them that you committed a murder—
A: Go ahead.
Q: —obviously they are going to think differently whether they are going to give you immunity for some financial crime, correct? Isn't it a fact that you wanted to make certain that whatever you said they wouldn't use against you in determining whether they were going to give you immunity? Do you understand that?

A: I mean, is it fair to me to be able to explain it the way I understood it.
Q: I just want to ask you that question?
THE COURT: If you can't answer the question, say so.
A: I can't answer the question, I really don't understand.
Q: I any event, didn't you understand that you had to hold back a little bit at these meetings, if you told them everything that you really did, they might not go along and give you immunity?
A: I have no idea. I didn't know what the Government's intention was. They didn't tell me.
Q: I'm asking you about your state of mind. Isn't it a fact that you believed from May of 1990, if you told them the full range of your criminal activity, you might not get immunity?
A: I don't know if that is true or not.
Q: I'm asking you, isn't that the way you felt about it?
A: I don't know how I felt at that time.
Q: You don't remember?
A: How I felt at that time, I don't know.
Q: Well, do you remember your attorneys asking the Government for a deal, while you are talking if you should say something bad that they would not use it against you, whether or not you would get immunity or not.
A: That was between my attorneys and the U.S. Government. I was not present.
Q: In any event, you didn't tell them in May or in June everything, did you?
A: No, I didn't.
Q: You were holding things from them, right?
A: Yes, I did.
Q: So now we're talking about statements made to the United States Government and you are withholding things from them, right? You are trying to deceive them, aren't you?
A: Oh, no, absolutely no. Why should I deceive them.
Q: Because you were afraid if you told them the truth about everything you would not get immunity, correct?
A: I don't know if is correct, no.
Q: You were holding things from them, you agree with that?
A: I withheld things from the Government. Yes, I withheld things from the Government. Excuse me, you are asking—

Q: Let me ask you about withholding?
A: Can I ask you to rephrase that question?
Q: If there is something that you wish to bring out, Mr. Fishbein can bring out?
THE COURT: I did not hear what he said.
A: I don't understand.
THE COURT: If you don't understand a question, say so. Mr. Lefcourt will oblige you and rephrase the question. Go ahead, Mr. Lefcourt.
Q: Thank you. Do you believe, Mr. Cohen, that it is deceiving when you withhold important information from people?
A: Yes, it is.
Q: And even though you don't say something that is untrue, you can deceive somebody by not telling them the whole story, correct?
A: That is correct.
THE COURT: Louder, please.
A: Yes, that is true.
Q: And while you were trying to negotiate this deal for your freedom, and to save all your money, you were withholding things in the Spring of 1990, correct?
A: Yes, there were certain things I was withholding.
Q: Because you were trying to sucker the Government in, to give you immunity, right?
A: No, that is not correct.
THE COURT: Can you hear him? We'll try the microphones. You may not be conscious of it, I see everybody's neck moving forward, shoulders turning, and it is a sign to me that you are having difficulty hearing the witness.

* * *

Q: Mr. Cohen, we were talking about these meetings in the Spring of '90, and I think you agreed that you were withholding things from the Government during that time. My next question is, isn't one of the things that you withheld this business about 200 in cash to buy a piece of property, is that one of the things that you withheld?

A: Yes.
Q: And isn't it true that you didn't give them the information about your tax fraud and your lying on your tax returns, correct?
A: Which years are you talking about?
Q: Did you give them the full story about your lying every year on your tax returns?
A: I wasn't asked about it.
Q: You didn't volunteer it?
A: I didn't volunteer it and I wasn't asked.
Q: Did you tell them in your first or second meeting that you had forged documents, or is that something that they didn't ask you about?
A: I don't know which meeting I told it to them, but I remember one of those meetings it was mentioned, maybe the second or third. I don't remember exactly which meeting.
Q: In fact, Mr. Cohen, the true investigation of you started, did it not, after these charges were brought, and the investigation has been done by the defense, isn't that true?
A: The true investigation of me started when it was brought by the defense?
Q: That's right, by subpoenas issued pursuant to law by Mr. Miller's defense, correct?
A: That is not true.
Q: There have been lots of things subpoenaed from you in the past several months, correct?
A: Yeah, that is correct.
Q: And it wasn't until August of this year that you brought in your tax returns, where all of these crimes were committed, to the United States Government.
A: That is correct.
Q: In fact, it was August 22, 1992, right? Does that sound right?
A: Maybe it's around that date. I'm not sure of the dates.
Q: They didn't ask for it, right, so you didn't give it?
A: They never asked me, and I never told them about it.
Q: And the reason why you brought it in, in August of 1991, was because of your fear that one of the subpoenas that was issued by Mr. Miller's defense was going to unearth it and the Government would find out about it, right?

A: That is not true at all.

Q: You brought it in voluntarily in August of 1991, correct?

A: I don't remember the circumstances, but it wasn't because of your investigation.

Q: You just decided one morning, I better bring my tax returns to the Government, is that your testimony?

A: Mr. Lefcourt, once I had immunity there was no reason for me not to tell the Government about it. It wasn't because of your investigation that I gave it to them.

Q: But you waited until August of 1991, right?

A: That's when the Government asked for it.

Q: That's when they asked for it?

A: Sure.

Q: Isn't it a fact, it was because we had subpoenaed your prior attorney who had these amended returns?

A: I don't know if that is a fact or not.

Q: Isn't it true that you knew he was about to turn them over so you ran in and turned them over?

A: I—

Q: Withdrawn. Did you know he was going to turn them over?

A: I have no contact with him. How did I know?

Q: Did you know through any other source?

A: That he was going to turn them over?

Q: That's right.

A: It's possible.

Q: It's possible?

A: It's possible.

Q: Aware talking about August of this year, we're not talking about '84?

A: I understand.

Q: Didn't you know this summer that he was going to turn them over?

A: It's possible. I don't remember 100 percent.

Q: It's possible?

A: Well, I don't know. Why he would turn them over without informing me first? He was my prior attorney, shouldn't he inform me first?

Q: When you realized this would be unfolded and the Government would learn that, you made a speedy entry to the U.S. Attorney's office with these tax returns, is that possible?
A: I don't know if that's the fact at all. I don't know if that is the fact. Once I had immunity, there is no reason—
THE COURT: Just wait for the next question, if you would, Mr. Cohen?
Q: I know you are going to say that over and over again. Isn't that your plan, 'once I had immunity,' you are going to say that?
A: This is not my plan, that is the truth.
Q: But the fact of the matter is, that you knew your prior attorney had been subpoenaed for these documents, right?
A: That I think I knew.
Q: That you think you knew?
A: Right.
MR. LEFCOURT: Thank you.
Q: And it was after learning about the subpoena to your prior attorney for these documents that you came in with the tax returns, right?
A: Again, I don't remember the facts the way you do. This way you are suggesting to me the facts, I don't remember this.
Q: You told me that you knew your prior attorney was subpoenaed for these documents, and I'm asking you, wasn't it after you learned that that you came in with the tax returns? You remember those facts?
A: It could have come the same time, but I don't think that is the reason why they were turned over to the United States Government, because you subpoenaed my previous attorney.
Q: At that time in August of 1991, is it fair to say that you had about 20 or 30 meetings with the Government prior to August of 1991?
A: Yes, that is correct.
Q: But you chose until after you knew that the prior attorney was subpoenaed to actually produce them, right?
A: Again, Mr. Lefcourt, I was not asked about it. If I would have been asked about it month earlier I would have gladly given it over on my own volition.
Q: That was something that you had withheld, Mr. Cohen, right?

A: Absolutely not.
Q: It was withheld until August 22, 1991, that's when you gave the returns, right?
A: That's when I gave in the returns, but it wasn't withheld intentionally, that's for sure.
Q: This was a matter that was so important to you, your taxes, and what effect it might have on your life, that you amended your 1985 tax return twice within eight months, right?
A: That is correct.
Q: And it was so important to you, that you had to pay $700,000 in taxes, right?
A: That is correct.
Q: And, in fact, some of these tax monies weren't paid until August of this year, right?
A: That is correct.
Q: Is it you forgot from 1985 to pay it?
A: I purposely didn't pay it.
Q: Isn't it a strange coincidence, Mr. Cohen, in August of 1991, you wrote a check to the IRS for $100,000—$141,000?
A: That is correct.
Q: Isn't it true, the reason why it was done in August of 1991 is you knew that your attempt to conceal was unraveling, and you were trying to cover the bases, right?
A: That $141,000, was, I think, late fees of filing the second amendment in April of 1990.
Q: But you knew since April of 1990 that the money was due, right?
A: And I paid it.
Q: But you waited until August of 1991, more than a year, to pay it, right?
A: That's when I got the bill—I got the bill a little earlier. That's when I made it, sure.
Q: Didn't you know when you filed an amended tax return on April 2, 1990, picking up another $650,000 worth of income there would be late fees, interest penalties, and other penalties, didn't you know it then?
A: I didn't know what they were going to be.
Q: Just a coincidence that you waited until August of 1991, at the time when you knew that your prior attorney was subpoenaed

for these documents, that you issued a check, correct? All a coincidence?
A: That is absolutely not right.
Q: Not right?
A: No, absolutely not. The IRS, I owed them money, and I sent it in. I paid $700,000 to the IRS. As Mr. Fishbein showed yesterday, at least ten checks I sent in, and that had nothing to do with your subpoenaing my previous attorney.
Q: You are saying that you got a bill in August of '91?
A: I'm not sure of when the bill was.
Q: You aren't. Was there a bill in August of 1991?
A: I don't think so, but I don't remember.
Q: Welcome back to the tax returns. You recall testifying yesterday that your wife Elaine signed Dorothy Segal's name on a variety of documents?
A: She signed one of the proprietary interests.
Q: Have you ever testified in the Grand Jury in this case?
A: Yes.
Q: Did you appear in the Grand Jury and did you take an oath to tell the truth?
A: Yes, I did.
Q: Just like the same oath that you took in the Courtroom?
A: That is correct.
Q: And instead of having trial jurors, they were grand jurors?
A: Correct.
Q: Didn't you lie to the Grand Jury when you went into the Grand Jury about signing Dorothy Segal's name?
A: That was not a lie, that was an honest mistake. At the time I thought I was the one that signed it.
Q: Isn't it a fact that you told the Grand Jury not only that you signed it, but, elaborately, how it was done?
A: Yeah, that was the way I just happened to remember the facts at that time. I thought that was what took place.
Q: You are under oath in the Grand Jury and you are telling the grand jurors, swearing to them, how it took place, right?
A: That is correct.
Q: You recall being asked these questions and giving these answers, pages 74 and 75.

Q: Who actually wrote the signature of Dorothy Segal on that day?
A: I did.
Q: Is that true of the other proprietary leases as well?
A: That is true.
Q: Where did you sign these leases?
A: In the office of Tiara Realty.
Q: This was before the closing of April 1?
A: Correct.
Q: What did you do with these proprietary leases after they were signed?
A: I gave them back to Mr. Miller and Mr. Adolf. I sent them to them.
Q: Do you recall how you sent them?
A: I can't recall.
Q: Now, do you recall that testimony before the Grand Jury?
A: Yes, I do.
Q: And that was false, right? You did not sign these proprietary releases in the office of Tiara Realty as you swore to the grand Jury, correct?
A: At that time I thought that was the fact. Remember I didn't see any documents at the time that I said that.
Q: You didn't?
A: I saw the documents afterwards.
Q: Weren't you being shown the document at the very time that you said that?
A: No, I was not shown any documents at all when I was asked that question.
Q: I'm going to go back one question and answer, before what I just said in the Grand Jury, on page 74.
Q: And to shortcut this, I'm going to show you Exhibit 149, and I'm going to ask if your testimony is also true for the other proprietary releases which were with Exhibits 150 through 154? I'm showing you page 30 of the Exhibit 149. Who actually wrote the signature of Dorothy Segal on that page.
A: I did.
Q:That's your testimony?
A: I thought that was my signature at that time.
Q: You thought. And you told a story about where you signed it, right?

A: At that time that is what I thought, how the signature took place.
Q: Weren't you just trying to protect your wife? Your wife signed them, right?
A: My wife and myself are like one person, why should I protect her?
Q: You didn't want to get her involved?
A: She has the same immunity.
Q: How did she get the same immunity that you have?
A: That is the agreement that my attorneys worked out. It doesn't matter if I signed it or she signed it. It's a big difference if I signed it or she signed it?
Q: You told the grand jurors, not only that you signed it, when you signed it and where you signed it, right?
A: Correct.
Q: And you were thinking about it?
A: That is correct.
Q: But none of that happened, what you swore to them?
A: That's the way I thought it happened at that time.
Q: But none of it did happen?
A: It's not the way it happened, but that's the way I thought it happened.
Q: But what happened is your wife signed them. You brought them home. Where was it done at home?
A: I don't remember exactly where, but it was done at home.
Q: You are capable of telling a story that was totally false, right?
A: At that time that is the way I remembered it, sir.
Q: And it was under oath, right?
A: It was under oath.
Q: By the way, that's not the first time you made that mistake, is it? Hadn't you told the Government that in previous meetings before that sworn testimony, over and over again?
A: I don't understand the question, I told the Government what?
Q: In the Grand Jury you said you signed Dorothy Segal's name, right?
A: That is correct.
Q: And isn't it true. Not only did you swear to it in the Grand Jury, but that you told Government agents that on prior occasions, before going to the Grand Jury?

A: At that time that was the—my best recollection is that I was the one that signed it.

THE COURT: The question you are being asked is if that is what you told the Government as well, prior to your appearance in the Grand Jury?

A: It's possible.

Q: Isn't it a fact that you now recall that your wife signed it, right?

A: That is correct.

Q: And didn't that recollection come about because the Government sought to take handwriting exemplars from you and your wife?

A: Yeah, that is correct.

Q: So you realized, again, when they were going to find out, because of handwriting exemplars, what the truth was, you said you made a mistake, correct?

A: If they find out it means at that time I was mistaken.

Q: But it's not until that you knew that the handwriting would show that you were telling a lie, before you fessed up and told the truth, right?

A: It's not right. You are classifying it as a lie and I'm saying it's an honest mistake. I thought at first I was the one that signed it.

Q: When they asked to take the handwriting exemplars from your wife, you had a new revelation?

A: It wasn't a new revelation. I made a mistake. I wasn't the one, my wife signed it. I thought I did because I was the one that was handling the deal. I was doing everything else. I thought that I was the one that did it.

Q: How did you realize that you made the mistake, when the Government was asking for the handwriting or when someone from the Government said, isn't it true that you didn't sign it?

A: I don't know how it came about. Once they took the handwriting test, then it was my wife's signature and not mine. Very simple. Very simple.

Q: Very simple?

A: Yeah.

Q: But you told the Grand Jury under oath how you did it, where, the circumstances, what you did with it, right?

A: At that time, that was the best of my recollection, sure.

* * *

Q: Isn't it a fact that you had an arrangement with Mr. Rokowsky in which you were going to be paid by him if certain apartments subscribed, and Philip Howard Apartments were therefore able to become a co-op?
A: Yeah, that was true.
Q: You didn't tell us about this arrangement on direct examination, did you?
A: I said I received three apartments when I left. Mr. Fishbein asked me.
Q: I'm asking about an arrangement. Wasn't it the understanding between you and Mr. Rokowsky that you were going to help see to it that the Philip Howard Apartments became a co-op by helping to get tenants to subscribe?
A: I should get—I should help the tenants subscribe?
Q: Yes.
A: That's possible.
Q: I'm not asking what is possible. Isn't that the fact?
A: Let's say that is the fact.
Q: And isn't it also a fact that you were being paid by Mr. Rokowsky for each tenant who you could deliver who would subscribe to the co-op, isn't that a fact?
A: You mean when I got the apartment at the end? That is true. I got the three apartments at the end, correct.
Q: I know you got three apartments at the end. I'm asking you whether it is a fact that you and your boss had an agreement that he would pay you money for every tenant who signed on the dotted line and subscribed the co-op, because this co-op conversion would mean millions of dollars, isn't that true?
A: Yes.
Q: And that's a fact, right. It's not only possible, that occurred, right?
A: It occurred, sure.
Q: How much were you supposed to get for each tenant that ultimately subscribed?

A: I don't recall the exact figure. I think it was maybe $300 an apartment.
Q: Was it more like a thousand dollars an apartment?
A: No, it wasn't.
Q: So you were doing a job for the landlord, the boss, getting people to sign on the dotted line, correct?
A: Correct.
Q: You were being paid for everybody who would come on board, right?
A: That is correct.
Q: Was that part of your strained relationship with Mr. Rokowsky?
A: The agreement was that I would be leaving, like I told you yesterday.
Q: Was the arrangement that we just discussed part of your strained relationship?
A: Part of the strained relationship? I don't know what you mean by that. Can you rephrase that question?
Q: You said that you had a strained relationship with Mr. Rokowsky?
A: That's what I said.
Q: Isn't it a fact that you had a deal with him, he was going to be paying you lots and lots of money?
A: Well, I didn't know if it was lots of money, because we didn't know how many apartments we were going to sell. How do you know it's lots of money.
Q: How about $200,000, isn't that a lot of money?
A: When did he give me $200,000?
Q: When? What was the value of the three apartments that you were given by the landlord, the one you had a strained relationship with; what is the value?
A: I sold them—I got them—I sold them for about 150, $160,000.
Q: It's a lot of money, isn't it?
A: Oh, yeah, sure.
Q: You didn't testify to this arrangement on your direct examination, did you?
A: I wasn't asked.
Q: You weren't asked. Have you ever told them about it?
A: Sure.

Q: They know that you had a dollar figure for each subscription agreement that you could turn in, that you were going to get by your boss?
A: I told them of the three apartments. I don't know if I told them—this deal, I don't know if I told them.
Q: You never told them about this?
A: This I never told them.
Q: It's coming out for the first time in front of these jurors today, right?
A: Yeah, I think that is correct.
Q: Is that something that you withheld?
A: Withheld?
Q: No?
A: I wasn't asked about it. We didn't discuss it.
Q: If you are not asked, you don't tell, right?
A: I don't see what the point of that was. I got the three apartments and I told it to them and I told them what I sold it for.
Q: You had 200 thousand reasons why those apartments could not be in your name. Had nothing to do with a strained relationship, did it?
A: The other apartments that I acquired?
Q: Yes.
A: When talking about whose name we should use for the six apartments, correct.
Q: And you chose your sister-in-law. It wasn't because of a strained relationship, was it?
A: It was because I did not want him to know that I had anything to do with that deal.

* * *

Q: When you first told the story to the Government, you agree you didn't tell them about the four nominees. When you first told them the story, the business about already using four nominees wasn't in the conversation, correct?
A: That is correct.
Q: So this was a new addition to the conversation that you gave the Government, approximately a year or so after you got immunity, right?

A: When I reminded myself of the conversation, I told the United States Attorney, that is correct.
Q: When you first told them about the conversation, you told them like it was very difficult for you to come up with a nominee and how upset you were; isn't that right?
A: Yes.
Q: You made believe in the first telling of it that you were not somebody that would use nominees, you didn't know how to do it, you got hot under the collar.
A: That's not what I said.
Q: Did you make it appear this was a difficult thing for you to get involved with?
A: I made it appear that it was difficult for me to come up with a nominee, correct.
Q: Do you recall testifying in the Grand Jury '70 to '71, being asked under oath the following question and giving this answer.
Q: Now, after she agreed to do—let me stop back for a moment. You said you had some heated discussion with Mr. Miller and Mr. Adolf during this period of time, is that correct.
A: I don't know if it would be discussion or a discussion, it was just this thing that I remember. I got a little hot under my collar, because I didn't think it was right for me to have to come up with a name when I really didn't have one.
Q: Do you recall giving that answer?
A: Yes, sure.
Q: That answer doesn't include anything about, I told him that I was already using four nominees, does it?
A: No, it doesn't say that.
Q: But that was added yesterday, right, in your testimony here in Court, correct?
A: That was added quite a while ago.
Q: This year, 1991, this summer?
A: When I told it to the U.S. Attorney, I don't know.
Q: This summer, correct?
A: Yes.
Q: And the grand jurors listening to this didn't know about your list, did they, because you didn't put in that part of the conversation, did you?

A: That is correct.
Q: And the grand jurors didn't know that you and Rokowsky had this deal where hundreds of thousands of dollars were at stake if he found out that you were making an investment in these six apartments, correct?
A: At that time didn't know about it. I wasn't asked about it.
Q: Right.
A: Right.
Q: And you withheld it?
A: I didn't withhold it at all.
Q: You withheld it until today, the deal?
A: That's not true.
Q: Didn't you tell us this morning that the Government didn't know that you were getting a price per head, yes or no, that the Government didn't know that you were getting a price for each tenant who subscribed?
A: That translated into apartments.
MR. LEFCOURT: Your Honor, may I have a direction that this witness be responsive?
THE COURT: Please, Mr. Cohen, it will save us a lot of time. You have information that you want to impart. Your whole role here is to respond to the questions.
A: I never told them about this money per unit deal, okay.

* * *

ON RE-CROSS-EXAMINATION

Q: And it is the Government who decides whether you get prosecuted for any perjury, correct, not me, isn't that right?
A: If you say so.
Q: Isn't that true?
A: That's true.
Q: And it is in the Government's hands as to whether you get prosecuted for lying in any way, correct?
A: I imagine so.
Q: And in August of this year, August 22, when you first brought them the tax returns that were amended, you for the first time told them about it and showed it to them, correct?

A: My attorneys may have showed it—

* * *

Q: You brought it in August 22nd, this summer, 1991, correct?
A: Is that—I don't know if that was the date. I brought it in.
Q: It was this summer, right?
A: I think so.
Q: **And in fact, you knew at that time that the defense had subpoenaed . . . Robert Goldman, correct?"**

As was apparent from the cross-examination, when Cohen learned that possibly some documents were to be released that had previously been withheld from the government, he revealed significant new information to the government. That, in turn, led to the Government turning the new information over to the defense which in turn led to the following cross-examination of the "victim," Meyer Rosenbaum:

Q: You told us that you arrived at a price that you were happy with of $71 a share, is that correct?
A: Yes.
Q: Once you arrived at that price, it was your understanding with Mr. Miller, correct me if I am wrong, that he should go in there and get the best deal they could get and he could keep the differences as long as you got your 71?
A: Qualify that. As long as we got the price—as long as we got the price that ultimately we would agree on.
Q: But the price that you ultimately agreed on that you wanted to pay was 71?
A: Correct.
Q: You discussed and you came to that price by discussing this matter with Mr. Beigeleisen, your accountant, Mr. Cohen, is that correct?
A: Mainly Mr. Cohen.
Q: So when you and your partner arrived at the price it was your understanding with Mr. Miller that he was to go get the price and he could keep the difference, whatever he got?
A: That's correct.

Q: You don't recall any conversation you ever had with Mr. Miller other than that brief one and you don't recall what was said in that one?
A: That's correct.
Q: Isn't it true that as long as you got your 71, you didn't care what Mr. Miller got?
A: True.
Q: And other than, putting aside feelings that everybody wants money, putting aside those feelings, isn't it true you didn't care whatever he got?
A: Even though I like money I didn't care.
Q: In effect, your understanding with him in the beginning, whatever you can make you make?
A: Correct.
Q: Wasn't it true that the price of 71 you believe based on what you knew of the insider price and outsider price and the market you thought was an excellent price?
A: Yes.
Q: Also, wasn't this a kind of unique arrangement for you to have with somebody to say in effect go out and get this price for you instead of you doing it yourself?
A: Yes.
Q: In effect Mr. Miller was acting as an intermediary or surrogate getting this money for you?
A: That's correct.
Q: Indeed would it be fair to say that he was doing the things that you would normally do as a businessman, an investor going out and getting the prices, is that correct?
A: Something similar about it.
Q: So, isn't it fair to say you were prepared to accept even if Mr. Miller was able to get a phenomenally good price you were prepared to let him have the difference?
A: Correct.
Q: Is it fair to say that the price of 71 which is the price he ultimately negotiated was not something that you ever thought about, to what he got?
A: Until later on.
Q: Until much later on?

A: Until the time of the investigation.
Q: At the time you didn't care, you didn't think about it?
A: I didn't think about it.
Q: Okay. Is it fair to say the first time you were asked to think about it was by the Government?
A: I rather put it by saying that was the first time it was brought to my attention and it got me thinking.
Q: And in fact, at the time, whatever he got you viewed essentially as a markup that you were paying, is that correct?
A: Correct.
Q: And indeed you then turned around and took the price you got and marked it up one step forward to $80 a share for occupied apartments?
A: Correct.
Q: In arriving at this price did Mr. Cohen tell you the price or did you work it out from the book in general conversation?
A: It was a combination of the two.
Q: Do you believe that Mr. Cohen misled you in these conversations?
A: Yes, I did.
Q: Is it fair to say you trusted him?
A: Yes, I did.
Q: Even though he misled you, in terms of the deal you got what kind of deal was it?
A: Great. Great.
Q: One more time?
A: Great.
Q: In fact, Mr. Rosenbaum, the investor group made millions?
A: I don't want you to count my money, but we did very well."

Messrs. Miller and Adolf were acquitted on all charges which depended on the testimony of Aviezer Cohen. All of the remaining charges upon which the jury convicted Messrs. Miller and Adolph were dismissed by the United States Court of Appeals for the Second Circuit. The basis of the decision reversing the conviction was that the charges could not be sustained based on the testimony of Meyer Rosenbaum elicited on cross examination.

The Theme 7

§7.1 INTRODUCTION

There is a reason for writing the summation first, a method highly valued by experienced trial lawyers. It is not enough, in presenting a case or rebutting an opponent's case, simply to focus on the essential elements and make sure that every "t" is crossed and every "i" is dotted. A story line needs to be developed, and this development is referred to as developing a theme. Without a theme, a finder of fact has little or no basis to relate one fact to another. If the overall theme makes sense, then all of the specific facts which have been presented in support of that position attain credibility and seem reasonable in the context of the overall story. If all of the facts marshalled have a logic, internal and external, other facts are dispelled which interfere with the overall theme. Then you have woven a fabric which can stand up to a lot of wear and tear and can result in a favorable verdict.

Establishing a theme also establishes the context in which particular questions on cross-examination are asked and the answers given. Outside of the courtroom, this has been a long-recognized technique which only recently has been given the word "spin." As now commonly seen, a person in public life makes a statement and; thereafter, a spin doctor emerges to create a context so that the public perception of the statement will be in accord with the intended impression, although, taken by itself, the meaning would appear otherwise. Serious gaps are explained away by creating a context in which the alleged misstatement seems to have a different meaning and constitute less of a mistake.

The development of a context in a theme is critical in the preparation of cross-examination. To demonstrate that a witness is lying or mistaken serves little purpose if there is not immediately incorporated upon cross-examination questions that bring out facts or inferences to support your theme. The selection of a proper theme which is perpetuated and enhanced in cross-examination can turn a trial completely around and result in verdicts which are 180 degrees apart.

§7.2 MARCOS AND HELMSLEY CASES

As an example, to all but the most literal-minded person, the trials of Leona Helmsley and Imelda Marcos were remarkably similar. Both were women that were charged with crimes that came to trial in the United States District Court for the Southern District of New York. Thus, we have an excellent example of all things being equal.

Both women, when they first came to public attention and for many years afterward, were highly regarded. Leona Helmsley was perceived to be somebody whose fondest wish was that every person in the world should have a good meal and an excellent night's sleep. When word filtered to the public that, on occasion, she was somewhat testy, it was only because of her dedication for the well-being of her guests.

For many years, Imelda Marcos was regarded as the epitome of Oriental grace and charm. She made a lovely demure appearance and was considered kind and caring of the people of the country over which her husband ruled.

By the time that they came to trial, all that had changed. Leona Helmsley was characterized as a nasty, irascible person who abused her privileges and allegedly thought "that only the little people pay taxes."

Imelda Marcos was cast as a vain, pretentious woman who thought nothing of endless extravagance while her people starved, as evidenced by her owning 800 pairs of shoes.

In both cases, their husbands, albeit indicted, were not available for trial—Ferdinand Marcos, through death, and Harry Helmsley, by virtue of illness. It was left to the women to shoulder the burden for the wrongdoings that the government charged.

The lawyers for Leona Helmsley developed a theme that, in fact, she was as bad as her then public image and seemed to delight in pressing that image even further, developing the position that being irascible did not equate with tax evasion.

Her attorneys were the epitome of New York sophistication. The success of such a defense if it ever works can only succeed among the most sophisticated people who live in the fast track where even the most heinous criminals can have their good points that overshadow the offense with which they are charged.

Conversely, Imelda Marcos' attorney, Gerry Spence, could not have been more different. He lives and practices in Jackson, Wyoming. He arrived in New York for the trial projecting the frontier and the old west with all that that entails. His theme was consistent with the image that he could credibly project.

The Helmsley defense team, tuned into the pace and tempos of New York with its great tolerance for nasty persons who are interesting and have status, attired in pinstripe suits, projected the theme that there was no relationship between obnoxiousness and tax evasion. They believed that, in New York, it would have been politically incorrect to suggest that a wife would routinely defer to her husband and simply carry out his instructions.

Gerry Spence was not encumbered by such considerations. He came from the old west where women are to be protected and the husband is still the dominant spouse in the world of commerce. On the frontier, women were not diminished if they accepted their historical role.

Consequently, he presented a defense which he pursued in cross-examination that Imelda Marcos was the dedicated, loyal wife of Ferdinand for which she was to be praised rather than censured or, in other words, "let's give the little lady a hand." No matter what wrongdoings were proven, she was not to be penalized for being a good and loyal wife.

It is quite possible that only someone like Gerry Spence could have ever sold that theme in the City of New York. But, sell it he did; and Imelda Marcos was acquitted. Gerry Spence blended a theme that had absolute marketability and which played off his natural abilities, talents and, probably, deep-seated attitudes. He apparently felt that a jury still believed or wanted to believe that a woman is to be forgiven for deferring to her husband and that a wife is to be protected rather than sharing the heavy blows.

Spence also demonstrated the critical attributes of a trial lawyer, flexibility and instinct. As noted in the media at the inception of the Marcos trial, it appeared that Spence and the Judge, John Keenan, were experiencing certain difficulties. From all appearances, it seemed that Spence had not quite picked up on the tempo and methods of the ''Big Apple'' which led to certain tense colloquies between lawyer and Judge. But Gerry Spence is nothing if not the epitome of a superb trial lawyer and, as John Keenan subsequently noted in a conversation with me, ''he started slow, got the feel of things as he went along and, by summation, was absolutely brilliant.''

The perpetuation and development of the theme on cross-examination is critical, and the questions so designed to be effective must be a theme which is consistent with the temperament and personality of the cross-examiner.

§7.3 TYSON CASE

A case in point in which a number of the principles of cross-examination can be reviewed is the recent trial of Mike Tyson, charged in the State of Indiana with multiple counts of rape and sexual assault. Under Indiana law, it is a defense to rape if the female consents or if the male reasonably believes that the woman is consenting. Thus, at the outset, a tactical decision would have to be made as to which of the two alternatives would provide the stronger theme or, if both, which was to be stressed.

While it is possible to proceed arguing both lines of defense, it is necessary to place one in a more paramount position and focus efforts upon that. In criminal cases, it is extremely difficult for a jury to accept alternatives such as ''I didn't do it'' or, if I did, ''it was self-defense.''

While clearly the defense of consent should not be abandoned, it is a defense which is dependent on one person's word against another. As such, it is speculative and contains many more risks than a defense premised upon a reasonable belief that consent has been given, which is singular to the accused. In that case, it is not one person's word against another but one person's actions which are documented and not subject to revision which supply the defense rather than winning a credibility contest. Thus, the defense could be made out based upon a witness' prior actions despite contradictory testimony rendered by an alleged victim.

With regard to the theme of "reasonable belief," there were two options. The option selected by the defense was to establish that Mike Tyson was an oaf who indiscriminately fondled women and made crude sexual proposals in order to establish that any woman who went out with him should be aware that he had only one interest in mind. Consequently, a consent to go out with him was an implied consent to engage in sex. This is completely dangerous in that en route to such defense there would be established that the defendant was not only capable of the act of rape but would likely commit it whenever given the opportunity. That gives the prosecution two bites at the apple. There is the opposing testimony regarding lack of consent; and, if not given, the defendant would not be deterred by its lack.

On the other hand, a simple cross-examination which did nothing but track the actions leading to the scene of the alleged rape would let the actions speak for themselves and control the cross-examination to exclude the personalities of the parties, i.e., Tyson's alleged nature and the complainant's innocence. Such simple questioning would be as follows:

Q: When you met him earlier in the day he asked you if you would be interested in going out with him?
A: Yes.
Q: And you encouraged him to call you?
A: Yes.
Q: He called you at 2:00 a.m. after you had retired for the evening?
A: Yes.
Q: You agreed to come down and meet him?
A: Yes.
Q: Did he force you to come down?
A: No.
Q: Was he waiting in a car?
A: Yes.
Q: Did he force you into the car?
A: No.
Q: Did the car go directly to his hotel?

A: Yes, but he said -
Q: No, not what he said, did the car go directly to his hotel?
A: Yes.
Q: When it arrived at his hotel, did you get out of the car?
A: Yes.
Q: Did he force you to get out of the car?
A: No.
Q: When you voluntarily got out of the car, did you know that you and he were going to his hotel room?
A: Yes.
Q: Did he force you to go to his hotel room?
A: No.
Q: When you entered his hotel room did you go into his bedroom?
A: Yes.
Q: Did he force you to go into the bedroom?
A: No.
Q: Thank you, no further questions.

All of the affirmative responses recited above were actually testified to by the witness; and, as to each "yes," there was no contradictory testimony.

Clearly, had cross-examination confined itself to the straight line from her bedroom to his and excluded personalities, there was a substantial likelihood that no jury would conclude beyond a reasonable doubt that she did not consent to what happened next. Just cataloguing the conceded actions would have established the theme of reasonable belief that there was consent.

Smaller issues which added flavor to the prosecution could have been easily deflected by "changing the lighting."

Much was made of the fact that the young lady brought along a camera allegedly to photograph celebrities at various parties they were supposedly to attend. The bringing of the camera was proclaimed to confirm the belief that they were going "star gazing" rather than to engage in a sexual act. The point was basically unchallenged.

A few questions could easily have negated the impression created and turned it to the advantage of the defense.

The camera could easily have been brought to get a picture of Tyson himself who was a "star" or, more likely, to get a picture of the two of them together so she would have a photograph to show her friends that she was out with Mike Tyson. In other words, a "photo opportunity."

Two simple questions would have achieved the purpose.

Q: The camera you brought with you—was it not capable of taking a picture of Mike Tyson and you together.
A: Yes.
Q: And then you would have a picture to show that you were out with Mike Tyson.
A: Yes.

The two above questions are examples of the only answers that a jury would accept. The camera takes pictures of anything at which it is pointed, which could include Mike Tyson. Thus, a "no" answer would have been unacceptable. It follows that a picture would be produced that could be "bragged on." Again, a "no" in the face of the rhetorically obvious would have damaged the witness' credibility. Yet, the two rhetorical "yeses" would have negated the prosecution's inference to be drawn from bringing the camera and shown the jury a reasonable alternative, consistent with the defense, which, in view of the earlier voluntary conduct, would have been easily accepted.

Such a cross-examination would have deprived the witness of credit for withstanding an attack as well as depriving her of the opportunity to make a number of statements which established in the minds of the jury that she was a naive, unsophisticated Sunday school teacher. It would have provided no opportunity to use phrases such as "yucky" to describe her distaste for Tyson's conduct or comment upon the fact that his breath smelled bad. In other words, the facts would speak for themselves and would have provided a basis for Tyson to reasonably believe that she was consenting to have sex with him or at least a reasonable doubt as to whether she generated a reasonable belief.

§7.4 TRYING TWO DIFFERENT CASES

In the development of themes, it often happens that the opposing sides are trying two different cases.

Several years ago I represented a defendant from whom two banks were seeking $20 million based on personal guarantees that he allegedly signed. There were two guarantee documents at issue, both signed by the defendant. One, by defendant's bankrupt corporation was conceded, the other, alleged to be personal, was in Hebrew and contested.

Opposing counsel anticipated that the defense would contend that defendant would claim that he was not conversant in Hebrew and did not know the nature of the document that he was signing. He prepared his case to rebut that theme.

To the plaintiff's surprise, the defendant contended that he understood the document and the language in which it was written (Hebrew) perfectly and that, in fact, it was not a personal guarantee at all but, rather, a translation of the corporate guarantee and, therefore, the defendant was without liability. The cross-examinations of the plaintiff's witnesses addressed the nuances in the Hebrew language, and the witnesses were forced to admit that a single word often can have several meanings. The jury, left to decide upon conflicting interpretations of a document written in a language with which they were unfamiliar, had to resolve their uncertainty in favor of the defendant.

Control 8

§8.1 INTRODUCTION

When asked the three most important things that an investor should look for when purchasing real estate, the answer is "location, location, location." When asked the most important three things to remember in cross-examination, the answer is "control, control, control."

Preparation is invaluable; but, the best preparation in the world is invalidated by permitting a witness to get out of control, thereby inflicting great harm to your case. Every trial lawyer is aware of the disaster that occurs when the witness gives a devastating, unanticipated answer and catches the lawyer by surprise. It is only through control that this disaster can be avoided.

§8.2 INTIMIDATION

A dirty word by which control is exerted is intimidation. Intimidation is not meant as battering or arguing forcibly with the witness. Intimidation starts from the fact of cross-examination. The lawyer gets to chose the questions, the sequence in which they will be asked and the point of view from which they will be generated. Lies or errors can be uncovered and the potential for the witness to be embarrassed or, worse, is a sword of Damocles. If there are any surprises, they are more likely to come from the lawyer who may have prepared or come from a different direction to an extent unanticipated by the witness.

The courtroom, its procedures and surroundings add to the effect. It is not a place in which infrequent visitors who find themselves under oath are comfortable.

A lawyer conducting a cross-examination should never give up that advantage. Rather, he should build on it in the course of the examination each time that a witness is shown to be mistaken, telling less than the truth or testifying differently than he had on a prior occasion. All of the methods under consideration here have, at their base, an element of intimidation. With one exception, none depends on yelling or arguing with the witness or bashing him.

§8.3 ACTION AND REACTION

Another element of control and its progeny, intimidation, is the fact that, upon cross-examination, the lawyer acts and the witness is forced to react. As indicated, the lawyer chooses the topic or area, the form of the question, the pace and the tempo, and even the sequence which is designed to maintain the advantage and reveal flaws in the testimony. To all of these things, a witness is required to react rather than initiate any of the above. A few wrong answers or an error in anticipating the direction from which the lawyer is coming can confirm a feeling of insecurity. Conversely, an uncontrolled witness is one who forces the lawyer to react. Once a lawyer is placed in the position of reacting, rather than initiating, the witness has gotten away from him.

§8.4 THE DUEL

What takes place between a witness and a cross-examiner is a duel or fencing match. While the repeated admonition, "stop fencing," is often heard in the course of a trial, the admonition is as valid as it would be if it were directed at the two finalists in the National Fencing Championships. A chess grand master would refer to it as a chess match, but the basic elements of all three are the same. Whether physical or mental, control is exerted by forcing a reaction or capitalizing on the lack of one.

In a fencing match, two opponents face each other each seeking to score points by hitting the other. Your opponent approaches you with his arm held in a position so as to provide the greatest protective shield of the target, which is his torso. In order to score a point, you must get the opponent to move his hand and arm out of the way giving you an opening to the torso. Obviously, you must make several feints by which you hope to induce him to react or, if he fails to react, adjust your strategy accordingly. If your opponent does not react, you must try something else or resort to a feint in a different direction. The one thing that is clear, however, is that you cannot attack until you have induced the movement of your opponent's arm out of the way.

The first feint that you make may induce movement, but not enough. A second feint is required and sometimes a third and a fourth until there has been sufficient movement of the arm to open up the target. Thus, you are setting up the attack by an initial series of feints.

Another purpose served by the feint is to get your opponent into a tempo or rhythm that you can track. If you feint to the right, they move to the right a certain amount. A movement to the left will bring a countervailing response to the left. Soon you will have your opponent's arms swinging left or right depending on where he perceives the feint is going and which side he believes the attack is coming from.

The secret of a successful feint is to convince your opponent that it is an attack that, if unanswered, will result in a touch being scored against him. If it is clear that the feint cannot conceivably be successful, it is no feint at all. Thus, if one was standing ten feet away from an opponent and made a movement which, if made within five feet of the opponent, would be serious since that is the maximum range, it will be ignored and no purpose served.

It is necessary to get your opponent to commit to a position that is less defensible than the one that he is in at the outset, which is his best position. Getting him out of position may mean having the arm too far to the side to protect the target or even having the person's weight on the wrong foot. If a person's weight is on the front foot, he cannot launch an attack since an attack is launched by pushing off from the back foot.

By the same token, an opponent is most vulnerable when he is attacking to an area for which you are prepared, being induced by your movements or feints to attack to a particular area. It is clear that success in a fencing match depends on planning several moves ahead and taking several steps along the way which are not designed to be capitalized upon until some time later. Thus, some early movements are not designed to score a point but to set up the possibility of scoring a point later, provided the proper responses can be obtained from the opponent.

By analogy, cross-examination functions in the same manner. Substitute the words "probing question" for "feint." The purpose of the probing questions is to get the witness to move from the position which he has asserted on direct examination and, if possible, to commit to a position that is less defensible. Thus, once he is out of position or has his weight on the wrong foot, by taking positions in response to your questions or exaggerating his answers, he has exposed a target for your attack. As in fencing, setting up the witness by the pace and tempo of questions as well as the sequence are all earlier maneuvers designed to produce rewards at some subsequent point in the examination.

Probing questions may simply serve to see how the witness responds. Does the witness stubbornly persist in an answer even if it is demonstrated to be less than acceptable?

How does the witness respond to a question phrased belligerently or antagonistically? Does his spine stiffen or does he back off? What response is there to showing the witness to be wrong even on a minor insignificant point? What causes the witness to become defensive and begin to defend himself rather than his testimony?

Does the witness become confused if questions are asked out of sequence instead of in an orderly chronology or tracking direct examination? This will tell the cross-examiner how to proceed with cross-examination by varying the sequence of the questions.

Once the witness has been moved out of position and the target is then in sight, the cross-examiner can then proceed to exploit the opening with a series of leading questions in which the witness can do little more than answer "yes" or "no" as demanded. That the witness, by a series of earlier questions, is being set up for a future reward is also analogous to fencing in that much of the questioning on cross-examination is to set up summation or to bring about a subsequent contradiction by the witness on the stand or even to provide a contradiction to a future witness.

The dynamics of the chess game or the fencing match are demonstrated in a common occurrence which occurs with regard to most criminal trials. As an example, the prosecution attempts to anticipate whether or not the defendant will testify. The defense is equally committed to withholding that information until the defense commences. It is important for the prosecution to anticipate correctly since they are faced with the prospect of producing evidence upon their direct case or, if they believe that the defendant will testify, withholding it until cross-examining such defendant where the evidence will produce a much greater effect. If the prosecutor guesses wrong and withholds the damaging evidence and the defendant never takes the stand, valuable evidence is never produced at the trial.

§8.5 MISDIRECTION OF ATTENTION OF WITNESS

An example of a feint in the courtroom is the probing question or the question which suggests a direction which is misinterpreted by the witness leading to the giving of answers devastating to the witness' position.

An example of how a carefully worded question can misdirect the attention of the witness leading to the giving of testimony adverse to the party on whose behalf he appeared is demonstrated by an example from a military trial that took place a number of years ago.

A mail clerk was charged, while monitoring prisoners' letters, with removing any cash that had been sent to the prisoners by their friends and families. Charges were brought against the airman; and, pending trial, he was confined to quarters under base arrest. Violating base arrest and going beyond certain limitations upon the base was itself a serious offense.

Three weeks prior to the trial, it was reported to the airman's commanding officer that the airman had disappeared, having been last seen on Friday, the preceding day. Despite vigorous efforts, the airman could not be located. On Sunday night, it was reported to the commanding officer that the airman had been located, asleep in his barracks. When questioned, the airman stated that he had no recollection of the events of the weekend since he had gone to the Noncommissioned Officers Club and apparently had too much to drink, remembering nothing until he woke up in his bed on Sunday evening. Although there was no direct proof, violating base arrest was added to the charges at the forthcoming court martial.

At the court martial, the defense brought in the father of the airman to offer some testimony which would serve to refute the charges of theft of money from the prisoners' mail. It was clear that this witness was unfamiliar with the charges as filed and was focusing on what he understood to be the nature of the problem, i.e., the larceny.

Nearing the end of the cross-examination, after a few probing questions were asked which established that the witness was not familiar with all of the specifications of the actual charges brought, the cross-examination concluded as follows:

Q. Are you aware, sir, that your son has a habit of getting in trouble?
A. I'm aware of no such thing.
Q. Well, are you aware of the fact that he has gotten in trouble recently?
A. The only trouble of which I am aware is these false charges of calling him a thief.
Q. Are you not aware that he got in trouble three weeks ago on the weekend of April 6?
A. That's impossible.
Q. How can you say it's impossible?
A. Because I was with him the entire weekend.
Q. Are you saying you were with him the entire weekend?
A. Yes.
Q. And are you saying that he was not out of your sight during the entire weekend when he could have gotten in trouble?
A. That's what I am saying.
Q. Please tell us then what occurred that weekend by which you can come before this tribunal and testify that he could not have gotten into trouble that weekend.
A. I picked him up at the base at 6:00 p.m. and we drove to his sister's house for dinner. After dinner we went to a movie and returned to my house. Saturday we returned to his sister's house and spent the entire day there until about 9:00 in the evening. At that time we returned to my home where he slept over. On Sunday we laid around the house until about 2:30 and went over to a friend's house. I personally drove him back to

> the base at 6:00 p.m. So, you see, he could not have gotten into trouble that weekend.

Of course, the witness having misinterpreted the word "trouble" delivered conclusive testimony of the violation of base arrest.

Control by Leading Questions 9

§9.1 INTRODUCTION

If control is the objective, the leading question is the most effective way of reaching that goal. The reasons are more numerous than are readily apparent.

At the first level, the leading question limits the parameters by which an answer can be responsive and to that extent serves a basic purpose. Recognition of what other elements are brought to bear not only makes the question more effective but even assists in the formulation of the question.

A leading question also intimidates. "What happened next" is a passive question that does not suggest to the witness that you know the answer or have any basis to challenge whatever the witness' response may be.

Conversely, "isn't it true that on February 15, 1992 you gave $10,000 to William Jones" is an aggressive question that challenges the witness. The question suggests that you have particular information in your possession that he will be confronted with if he should answer in the negative. At the least, it conveys that you may be lying in wait to pounce on a negative answer.

Even the uncertainty as to whether or not you are possessed of valid information to support your question or only an educated guess made in good faith is sufficient to generate apprehensiveness in the witness about disagreeing with you.

Assuming a level of conservatism in the wording of such leading questions so as not to appear to be grasping at straws, the witness will generally agree or answer with a qualified negative to protect himself. That retreat to the qualification is often all that needs to be accomplished by that area of cross-examination.

§9.2 PROVIDE AN EASY WAY OUT

The object of control is to steer the witness in a particular direction. It would make no sense to exercise such control that the witness simply makes figurative circles within a four-walled fortress. It is important to provide an exit that constitutes the easy way out. The exit may be general or specific.

The witness may simply want to get the examination over with. It is enough simply to telegraph in the questions that the quickest way to end the examination is just to agree with you, particularly if you make it non-demeaning or non-humiliating to do so. An example would be not an admission of lying but, rather, the possibility of error.

The leading question can also convey that unequivocal disagreement will lead to lengthy and difficult examination that can demonstrate false testimony or biased exaggeration.

Nobody knows better than the witness what he is hiding, avoiding or shading. If it exists, the witness under cross-examination will go in the pointed direction, if you let him.

§9.3 BUILDING IN THE ANSWER

More direct control is exerted on cross-examination by leading questions that conclude with a built in answer such as, "isn't that right?" "yes?" or "isn't that so?"

Despite all efforts, witnesses try to deviate from the narrow path that you have set for them. On each occasion, the witness must be reined in and forced to stick to that path.

While a leading question narrows the limits within which a responsive answer can be given, affixing an "isn't that so?" or "is that a fair statement?" closes down the range even further toward "yes" or "no" without opportunity to wander.

Yet another advantage is that the subquestion can be the establishment of another issue which permits tighter control.

For example, where a witness is being confronted with a prior inconsistent statement, the object is to establish the existence of the statement without giving the witness a chance to explain the discrepancy. Thus, in questioning about a letter which appears to contradict the testimony presently being given to the effect that there was no contract with the Phillips Company at any time, cross-examination would proceed:

Q. Mr. X, on December 6, 1990 you wrote to Mr. Y, did you not?
A. Yes.
Q. Is this the letter?
A. Yes.
Q. And in that letter you stated, and I quote: "based on our meeting in San Francisco with the Phillips Company, I believe that a contract should soon be on the way." I read that portion of the letter correctly, did I not?
A. Well, you see—
Q. The only question is did I read the letter correctly?
A. Yes.
Q. Thank you.

The questioning only sought to establish the existence of the letter and the critical factor of its contents which is then before the jury. At no time was the witness given any opportunity to offer any reconciliation between the prior statement and the current testimony.

§9.4 THE ST. JOHNS' ATHLETES

A witness tightly controlled when cross-examination commences but who is free to roam in the later stages defeats the entire purpose. The control is gentle at times and at other times very tight. The primary goal is that control must be constant and unyielding.

Stephen Scaring, a former Chief of the Homicide Bureau in the Nassau County District Attorney's Office, now a leading defense attorney, recently defended several college athletes who were accused of sexually abusing a young lady at a campus rifle club at St. Johns

University. The defendants were acquitted, and there could be no question but that it was the cross-examination by Scaring that accomplished that result.

It was recognized at the outset that the first visual impressions the jury would receive were "three jocks sitting at one table and one young woman at the other." Scaring knew that, if he leaned too hard on this woman at the outset, his clients would suffer; yet, if he did not tightly control her, her testimony and the sympathetic figure that she would cut would be devastating. Thus, during the course of cross-examination, while his tone was courteous and considerate, his exercise of control was relentless.

The cross-examination consumed several days. There was always the temptation to wear down at the end in which case a witness would start to recall the statements from which they had been repressed during the preceding examination. The transcript demonstrates from start to finish that Scaring never provided that opportunity.

It does not matter what the question was or the issue that was being explored. If the witness did not respond directly to the question as phrased by Scaring, the witness was brought back by several means.

Q. So, you went to the DA's office by yourself?
A. There was a misunderstanding. I was told that . . .
Q. I'm sorry, Ms. Jones. Did you go by yourself or did you go with somebody?
A. I went alone.

* * *

Q. And how long did that session that you had with Mr. Gonzalez take?
A. It's over the same forty-five minutes.
Q. Did Mr. Gonzalez write anything down?
A. No, Mr. Scaring. May I explain something to you?
Q. I'll be very specific, Ms. Jones, if you don't mind. Did Mr. Gonzalez have a stenographer like we have here take down what was said?
A. Not that I remember.

* * *

Q. Did he take any notes during that session?
A. No, I was being difficult.

Q. You were being difficult so he didn't write anything down, is that what you are saying?
A. No, you know, what I am trying—
Q. Let me be specific. The question is very specific, Ms. Jones. Did he write anything down?
A. No, Mr. Scaring.

* * *

Q. So, this is what you said to Dean Thomas you told Sister Faith, yes?
A. Yes. Could I explain something to you?
Q. Well, let me ask the questions and the District Attorney can come up later. And did you tell Dean Thomas that Sister Faith then said, "I'm beginning to get the picture?"
A. I told her that.

* * *

Q. In fact, you told this jury just a few minutes ago or maybe it was yesterday that you had consumed two full glasses or cups or whatever the item was, I think you said six ounces and almost a third, isn't that so?
A. Yes, Mr. Scaring.
Q. And you said to Sister Faith that, "I don't have much to drink. I only had a cup and I didn't finish my cup" and she started telling me—That was your testimony yesterday, isn't that so?
A. May I see that? It was my testimony yesterday.
Q. So you lied to Sister Faith about how much alcohol you had consumed regarding the incident of March 1, isn't that so Ms. Jones?
A. Yes.

* * *

Q. Now, you said in this courtroom (your answer was on page 53) that you actually had two cups, two full cups over six ounces and most of the third, isn't that so?
A. Yes, Mr. Scaring. You know, I can explain why I minimized the drinks.
Q. Ms. Jones, the District Attorney can ask you as many questions as he chooses. Now, Ms. Jones, you also told different stories about what you had to drink to different people, isn't that so?

* * *

Q. And so we are clear, Ms. Jones, when you spoke to Detective Navarro, you said that you had one drink and you couldn't finish the second one, isn't that so?
A. May I explain something?
Q. Just tell me if that is so, Ms. Jones.
A. That's so.

* * *

Q. Was Todd Miller asking you what happened and did you tell Dean Thomas that you didn't answer him because you were sick and tired of him bothering you?
A. Oh.
Q. Did you say that?
A. Yes, Mr. Scaring. May I please explain something to you?
Q. Ms. Jones, the District Attorney may ask you whatever he chooses.
A. I know.
Q. I'm allowed to ask questions on cross and I would like you to be as specific as you can. If you can't answer my question, just say you can't answer the question. Was Mr. Miller, Todd Miller, friendly to you?
A. Yes, he was.

* * *

Q. So, you made an excuse for him to give it to you, isn't that so, yes?
A. I had to have a good reason, a solid reason.
Q. So you made up a reason?
A. It was pretty made up, that reason.
Q. It was a pretty made up reason, yes?

* * *

Q. What you told Bill Collins was not true, isn't that so, Ms. Jones?
A. Mr. Scaring, if you would let me explain, I can answer.
Q. I'm going to ask you a very specific question. You told Bill Collins as an excuse to get the number that somebody was going to kill Michael Calendrillo, didn't you say that?
A. Yes, Mr. Scaring.

* * *

Q. You went to Bill Collins to get the number for Michael Calendrillo, yes?
A. Yes.
Q. And as an excuse to get it—that's the word you used yesterday, you told Bill Collins that somebody was going to kill Michael Calendrillo?
A. Yes, I told Bill Collins that.
Q. And that wasn't true, was it?
A. Mr. Scaring—
Q. Ms. Jones, can you tell me whether or not that was a true statement when you said it?
A. That's very difficult to answer yes or no.
Q. You mean whether or not your statement to Bill Collins that somebody was going to kill Michael Calendrillo? You can't tell this jury whether or not that was a true statement or a false statement?
A. That's not what I'm saying, what I'm trying to tell you.
Q. Well, the question to you, Ms. Jones, is was it a true statement or a false statement?
A. It was a false statement. Michael wasn't going to be killed.
Q. But you told a false statement to Bill Collins as an excuse to get the phone number, yes?
A. Yes.

* * *

Q. Well, how long after was it that you finally told Dean Rodriguez that the story you told Bill Collins was false and the story you told Dean Rodriguez was false?
A. It's not so much that its false, Mr. Scaring. It's more like—
Q. It is not true, Ms. Jones.
A. Can I explain?
Q. Ms. Jones, you said way, way after you told him. When was way, way after? Tell me, please.
A. Mr. Scaring, I'm very harmless and my friends are very harmless.
Q. Excuse me, Ms. Jones, I'm not concerned about whether you were going to do it or not. I'm only concerned about whether or not you told him a false story. You said that you corrected it at some time way, way after. You tell this jury and myself and

everybody else here when you told Dean Rodriguez about this false story.

A. I told Dean Rodriguez March 26 that I'm going to go to the police and I wasn't going to hurt Michael in the first place. I have too much consideration for his mother.

Q. So you told Dean Rodriguez that you weren't going to hurt him in the first place because you have too much consideration for his mother, yes?

A. Well, words to that effect.

Q. Did you tell him, "I lied to you, Dean Rodriguez, when I said I was going to kill or somebody was going to kill Michael Calendrillo?"

A. Well, I don't recall lying much. I'm trying to explain to you the statement, how it came about. You didn't give—

Q. Well, did you tell him specifically, Ms. Jones, that "I lied to you. I spoke to you earlier and told you that somebody was going to kill Michael Calendrillo."

A. No. No, Mr. Scaring.

* * *

Q. You told this woman that Bill Collins said you can have the number, isn't that so. Did you say that Ms. Jones?

A. Yes, Mr. Scaring.

Q. And that wasn't true, was it?

A. Well, you know, Bill Collins—

Q. Ms. Jones, that is a simple question that was either not true or it was true.

A. It's not true.

* * *

Q. And when you used the name Lisa that was a lie, isn't that so?

A. An excuse, yes, Mr. Scaring.

Q. An excuse or a lie. Was it true, Ms. Jones, or not that you were Lisa?

A. I am not Lisa.

Q. So it was a lie, yes?

A. I had to get to Michael.

Q. I see. If you had to get to Michael, you can lie to get to Michael.

A. Michael was lying on me and lying about me and no one is saying anything.

Q. Well, I haven't heard your answer. Did you lie or not when you used the word Lisa?
A. I lied.

* * *

Q. You can't attempt to pronounce her last name for us?
A. I will look back for it. I'll try for you the next time.
Q. What next time, Ms. Jones? This is my last time to speak to you.
A. You are not going to speak with me tomorrow?
Q. Maybe, maybe not.
A. I can't do it for you.
Q. You don't want to do it for me or you can't do it?
A. I said I can't do it for you.
Q. Are you saying you will get it for me tomorrow, not today?
A. Mr. Scaring, I'll do my best.
Q. That's all I'm asking, Ms. Jones.
A. Thank you; I'll do what I can.

* * *

Q. And did you say to her, "I shouldn't have gotten in the car. I shouldn't have said yes to the ride. It's no big deal."
A. I was being a typical victim; I was blaming myself.
Q. Ms. Jones, I don't want you to tell me about a typical victim, just tell us, is that what you did?
A. That's what I did.

* * *

Q. Did you assume it, Ms. Jones? May I have an answer to that question?
A. I'm trying to explain, Mr. Scaring. The way Walter abused me, yelled at me—
Q. Excuse me.
A. I thought—I'm sorry.
Q. You had the opportunity to say that to this jury and they heard you say that.
A. I was trying.
Q. I'm going to ask the question. If you don't understand it, please tell me okay.
A. Okay.

* * *

Q. Did Dean Thomas—didn't you say that about that screaming incident the following—on page 37 and 38: they are pulling at your—that is by Dean Thomas—they are pulling on your pants. Somebody pulled your hair.
A. Right; they grabbed me by my hair and pulled it.
Q. And then the interviewer: grabbed you by your hair and then you said and there and that "yeah, I did scream. I did scream and Walter said something about me screaming all night."
A. Mr. Scaring, that—
Q. Excuse me. Isn't that the same incident you were talking to Dean Thomas about?
A. No, that's when I just came in. This is when I came in and Walter started impressing his friends by abusing me in front of everyone on the floor.
Q. Did I misread this wrong?
A. You are doing—well, never mind.
Q. I'm sorry.
A. I won't answer you, Mr. Scaring. That is when I first came in and, well, that is when I first got there and Walter picked up my shirt and made his comment over my breasts.
Q. Did I misread what you said to Dean Thomas, Ms. Jones?
A. You are reading very conveniently, and I'm trying to explain to you.
Q. Is there something that I misread?
A. Mr. Scaring, it's in the wrong place. You weren't there, Mr. Scaring. And I'm not on trial and I'm trying to explain to you that Walter—
Q. Ms. Jones, did you say what I said to Dean Thomas?
A. Right. When I first got in.
Q. Thank you. I'll go to the next question.
A. You're welcome.

* * *

Q. By the way, when Walter was speaking about hooking up with people, do you realize that he was talking about—at some point do you realize that he was talking about sexual activity among different people; isn't that so?
A. Yes.
Q. And did you ever tell him that's not what you were talking about?

A. I was too embarrassed to open my mouth. I mean—
Q. The question was, Ms. Jones, did you ever say to Mr. Grabinowitz that's not what I mean by hooking up?
A. I was too uncomfortable to talk.
Q. So the answer is you didn't say that?
A. I'm sorry.
Q. So the answer is you didn't say that to Mr. Grabinowitz and that's not what I mean by hooking up to Mr. Grabinowitz?
A. By my reaction, he knew the answer.
Q. But you didn't say that, Ms. Jones, that's the question. Can you simply answer that question, please, for us?
A. I will do my best for you. I have been doing my best for you all morning.
Q. I just asked for a yes or no. Did you say it to him or not?
A. No, I didn't tell him. I never heard the term used like that before.

* * *

Q. You reviewed the transcript before you testified, didn't you? There is nothing wrong with that.
A. I'm trying to remember for you. Yeah, I recall that.
Q. I'm sorry.
A. Yes, Mr. Scaring. Mr. Scaring, I don't know where to find it.
Q. I'm sorry.
A. I don't know where.
Q. Are you finished or would you like to look at it some more?
A. I haven't found it.
Q. You can look at it as long as you wish, Ms. Jones.
A. Okay, it's not there, Mr. Scaring.
Q. Isn't that what she said? Did she say let's start then, Ms. Jones, with the story and I would like you to tell me from the very beginning to the very end all the details. You tell me everything. Don't eliminate anything from start to finish. Isn't that what I just read what you told her?
A. She is only a Dean but that's what she said.
Q. I'm sorry.
A. Mr. Scaring, she was only a Dean.
Q. I can't hear you.
A. I'm sorry.

Q. Please repeat your answer if you would.
A. That's what she said, that she is only a Dean. She wasn't looking for detail.
Q. She is only a Dean, is that what you said, I didn't hear you.
A. I mean, Mr. Scaring, at this point in the investigation, no one was thinking of court. I mean I didn't think I would be here today. I have to explain every little detail. I'm being put on trial and being practically accused of lying, you know, I mean . .

Q. Ms. Jones, would you like to answer my question?
A. I'm sorry, please repeat your question.
Q. Yes. Did Dean Thomas tell you: let's start then, Andrea, with the story and I would like you to tell me from the beginning to the very end all the details. You tell me everything. Don't eliminate anything from start to finish, okay? Isn't that what she said?
A. She said that.

* * *

Q. Did he ask you if you were alright and did you say to him I'm fine. Why shouldn't I be alright.
A. Because if Michael wanted to play a game I'll play along in what happened March 1 and if Michael doesn't want to admit it—
Q. Ms. Jones, would you respond to the question.
A. I'm sorry, okay.
Q. If you can't respond to it just say so. Did you say to Michael in a phone conversation—I'm sorry. Did he say to you or ask you if you were alright? Did you respond by saying: I'm fine. Why shouldn't I be alright?
A. I was becoming sarcastic. Yes, I said that.

The last exchange took place one question prior to the end of the cross-examination. It demonstrated that the control over the witness was being exerted right to the very end and that at no time was the witness permitted to wander from the very precise questions that were being put to her. Time after time, the witness attempted to modify her story or to insert matters which would have put her in a more sympathetic light and would have been adverse to the defendants. On each occasion, Scaring's unyielding control thwarted the effort; and, he extracted a series of admissions that she had repeatedly lied in telling the story on a number of other occasions.

§9.5 CONTROLLING THE MOST DIFFICULT WITNESS

In *U.S. v. Mangano*, the main government witness was not one to be chilled or intimidated by the concept of cross-examination.

Nevertheless, Fred Hafetz, former Chief of the Criminal Division of the United States Attorney's Office for the Southern District of New York, utilized the leading question ending in a short direct question and held the witness in check.

Q. Mr. X, is it your testimony, that having not hesitated to commit the crimes of murder, sir, that you would hesitate to commit perjury in this Courtroom if it served your interests to do so?
A. I will not commit perjury.
Q. You would not commit perjury?
A. No.
Q. You would commit murder, but you would not commit perjury. Is that your answer sir?
A. Yes.
Q. You have a higher regard for the laws of perjury then you do for the law against taking someone's life; is that correct?
A. No.
Q. No, you have lied before in your life, have you not, Mr. X?
A. Yes.
Q. And you've lied to City, State and Federal officials; am I right, sir?
A. Correct.
Q. You have submitted false affidavits to New York City with regard to the window program. Am I right, sir?
A. Yes.
Q. That was perjury, was it not?
A. Collusion, I don't know if it was perjury.
Q. You submitted false statements to New York City, am I right, in connection with the window program, documents your company signed?

A. Perjury is when you're on the road, Mr. Hafetz, any other document is collusion, I was colluding to bid rigging.
Q. Did you sign documents submitted to the City saying that you were not participating in collusion, sir?
A. Yes.
Q. So you were submitting false statements to government officials; am I correct?
A. Yes.
Q. You also submitted false Federal tax returns. Am I correct, sir?
A. Yes.
Q. Submitted under penalty of perjury, am I right, Mr. X?
A. I can't answer that because I don't know if that is the truth or not. If it is perjury, I don't know.
Q. But false?
A. False, yes, they were false.
Q. False statements submitted to governmental authorities, am I right?
A. Yes.
Q. They are lies. Is that right, sir? You lied in the documents you were submitting under your signature to the Federal Government? Am I right?
A. Yes.
Q. And you didn't hesitate to do that. Am I right, sir?
A. Right.
Q. You lied to the bank with regard to bank applications throughout your career for loans?
A. Yes.
Q. And you've lied, and you've lied and you've lied with regard to statements that you have made concerning your affairs. Am I right, Mr. X?
A. Well, I wouldn't say I lied and lied and lied but on—
Q. There were breaks in between, some days you didn't lie and some days you did lie? Am I right?
A. No.
Q. Pardon me.
A. No.
Q. But there were many days when you did lie. Am I right, sir, throughout a long span of time?

A. There are days that I lie.

* * *

Q. When he came in, did you have some conversation with him?
A. Yes.
Q. Say hello Richard, how are you Richard?
A. We had conversation.
Q. You had some small talk with him; is that right sir?
A. Yes.
Q. And then you led him down to the basement, am I right, sir?
A. I did not lead him down to the basement.
Q. But you knew he was going down into the basement?
A. Yes, I did.
Q. Into his death trap. Am I right sir?
A. Yes.
Q. That was going to be the execution chamber the basement of your building?
A. Yes.
Q. That was your mother's building. Am I right, sir?
A. No, it was my mother's building and another person, two people in that building.
Q. Excuse me.
A. Two people owned that building.
Q. Your mother was one of them.
A. It was my father and my father passed away, and my mother.
Q. So you were utilizing the building owned by your mother as an execution chamber. Am I right, sir?
A. Yes.
Q. For Mr. Scarcella?
A. Yes.
Q. For a planned hit on this man, right, sir?
A. Yes.
Q. And your standing upstairs in the office was helpful so that he would not think there was anything out of the ordinary; am I correct?
A. No.
Q. No, it was not helpful?
A. No.

Q. Did you tell him before he went into the basement that there was somebody waiting down there with a gun who was going to kill him?
A. No.
Q. Did you point out that small fact to Mr. Scarcella, sir?
A. No, I did not.
Q. You didn't bother to point that out, sir?
A. No.
Q. Am I right?
A. No, I didn't.
Q. Would you regard that as concealing something material from Mr. Scarcella, sir?
A. Yes.
Q. But that is something you wouldn't do any more. Am I right Mr. X, you would not conceal any material information, am I right, sir?
A. You are right.
Q. Because you have turned a corner in your life and you don't do any of those things anymore. Am I right?
A. You are.
Q. It is the new Mr. X?
A. Yes.
Q. A brand new character?
A. Yes.
Q. You are a transformation. Am I right, sir?
A. Yes.
Q. Did you hesitate for one second before Scarcella walked down in the basement to be killed?
A. No.
Q. So you freely, willingly, voluntarily participated in a plan to have Scarcella come to your office and go down into the basement under false pretenses where someone else was waiting to kill him. Am I right?
A. Yes.
Q. By the way, before Mr. Scarcella arrived to be executed, his grave had already been dug in the basement. Am I right?
A. Yes.

* * *

Q. You had undergone a conversion between the time of the six murders in 1987, in those seven years you have become a better individual, is that correct, sir?
A. I think that I did.
Q. You have stopped violating the law, correct?
A. No.
Q. You were still scamming and cheating and lying and bribing and participating in other crimes between 1980 and 1987, am I correct, Mr. X?
A. Yes.
Q. But yet you say you were a changed individual, am I right?
A. Yes.
Q. You had become a better individual, am I right, sir?
A. I'm trying.
Q. No, no, no. In November, 1987, when law enforcement came to you on that day at the point when they came to you you had become a better individual than you were in the past, is that right, sir?
A. Yes.
Q. But you were still participating in cheating the government, were you not?
A. Yes.
Q. You were still participating in bribery, correct?
A. Correct.
Q. You were still participating in other criminal activity am I right, sir?
A. Yes.
Q. You were participating according to your testimony on duress and extortions, am I correct?
A. Correct.
Q. But you had become a reformed individual, is that your testimony?
A. Yes.
Q. Was it because you had become a better individual because you no longer did murders?
A. Yes.
Q. You were still willing to participate in many other criminal activities, am I correct?

A. Yes.
Q. Which included lying and cheating, am I right, sir?
A. Correct.
Q. And including, if necessary, making false statements to the Government, correct?
A. Correct.
Q. And all for your self-interest, am I right?
A. Correct.
Q. These crimes were all for your self-interest, am I right, sir?
A. Correct.

Obviously, there was little left to the credibility of the witness. The clear effect was achieved, as evident from the short answers that were hemmed in by the wording of the questions. The witness had no choice but to give those answers, even though when viewed in their entirety, the position was beyond the bounds of reason.

Control: Stripping Away the Mystique 10

§10.1 INTRODUCTION

The initial way to approach the subject of controlling a witness is to strip the process of its mystique. People routinely control others in daily conversation and think nothing of it.

Consider that you are in conversation outside the courtroom with a friend, acquaintance, business adversary or anyone else. There is no courtroom, no rules, no judge or person to pass upon objections to something that is said which may be inappropriate. In other words, the other person is free to say whatever he wants, however ignorant, offensive, outrageous, irrelevant, non-responsive or even false.

How would you seek to control the conversation? What is it that is actually meant by controlling the conversation?

The first thing to be considered is whether you want to control the conversation or just pass the time without friction. That decision would be made if the person does not say anything which forces you to respond and you have no interest in unnecessary friction or confrontation. In the courtroom, this is the first decision to be made. Should you cross-examine at all?

The person with whom you are in conversation may have said something mildly disturbing but to continue further would only induce further statements significantly more troubling. Under those circumstances, the shorter the conversation the better. Once again, it is no different in the courtroom. Don't risk a dollar to win a dime.

If you decide that you need to take control of the conversation, what result do you hope to obtain if you are successful? Do you want to challenge everything the person is saying or only parts of it?

The obvious goal of exerting control is to get the person with whom you are having the conversation to defer to you at that moment even if they do not fully agree with everything you are saying on a long term basis. Having assumed control of the conversation, the object would be to get the other person to discontinue pressing his point and stop opposing the point that you are seeking to make in order to achieve the result you want. This may be more true in the courtroom. In private conversation you may be interested in actually changing a person's opinion. In the courtroom the only opinion you want to influence is the judge or the jury, not that of the witness.

It is well to reiterate that the purpose of assuming control in our hypothetical conversation, as well as in the courtroom, is not for the purpose of guiding or influencing future action but only to have the person agree with you or stop opposing you for that moment. Thus, even if there is not general agreement, it is enough to get agreement or stem resistance at that moment for the purposes of the immediate conversation. It will be easier to achieve upon the particular issue in the conversation in accordance with the limited way that you define the point of the discussion which does not involve a complete reversal or withdrawal of everything that he is saying.

Using an everyday example, you may be engaged in conversation with a person who is absolutely adverse to the concept of abortion. Suppose, however, that the subject of abortion, for purposes of the discussion at hand, is limited to cases in which the procedure is necessary to save the life of the mother. It would not be uncommon to find somebody absolutely adverse to abortion generally who would concede that, under those circumstances, it might be appropriate or acceptable. The same is true in any other discussion provided one person can limit the issue and bring about a point of agreement even though there is general disagreement on a more expanded subject. It is also effective if the question is structured so that there is a diminished will to resist. That, in and of itself, will create the opening for going along with your lead.

Why would a person yield control of a conversation held in ordinary circumstances with no judge, jury or set of rules to force him to do so? What are the techniques to be utilized to obtain such control when the other person is not obliged to do so and is free to say anything he wants without fear of repercussion of any kind?

In ordinary discussion, if you demonstrate that you are more knowledgeable on the subject being discussed, it is a natural inclination for your opposing number to defer to you or, rather, to the greater knowledge that you seem to possess. Since he cannot go stride for stride with you on the facts and he is reduced to generalities while you are able to cite specifics, he will look for the easy way out of the discussion.

If the person refuses to yield, he is faced with the risk of being embarrassed by your superior knowledge and being called to account by a demonstration of his ignorance. The fear and avoidance of embarrassment is a great motivator to induce people to agree with you.

In other conversations, you have taken some earlier comments and extended them out to their logical conclusion, thereby showing that the original comment was wrong or not clearly thought through. Once shown that his earlier comments, when held up to the light of day, are either ludicrous or ignorant, a person will come over to your side or back away, particularly if you provide a path to your doorway.

Somewhere in the course of conversation, you may have demonstrated that you are in possession of or have access to facts that will demonstrate that he is wrong and, if he persists, there may be consequences attached to his being wrong, even if those consequences are only his being shown to be foolish or uninformed, let alone some actual penalty.

On other occasions, you exhibit a potential for belligerency or antagonism with which the person with whom you are in conversation does not wish to deal and so he agrees with you simply to avoid an unpleasant experience or to avoid confrontation.

Perhaps you have resorted to sarcasm or irony that again puts a person on the defensive to the extent that he wishes to avoid discomfort.

You remain focused and dismiss all extraneous comments as meaningless. Such an approach, even pleasantly delivered, would commence with statements to the effect "but is that really the point" or "that's not what we are talking about."

You might demonstrate that you understand that the only reason the person with whom you are having the discussion is taking the position he does is because of a personal situation which places pressure upon him to say what he is saying. This, again, has a way of leading people to agree that the circumstances of which they speak are limited to themselves and are not necessarily applicable to other people in other situations. Your failure to continue only suggests that they are more to be pitied than censured, but that little weight can be accorded their statement.

It is easily seen that control of a conversation can be taken without the imposition of rules enforced by a judge in the formal trappings of a courtroom. What is significant to understand is that it is precisely the same methods and techniques that permit a lawyer to assert control over a witness in the courtroom. It is not the judge, the presence of the jury, or the existence of evidentiary rules that establish control. It is the one on one approach of persuasion, intimidation, knowledge, sometimes humor and sometimes belligerency and the ever present element of human frailty that invariably seeks to avoid ridicule, embarrassment or being proven wrong or being shown up.

In some cases, attempting to earn your good opinion motivates and places a witness under control. Many people or witnesses try to do this and the price of your good opinion is that they cooperate with you.

When lawyers stop depending on the crutch of the courtroom with its trappings and rules to effect control, they rapidly develop the techniques by which control of a witness is accomplished.

Some examples of ordinary conversations transported to the courtroom illustrate the point.

§10.2 BEING MORE KNOWLEDGEABLE

Being more knowledgeable means knowing more about a particular subject or having the source of that knowledge handy to act as a "stopper" to the other person's comments so as to bring the conversation to a close on your terms.

a. An Every Day Conversation

You and a friend, having just been to the "West Side Story" engage in the following conversation:

Friend: What a great story. The guy that wrote that is a genius.
You: Who do you think that is?
Friend: Arthur Lawrence, the guy that wrote the book for the show.
You: He is certainly talented and clever, but he certainly didn't dream up that story.
Friend: Of course he did; we just saw the show.
You: Yes, but it's an old story that was simply adapted.
Friend: Oh, come on.
You: Have you ever read Shakespeare?
You: A little bit.
Friend: Well, are you familiar with his works. Have you ever read "Romeo and Juliet?"
Friend: What's the point?
You: Do you remember the story was about the two young lovers that came from families that hated each other and it led to both of their deaths?
Friend: Sort of, but there's no resemblance between Shakespeare and this play.
You: Well, wait a minute; I've got a copy of "Romeo and Juliet" here in the bookcase. Let's take a look.

[the two review portions of the book]

You: Well?
Friend: Well, I see certain similarities; but I'm still not convinced.
You: Do you still have your program?
Friend: Yes.
You: Why don't you take a look at it. Did you notice anything in it about Shakespeare when you read it?
Friend: No.
You: Well, look at it now.
Friend: I'll be darned. It says here the book is based upon "Romeo and Juliet" by William Shakespeare.
You: Now, what do you think?
Friend: I guess you're right.

b. In The Courtroom

The trial is one for medical malpractice. A psychiatrist has just completed testimony that the defendant misdiagnosed "post-traumatic stress syndrome" and, therefore, failed to render proper treatment, thus resulting in plaintiff's attempt at suicide. Defense counsel commences cross-examination with a series of books and pamphlets arrayed at counsel table, one of which he is holding in his hand. The questioning is a follows:

Q. Doctor, are you familiar with when post-traumatic stress syndrome first became a recognized medical condition?
A. I know it's at least thirty or forty years.
Q. Do you recall any particular events which prompted studies of the subject resulting in its identification as a medically recognizable emotional condition?
A. I don't recall any particular event.
Q. I take it you're familiar with the fact that in the 1960's and early 1970's this country was engaged in what is known as the Vietnam War?
A. Of course.
Q. Do you know of any study or medical identification of this condition which predates the Vietnam War?
A. Not off hand.
Q. Do you know who conducted the original research that resulted in this identification?
A. I don't know who originally did it but I do know that Doctors X and Y at some point have published writings on the subject.
Q. Yes doctor, but wasn't that in 1983 and 1987?
A. I believe you're right.
Q. Weren't there extensive studies published in 1972?
A. I'm not sure.
Q. Have you ever heard of a study performed at the Bethesda Naval Hospital during the years 1969 through 1972 which resulted in a change of listed ailments for which the Veterans Administration substantially expanded medical benefits?
A. I never heard of it in that context.

Q. And in fact doctor, in 1976 were there not substantial publications identifying ''post-traumatic stress syndrome'' as one of the significant by-products of the Vietnam War?
A. I never heard it put quite that way.
Q. Isn't it a fact, doctor, that the symptoms were first considered after the Korean War as a result of the brainwashing of American servicemen by the North Koreans and the Chinese?
A. I'm not familiar with any connection between the two.
Q. Well, doctor, you identified the study by Dr. X which was published in 1982. I have a copy of that here.
A. I see.
Q. Do you still contend that you are familiar with its contents?
A. Yes.
Q. I now hand you a copy of Dr. X's study of ''post-traumatic stress syndrome'' and direct your attention to page 89. Have you located that page?
A. Yes.
Q. Please read it to yourself. Is it still your contention that it has never been brought to your attention as to the connection between the brainwashing of the Korean War and the post-traumatic stress syndrome recognized as such in the Vietnam War?
A. That's what it says.
Q. Apparently you did not read that study very carefully, isn't that true?
A. I must have missed that.
Q. Now, as regards symptoms, are you familiar with the symptoms recited in both of the studies you mentioned by Doctors X and Y evidencing the existence of ''post-traumatic stress syndrome?''
A. Yes, I believe so.
Q. Do you believe so or do you know?
A. I think I know.
Q. I now hand you the study by Dr. Y so that you have both the studies of Doctors X and Y to whom you made reference. Will you review both studies and list for us the symptoms that they enumerate in those studies?
A. [the witness does so and lists eight symptoms which according to the studies the existence of five suggests a diagnosis of post-traumatic stress syndrome]

Q. Now, doctor, of those eight symptoms, how many have you testified were exhibited by the plaintiff in this case?
A. Two.
Q. But according to the studies which you enumerated, there is required at least five of the symptoms before a diagnosis is certain.
A. That's what the study says.
Q. But you only found two?
A. Well, I'm not certain I said only two.
Q. Do you recall testifying in this courtroom yesterday?
A. Yes.
Q. Let me hand you the transcript of your testimony yesterday.
A. I have it.
Q. Now, will you please review your testimony and tell this jury that of the eight symptoms that are set forth in the study to which you made reference how many you enumerated in your testimony in this courtroom yesterday?
A. I see only two.
Q. Do you have any reason to believe the transcript is inaccurate?
A. I guess not.

§10.3 EXTENDING THE ANSWER TO ITS LOGICAL CONCLUSION

An initial response may be superficially appealing only as long as it is not questioned. When ''played out'' to its logical conclusion, all substance fades.

a. An Every Day Conversation

You and a friend, the owner of a medium-sized business, are having a conversation when he relates that he just had to discharge three long time employees.

Friend: I hated to fire them, but I really had no choice.
You: Why not?
Friend: Well, business had fallen off slightly and we really had to conserve expenses.

You: Couldn't you have retrained them and put them to use in some other part of the business?
Friend: I guess I could, but that would have involved a lot of time and some reorganization.
You: But don't you have some employees that you believe will be leaving within a year and maybe it would have been better to work out some kind of deal with them rather than letting go long time employees with whose work you were satisfied?
Friend: I never thought of that.
You: Didn't you once tell me that you were thinking of revising your line and maybe taking a shot at service back up?
Friend: Yes, but our plans for that aren't firm.
You: Well, assuming that you were going forward, wouldn't these people have been important or useful?
Friend: Yes, but we hadn't arrived at that point yet.
You: Maybe it was a good time to arrive at that point rather than losing the employees and getting some strangers who may not be as satisfactory.
Friend: Well, that's a possibility, too.
You: I hate to tell you but it seems like you had a lot of choices.
Friend: Well, I guess you're right if you look at it that way.

b. In the Courtroom

The case was a vigorously disputed matrimonial in which the husband was a risk arbitrageur at a major securities house. He had consistently reported income in excess of $1 million per annum until the year the complaint in the divorce action was served. In that year, tax returns which had been admitted into evidence showed a declared income of $136,000 which he attributed to a bad year occasioned by unfortunate losses. The tax returns for the subsequent years up to the time of trial also reflected this vastly reduced income. There was also admitted into evidence extensive documents showing his business, transaction by transaction, documenting every loss he claimed to have suffered. The defendant presented himself as the victim of harsh economic reality so that the plaintiff unfortunately could not be awarded maintenance and support based upon a prior standard of living. The cross-examination was as follows:

Q. Am I correct that as to the hundreds of documents and transactions you've produced, each of the losses is recognized at the time there is a sale of a security which was originally purchased at a higher price?
A. Yes.
Q. So that each of these transactions represents a sale of a security at a loss?
A. Yes.
Q. Am I further correct that a profit would not be recognized until there was a sale of a security at a higher price than the price at which it was purchased?
A. Of course.
Q. At your firm how is X's compensation determined?
A. He receives a small draw and 18% of the profits.
Q. And for him to receive a percentage of the profit, that's the actual realized profit based upon an actual sale of the security?
A. Yes.
Q. And those profits would be reduced only by actual losses realized upon the sale of a security at a loss?
A. Yes.
Q. Let me show you X's tax return for the year 1987, the year preceding the commencement of this divorce action.
A. I have it.
Q. Do you notice his reported income is $1,456,000.27?
A. Yes.
Q. Since we have all of the documents representing the transactions conducted by his department, can you tell us how much of that $1,456,000.27 is attributable to draw and how much is attributable to his profit participation?
A. $125,000 is attributable to his draw and the balance is a share of the profits realized by his department.
Q. Now, please take a look at the schedule of loss transactions which you previously produced. What is the percentage of those loss transaction to the total number of transactions within that department?

A. Roughly 10%.
Q. And based upon those transactions the profit, as defined for our purposes here, was only approximately $200,000 of which he received compensation in the amount of $36,000?
A. That's right.
Q. Now, who gets to choose when to buy and when to sell?
A. X.
Q. And as to each of the loss transactions, that represents a deliberate choice made by X to sell that security at a loss?
A. Yes.
Q. And if he had not chosen to sell those particular securities at a loss, the profits of that department would have been far greater for purposes of computing his profit participation?
A. That is right.
Q. So that we are clear, the decision to sell those securities and realize losses or not sell and realize a profit was a matter of his sole choice?
A. Yes.

§10.4 ISOLATING THE ISSUE

The object of isolating an issue is to reduce the subject to a subtext that the person to whom you are speaking can least defend or be inclined to defend. Stripping away the extraneous matter and focusing upon the limited point will create the opening and make the witness more pliable.

a. An Every Day Conversation

A husband returns home at 1:00 a.m. to be met by his wife who is extremely upset.

Q. Where have you been, I've been frantic?
A. The meeting with the Acme Company went longer than expected and I ended up going out to dinner with the President and the Comptroller of the company and we got to talking.
Q. Okay, but why didn't you at least call me and tell me so I wouldn't worry?

A. Get off my case. They're a good customer, and I had an opportunity to get to know them better. In case you forgot, that's what pays the bills around here and feeds and clothes your children.
Q. I'm not saying you shouldn't have done it. Do you mean to tell me you couldn't have taken a few minutes to make a phone call?
A. Okay, I could have made a phone call.
Q. Well, that's all I'm talking about. I'm not talking about not doing your job.
A. You're right. I'm sorry. I should have called.

b. In the Courtroom

The issue is a union jurisdictional dispute. One union claims that it has the right to a particular series of jobs and that the other union should have removed all its employees from the job sites. The plaintiff union contended that its jurisdiction had been violated but conceded that if the persons working on the job were members of a union other than the defendant union that its objection was invalid since it only had control of its own membership. At issue was whether or not the defendant union violated its obligations in failing to clear the sites of persons who had historically been members of that union. The cross-cxamination was as follows:

Q. You agree, do you not, that you are only entitled to damages for violating an injunction if the persons remaining on the site who you did remove were members of your union, and that applies as of the time they were actually working at the site?
A. Yes.
Q. Is a person permitted to have more than one union membership?
A. Yes.
Q. And isn't it true that a person who has dual union membership can work at a site as a member of one union and not the other union to which he also belongs.
A. Yes.
Q. So, isn't the question here whether or not the people we have been talking about were working at the job site as members of the defendant union?

A. Well, I know that they were members in that union.
Q. That's not the question, isn't the question whether or not they were working at the job site as members of that union?
A. I guess so.
Q. Isn't it a fact that the persons at that job site, while they may have been members of the defendant union, also held membership in other unions?
A. It wouldn't surprise me; that's very common.
Q. How do you determine union membership?
A. The worker has to be registered and pay dues.
Q. So, it's a question of who the particular worker is paying dues to if one wanted to determine his union affiliation for purposes of a particular job?
A. That would be a way.
Q. How does the union collect dues from its workers?
A. By means of a check off.
Q. Isn't that a system whereby an employer automatically deducts the dues from a worker's wages and sends them directly to the union?
A. Yes.
Q. So isn't the real question to which union the employer is sending checked off dues?
A. Yes.
Q. To put it another way, isn't it a question of which union got the income represented by checked off dues on a particular job?
A. Yes.
Q. Well, now that we know what the real questions are, to whom did the employer send checked off dues of the workers on the various job sites that you're complaining about?
A. [the witness answers a different union than the one against which he had brought the complaint].
Q. So the real issue is not whether or not its the same individual that you saw there previously as a member of the defendant union, but which union was getting the income at the time that you're complaining of their presence?
A. If you say so.

§10.5 SUGGESTING ACCESS TO INFORMATION

Casey Stengel used to prevail in a lot of discussions by taking a position and closing out the conversation by stating, "you could look it up." Obviously, until someone looked it up, they were not in a position to dispute Casey's position. But, at the moment, Casey had his way.

a. An Every Day Conversation

We are back with our two friends who are arguing as to whether or not it was Vince Lombardi or Branch Ricky who coined the phrase "luck is the residue of design." The friend insists that it was Vince Lombardi while reciting a long list of character traits that support the likelihood that such a philosophy could emanate from Vince Lombardi. You are equally insistent that it was Branch Ricky, the former general manager of the old Brooklyn Dodgers, but have nothing but your recollection to substantiate that belief. The conversation is as follows:

Friend: I'm telling you, it was Vince Lombardi; he had a winning habit and he used to say that all the time.

You: No, it was Branch Ricky; and he said it while Vince Lombardi was still trying to make some high school team as a player.

Friend: For how much?

You: What do you mean?

Friend: How much you willing to bet it was Branch Ricky? Want to go for twenty bucks?

You: Okay, here's what we'll do. Call up Charlie, who's a sports freak, and see if he knows the answer; if he doesn't, we'll call up the New York Times information bureau because they can answer every question known to man, particularly anything to do with sports.

Friend: So, what makes you think it was Branch Ricky?

You: I know I heard that phrase years before I ever heard of Vince Lombardi.

Friend: Do you think the Times would have such an answer?

You: They have all the answers like that.

Friend: Okay, I'm curious. Let's call the Times just so we can get the answer, but we don't have to bet.

b. In the Courtroom

A breach of contract suit was brought by plaintiff as a result of defendant's refusal to accept delivery of several truckloads of perishable goods. The contract between the parties provided that the purchaser could cancel the order provided notice was given to the seller 120 days prior to the scheduled delivery date. Uniquely, the contract did not specify that such notice had to be in writing and as a consequence the defendant testified that notice was given verbally in the course of a telephone conversation during a particular week whose dates were in excess of one hundred twenty days before the anticipated delivery date. Plaintiff contended that no such notice had been given. The cross-examination was short but effective.

Q. Are you claiming that you telephoned Mr. X at the Y Company and advised you were cancelling the order?
A. Yes.
Q. Do you recall where you were when you made such phone call?
A. At my office.
Q. What is the area code of the location of your office?
A. 201.
Q. Do you know the area code for the office in which Mr. X works?
A. He is located in Massachusetts.
Q. Where in Massachusetts?
A. Boston.
Q. Do you know the area code for Boston?
A. I believe it is 617.
Q. I have here the Boston telephone book, would you take a look at it and see if you can agree with me that the area code is 617.
A. I've checked it and that's the area code.
Q. Are you aware that phone calls from one area code to another are toll calls that are recorded by the telephone company on your bills showing the source of the call and its destination?
A. [Pause].
Q. Well, aren't you aware of that practice?
A. Yes.

Q. So that if we were to look at your telephone bills for your office for the week of March 6, 1991, there should be recorded on that bill a toll call from your office to Mr. X during that week.
A. I don't know if I still have the phone bill.
Q. Well, we can get it from the telephone company if you don't, all I'm asking you is if you are telling us that if we produce that phone bill there will be listed a phone call from your office to Mr. X on the bill for that period.
A. Well, maybe I made it from somewhere else, I'm not sure, but I know I spoke to him.
Q. Now you're uncertain as to where you made the phone call from?
A. Well, possibly it was somewhere else.
Q. But you didn't tell us that on direct testimony, you were certain it was made from your office in the course of business.
A. Maybe I was wrong.
Q. But you did not admit you might be wrong until confronted with a phone record that would have confirmed or rejected your claim that you had made such a phone call.
A. Maybe I was wrong.

§10.6 DURESS DICTATES THE TESTIMONY

Often, an answer is dictated by an external pressure that is not immediately apparent. By recognizing and identifying the pressure, the position is diluted, if not negated.

a. An Every Day Conversation

In the course of conversation, you have just invited a friend of Japanese descent who works for a major Japanese corporation do dinner. His response demonstrates that his position has nothing to do with the invitation or even his feelings about whether or not he would prefer to have dinner with you. It is demonstrated that it is an external pressure which has little to do with the issues under discussion and, consequently, should have no significant effect upon them or your feeling toward him but which caused him to declare:

Friend: I really would love to have dinner with you on Saturday night; but, we have been spending a lot of time together and my company is not too thrilled with us when we spend too much time socializing with non-Japanese outside the company.
You: Are you serious? They really care about that?
Friend: They're very serious. They have this feeling that they don't want us to get too far from the Japanese community and maybe pick up some bad habits.
You: I understand, you can't jeopardize your career. We'll make it next month after a decent interval passes.

b. In the Courtroom

A commercial lawsuit is in progress. At issue is whether or not the defendant verbally agreed to certain terms of the alleged agreement. The comptroller of the defendant company has just completed testimony that he was present during the entire time that the parties met and that the subject did not arise nor was there any conversation indicating agreement to the terms as alleged by the plaintiff. The following cross-examination takes place:

Q. Now, it is your contention that you were present during the entire time that the parties were in conversation and that no such discussion took place, is that correct?
A. Yes.
Q. How long have your worked for X Company?
A. Twelve years.
Q. So it is the X Company that has provided the main source of your income during those twelve years, is that correct?
A. Yes.
Q. I take it you would not like to give up that income or take any chances on losing it?
A. It would put me in a very difficult position.
Q. I take it you understand that your testimony is very important to your company, is it not?
A. I would assume it is.
Q. Can we agree just as a general principle that you would not like to do anything that would jeopardize your position?

A. I'm telling the truth.
Q. That's not the question, the question is as a general principle you would not like to do anything which jeopardized your position?
A. Of course.
Q. And can we further assume that you would not like to do anything which displeased your employers?
A. No.
Q. And over the years you have probably avoided doing things which you believed would displease your employers?
A. Yes.
Q. And as a general principle would you also state that you would not like to do anything that might cause your employers to question your loyalty to the company?
A. Yes.
Q. And you understand that by appearing here and giving the testimony that you are giving you are helping your company?
A. Yes.
Q. By the same token, you appreciate that if you testified that you heard the conversation as alleged by the plaintiff that would not be helpful to your company?
A. It would not be helpful.
Q. In fact, if you testified that you overheard such an agreement, it might put you in an awkward position from here on out, isn't that true?
A. Its possible.
Q. Thank you very much, sir.

§10.7 AGGRESSIVENESS

Most people like the benefits of aggression, but few like to engage in it or be identified with it. When based on solid ground, if an opening is aggressively exploited, the witness, who doesn't know what's coming next, will likely choose to avoid confrontation.

Aggressiveness need not be surly or high decibel, only telegraph determination with more to come.

a. An Every Day Conversation

Your doorbell rings; it is your next door neighbor complaining about the fact that your dog has relieved himself on his lawn and that he intends to file a complaint that would result in your being fined. He also suggests that his grass is turning brown, and he might seek damages to his lawn. You are not certain as to whether or not your dog has used his lawn for the described purpose but tend to doubt it since your dog is rarely permitted to roam free. In any event, you simply don't want to put up with the bother that would be expended in dealing with this complaint. Thus, the conversation proceeds along the following lines:

Q. How do you know it was my dog?
A. Whose could it have been?
Q. I didn't ask you that; I asked you how do you know it was my dog?
A. Well, I don't know of anybody else whose dog it could have been.
Q. I really don't care what you think, I want to know what you know; and, I'm telling you now that, if you make a complaint and you can't prove it's my dog, the only complaint we're gonna have to worry about is the one that I bring against you.
A. Look, there's no sense in this thing getting out of hand. If it isn't your dog, okay. In the meantime, if it is, maybe you'll keep an eye on him.
Q. Look, I don't want my dog to mess up your lawn and you should have come over in the first place and just asked me to keep an eye on him instead of charging over here and threatening me with all kinds of complaints.
A. Alright, alright. Maybe I shouldn't have jumped the gun; I'm sorry.
Q. Come on in and have a drink.

b. In the Courtroom

A Federal agency has recently closed down a bank estimating that losses in its loan real estate portfolio had rendered the bank insolvent or below capital requirements. Several directors of the bank brought suit against the agency for prematurely bringing about the closing of the bank contending that it was that act that occasioned the losses of depositors rather than the state of affairs occasioned by the bank's operations. The agency auditor who prepared the initial report that led to the closure was under cross-examination:

Q. Now, it is your report that determined that the bank didn't meet its capital requirements?
A. Yes.
Q. How long did you spend on the premises of the bank?
A. Two and a half days.
Q. What did you do in the two and a half days?
A. I reviewed certain books and records.
Q. Did you ever go look at any particular building?
A. No.
Q. Did you ever speak to any particular real estate appraiser?
A. No.
Q. Have you ever owned any real estate?
A. My own house.
Q. Anything else beside that?
A. No.
Q. What made you think you were qualified to evaluate a real estate portfolio of the nature and extent possessed by this bank?
A. That's the way it appeared to me.
Q. What do you mean, appeared? How will this jury know how things appear to you?
A. I don't understand your question.
Q. Do you understand that this jury wants to know the facts, absolute accurate facts, and not the way things appear to you?
A. I don't understand the difference.
Q. Well, for all this jury knows, you could watch a football game and think its a rugby match.
A. How do I know what they think?
Q. You don't, maybe some of them like beer commercials and some don't. Maybe some of them think that Madonna appears to be a great artist and others think it appears that she's trafficking in sex, but you don't know which is which, do you, or even if any of them feel that way.

Objection.
COURT: Sustained.
Q. In any event, Mr. X, lets not talk about how things appear to you but what actually is the fact. Did you physically visit a single property contained in that real estate portfolio?
A. No.
Q. Did you actually obtain a real estate appraisal from a professionally qualified appraiser with regard to the value of that portfolio?
A. No.
Q. Did you know that your report would result in 286 people losing their jobs?
A. That's not my fault.
Q. Was your report the one upon which your agency relied in closing this bank?
A. Yes.
Q. Answer my question, did you know that your report would result in 286 people losing their jobs?
A. I did not consider that within my area of responsibility.
Q. Did you ever consider that hundreds of depositors would lose their money if this bank closed?
A. I did not consider that within my area of responsibility.
Q. That's not the question, I asked you if you ever considered that that would be one of the results that might occur as a result of your report.
A. I did not feel that I had to deal with that.
Q. In other words, when you wrote your report you never considered whether or not the positives would be heard, people would be unemployed or that families might suffer?
A. I certainly had no intention that those things would happen.
Q. But they did.
A. It's unfortunate.
Q. How much more unfortunate would it be if you were wrong?
A. That would be tragic.
Q. Don't you think under the circumstances you had an obligation to get appraisals?
A. It would have been better.
Q. Especially since you had no experience yourself, isn't that true?
A. I had no direct experience.

Q. So now we are dealing with the way things appeared to a person who had no experience.
A. I thought I was right.
Q. I'm not interested in what you thought, only in what you knew. Do you understand that?
A. Yes.
Q. Will you spare us your thoughts and restrict your answers to what you actually knew?
A. I'll try.
Q. Would you agree with me that if your failure to get independent confirmation of your thoughts led to your writing an inaccurate report so that people lost jobs and money, it would be a tragic event?
A. I wouldn't like to think that happened.
Q. Can we agree that if it did it would be a tragic event?
A. It would certainly be unfortunate.
Q. Can you sit there now and tell this jury that given the circumstances of this matter as we now know them it would not have been better had you checked and gotten independent confirmation of the facts as they appeared to you?
A. I guess it would have been better.

Control By Humor 11

§11.1 INTRODUCTION

Everyone is familiar with the legion of famous comedians who turned to humor as children as a defense against being beaten up by the "big boys." If they could make them laugh, the bullies would not hurt them. The twist in cross-examination is that, if you can make the jury laugh, the witness won't hurt you.

There is no question but that humor can reduce the most ponderous of testimony to trivia. It can also "lighten up" the nature of serious testimony rendered as well as the mood of the jury. As such, it is highly effective for those purposes as well as winning the regard of the jury.

Properly applied, it can always serve to deflate the opposition's position.

§11.2 CIRCUMSTANCES; EXAMPLES

However, an attempt at humor is always the most dangerous, not only for the reason that "he who laughs last laughs best," but also because, if an attempt at humor falls flat, it will seem clumsy and awkward, if not foolish. Under the circumstances, there are no suggestions here as to what will create a humorous event since it will always depend upon the circumstances of the moment, the instincts of the questioner and the speed at which the questioner responds to the opening. The humor may be self-deprecating, pointing out the irony of the situation or, in appropriate circumstances, have a biting edge at the expense of the witness.

Unlike the other areas of cross-examination where a universal skeleton can be developed, humor will always depend on the circumstances of the moment. It is governed by the context by which the humorist surrounds the event. Death, disease and mental illness are uniformly tragic events; but, there is no end to examples of books, movies or comedians who have treated the subject in a way that evoked the heartiest of laughs.

Like jokes that are soon forgotten, it is difficult to give a number of examples; but, one I recall occurred during a pornography trial. In earlier times, the defendant was referred to as the "king of the pornographers." His specialty was in print and film. The material was sexually off beat in nature as contrasted to simply violent and illegal so that the prosecution had to call a psychiatrist to give expert testimony as to the sexual implications of the material.

One of the themes that I was attempting to develop was that, like beauty, pornography was in the eye of the beholder. After a number of technical questions on the subject generally, I asked the witness:

Q: Doctor, if I drew a straight line on a psychiatric evaluation, are there any circumstances under which that line could have sexual implications?
A: Ycs, it could bc phallic symbolism.
Q: And if I drew a triangle could that be considered sexual?
A: It could be a vagina.
Q: And a circle, how about that?
A: It could be an orifice such as the anus or the mouth, both of which can have significant sexual implications.

I dropped the subject and concluded the examination shortly thereafter having obtained everything that was needed from the doctor.

On summation, prior to discussing the doctor's testimony, I took out a large sheet of oaktag on which I had drawn a straight line, a triangle and a circle. In holding up the paper, I apologized to the jury for drawing and subjecting them to "dirty pictures." I also advised them that I would hurry through the balance of my summation since I feared imminent arrest as a result of my drawing and possessing such obvious filth, particularly in the courthouse.

A great deal was not needed to be said to trivialize the doctor's testimony, especially since the entire time I discussed it I kept glancing furtively over my shoulder.

We know that humor can move mountains and is often the best medicine. It is to be used whenever possible but never when it would make the cross-examiner appear frivolous or insensitive. It is particularly effective for the cross-examiner who is anticipated to proceed in a heavy handed manner to surprise with a light, if not humorous, touch.

Closing the Escape Hatch 12

§12.1 INTRODUCTION

If one were training a horse that was not on a tether, the only way to insure that the horse would remain within your area of control would be to lock the gate to the corral. By the same token, everyone is familiar with the axiom regarding the ineffectiveness of "locking the barn door after the horse is gone."

The same is analogous to a witness that you are attempting to control if you have not closed the escape hatches through which the witness can wriggle out when directly confronted with a critical question. Closing these escape hatches can consume hours in cross-examination when it appears that nothing of significance is taking place. Do not be deterred by the time that it takes to seal these routes as failure to do so may render the most important part of your cross-examination useless. The process is absolutely vital.

§12.2 LEARNING THE HARD WAY

Early in my career, I did not recognize the necessity of blocking the exits although I had heard that it was a sound practice. I was representing an accountant alleged to be the mastermind of a complex financial scheme which resulted in deductions taken by the accountant's client which were alleged to be fraudulent. As often occurs, the client had turned government witness and had sought to place the blame on the shoulders of the accountant.

An agent of the Federal Bureau of Investigation testified upon direct testimony that the tax scheme was devised and executed by the client accountant on trial. Having previously obtained a copy of the agent's report which he filed at the conclusion of this investigation, I believed that I possessed "dynamite" to be used upon the cross-examination of the agent. The report stated that after investigation the agent found that the accountant was **not** involved. The report was consistent in all ways with the testimony of the agent with the exception of its inclusion of the word "not" prior to the word "involved" in the aspect that was the subject of the immediate questioning.

In my eagerness, the cross-examination on that point proceeded as follows:

Q: Now Agent X, at the conclusion of your investigation you filed a report of your findings, did you not?
A: Yes.
Q: And in fact your report indicated that you found that Mr. X was not involved, isn't that true?
A: No.
Q: Let me show you a copy of your report [handing the witness his report which had been previously marked for identification]. Doesn't that report state that he was not involved?
A: Are you referring to the sentence which says that he was not involved?
Q: That's what I'm referring to.
A: That's a typographic error.

It appeared that the most devastating bit of evidence which I had on cross-examination slipped away, especially since the contention that it was a typographical error was being rendered by an agent of the Federal Bureau of Investigation whose image was substantially different than exists today.

Fortunately, at that early stage, I had developed the practice of converting every answer to a walk through to see if it was internally logical. As a result, I was able to make a come back through the following questions:

Q: I take it that you wrote that report at the conclusion of the investigation?
A: Yes.
Q: And at the time you wrote the report the incidents and your observations were fresh in your mind, were they not?
A: Yes.
Q: And after you completed your report, I take it it was placed in the files of the FBI?
A: It was.
Q: And it remained in those files for the nineteen month period between the date on that report and the date of this trial?
A: Yes.
Q: I take it you are aware that the reports you write may determine whether a person is indicted and charged with a crime or not?
A: Yes.
Q: Do I correctly assume then that before you put such a report in the files you review it carefully?
A: Of course.
Q: Can I assume that you reviewed this report carefully?
A: I review all reports carefully.
Q: And you did not pick up that typographical error about which you now contend?
A: Obviously I missed it.
Q: If you had discovered the error upon your review, you would have corrected it, right?
A: Yes.
Q: And if you had discovered the error at any time between putting it in the files and this date you would have corrected the report at the time that you discovered the error?
A: Yes, I would be obliged to.
Q: Did you subsequently forward your report as part of the file to the United States Attorney recommending criminal prosecution?
A: Yes.
Q: And at the time that you forwarded such file, did you review the documents that you were sending forward?
A: Yes.
Q: And at that time in reviewing the file did you recognize your error?

A: Apparently not.
Q: And we know that because there is no correction in the file, isn't that true?
A: Yes.
Q: Did you, together with the United States Attorney, prepare for your testimony in this case?
A: Yes.
Q: And in the course of that preparation did you review any reports which you had written about this case or defendant?
A: Yes.
Q: Did you review this particular report?
A: Yes.
Q: And at the time that you reviewed this particular report in preparation for your testimony here, you did not discover the typographical error?
A: No.
Q: We know that because if you had discovered it at that time you would have been obliged to correct it?
A: That's right.
Q: So that after three careful reviews, with a man's life hanging in the balance, the only time you became aware of the error was when I confronted you with that document in this Courtroom and pointed it out to you?
A: Yes.

Fortunately, the jury apparently concluded that it was not a simple typographical error but, rather, a material prior inconsistent statement which threw the issue into doubt. It had never dawned on me prior to that time that a renowned government agency would ever admit to such a discrepancy in a material matter, even if it was true. That day I learned that, as to any witness, if you leave any possible escape route whatsoever a confronted witness will take it.

The lesson that was learned mandated that, with regard to such a document, the cross-examination prior to its use should have followed the following lines:

Q: I believe it is your practice, Agent Y, to prepare reports regarding the investigations that you conduct?
A: Yes.

Q: I further take it that such reports are truthful and accurate to the best of your ability?
A: Of course.
Q: And such reports are filed and maintained in the files of the Federal Bureau of Investigation, are they not?
A: Yes.
Q: And I take it that any report that goes into the file is carefully reviewed before it goes into the file?
A: Yes.
Q: And if any errors are discovered in those reports, the report is corrected so that the files do not contain false information, isn't that true?
A: Yes.
Q: Are you aware of any time that you filed reports which contained false information and were maintained in the files of the FBI?
A: Of course not.
Q: And as to your reports of investigation, they are reviewed from time to time by other people who confer with you about your investigation?
A: Yes.
Q: And if there were an error it would certainly show itself in the course of those conversations, would it not?
A: Yes.

With that kind of preliminary questioning, the subsequent confrontation regarding the report would have constituted the bombshell that I hoped it would be. Even the comeback was not the same as having the agent repeatedly assert the truthfulness and accuracy of his reports together with the built in system by which errors would surface. Without the comeback, the most dramatic bit of evidence to be used on cross-examination would have been dismissed as trivia.

§12.3 WHICH EVIDENCE TO PROTECT

The particular method of sealing the exits will depend upon the particular piece of evidence you wish to protect. There are a number of preliminary questions upon cross-examination that provide a general prophylaxis against the witness who in the face of being confronted seeks to modify, change or reconcile his testimony with a now identified discrepancy. These general methods are applicable to virtually all cases with nothing lost by their asking.

A great all purpose question to commence cross-examination is to ask the witness:

Q: In your direct testimony, have you told us everything you know about this incident?

The witness will invariably answer yes, since not being pointed in a specific direction he will generalize to insure that the jury does not feel that the witness has deliberately left anything of importance out of his testimony. Subsequently, when challenged, should the witness attempt to add to his testimony or make a particular answer better, he will be subjected to:

Q: But you didn't tell us that before, did you?
Q: You told us earlier that you had left nothing out.

§12.4 CERTIFICATION OF ACCURACY OF TESTIMONY

Another method of removing any possibility of the witness's contending error with regard to any testimony given and having the witness certify as to its accuracy before the subject comes up is, assuming the existence of a writing or statement which is inconsistent with the testimony and which you want to establish as the actual fact, is to ask a series of questions along the following lines:

Q: Possibly you were rushed when you wrote that letter?
Q: Possibly you were tired?
Q: Possibly you misunderstood what was going on and didn't appreciate the circumstances?
Q: Possibly you were thinking of something else when you made that statement?

The witness will invariably give such certification prior to confrontation since a witness will rarely admit a mistake, inaccuracy or lies in the absence of it being pointed out to him. Subsequently, when you confront him with the prior inconsistent statement be it oral or written he can no longer escape by contending that the words or acts attributed to them in your question are anything but accurate and it is his testimony that has now wavered in credibility.

Pace and Tempo 13

§13.1 SIGNIFICANT QUESTIONS

A witness can be controlled by varying the pace and tempo of the examination. If all questions are asked in the same tone of voice or at the same pace, the jury will never get the idea that something significant is taking place. Significant questions should always be asked in a manner that telegraphs to the jury that something important is occurring.

§13.2 INCREASING THE TEMPO

Increasing the pace and tempo serves to put additional pressure upon the witness. Thus, increasing the speed of the questions or even the intensity with which they are asked places a witness under growing pressure. The witness' efforts to keep pace often lead to answers which the witness had no intention of giving but which simply came out.

It is difficult to reproduce cross-examinations which demonstrate this technique as the printed word is read at the reader's pace and in a monotone. The ultimate book on cross-examination would be scored by some system similar to the system used in a musical composition. There, in the music there will be notations indicating ''largo,'' a slow movement, ''allegro non troppo,'' a more swift and thunderous movement or ''allegro moderato,'' melodious and moderate speed. More popular music may be written with notations indicating ''3/4 time'' or ''eight beats to a bar.'' The reader of the music not only knows what notes to play but the speed and intensity with which to play them. No such scoring has yet developed for cross-examination.

The reason may be that, as to pace and tempo, it is a matter of the moment and the personality of the cross-examiner.

A visual example of pace and tempo is the ''no-huddle offense'' of the Buffalo Bills professional football team. The Bills have developed a system of running their offensive plays without calling a huddle between each one. It has been found to be an effective device for putting pressure on the opponents who have less time to regroup or anticipate the next play.

In basketball, the concept is visually demonstrated by the ''fast break,'' conversely slowing the game down to run out the clock when a lead is in hand.

A case in which the technique proved effective involved eighteen indictments growing out of an investigation into practices in the supermarket industry involving alleged kickbacks to Moe Steinman who had allegedly arranged for sales to supermarkets on behalf of the Iowa Beef Company, the largest meat packer in the world. Of the eighteen men indicted, I represented three who were alleged to have received the largest amount of kickbacks among the supermarket executives. The other fifteen people either pleaded guilty or, in one instance, were convicted upon the testimony of persons other than Steinman who had turned government witness after being investigated for years as the ''kingpin'' of the New York meat industry and who had allegedly paid virtually millions of dollars in kickbacks to supermarket personnel. The trial to which I make reference was the first and only time Steinman was cross-examined.

In exchange for his testimony against supermarket executives and union officials, Steinman was permitted to plead guilty to a misdemeanor and was sentenced to a period of incarceration requiring him to serve approximately five months, virtually every day of which was spent at the office of the United States Attorney in preparation for the cases where it was anticipated he would be the star witness.

I represented the last three of the eighteen indicted individuals and those who were alleged to be the largest recipients of the kickback scheme. The actual charge was tax evasion premised upon their alleged failure to pay taxes upon the kickbacks they received.

I previously applied for and received an order severing the trials of the three defendants that I represented, and each was to be tried separately. It was at the trial of the first of the three defendants that the cross-examination took place.

The cross-examination was extensive and went through Steinman's prior history, appearance before Congressional committees, as well as racketeering associations. Early portions of the cross-examination focused on his plea bargain and the significant advantage that he had derived by testifying against the defendants.

The earlier portion of the cross-examination addressed his racketeering associations, which constituted his power base and who had not been indicted. The object was to make it appear that Steinman was only turning in those with whom he had no significant relationship.

The witness prided himself at keeping pace with me under what he believed to be a difficult cross-examination. As with most witnesses, particularly in view of his background, he felt an urge to beat me at my own game. As the cross-examination proceeded, I continually sought to speed up the pace and deny to Steinman the opportunity to give me a calculated, thought-out answer.

As the examination concluded, I turned my back and walked away from the witness and, without pause, turned suddenly and fired one last question:

Q: [while turning] And you wouldn't lie, would you?
A: I lie a lot.

In that one flippant comment, Steinman undermined any testimony that he had previously given and established the basis upon which the court dismissed the charges against my client.

The government was reluctant to proceed against my other two clients but was more reluctant to dismiss the charges against them. I then entered into a stipulation that Steinman's testimony would be the same on subsequent trials of the other two. The stipulation was submitted to the trial court as part of a motion for summary judgment seeking the dismissal of the remaining charges. The court, consistent with the outcome in the first trial, dismissed the charges, writing an opinion that Steinman's testimony lacked credibility.

The government appealed to the Second Circuit Court of Appeals claiming that credibility was not a valid basis upon which to order dismissal of the charges against the remaining two defendants, as well as pointing out that the Appellate Court similarly could not rule upon credibility.

The Second Circuit affirmed the decision of the trial court, apparently feeling that to go through the time and expense of subsequent lengthy trials on the credibility of such a witness was not a worthwhile endeavor.

Although there are many other areas where Steinman's credibility was called into question, it was clearly that one answer which provided his own evaluation of his testimony. The answer was obtained solely by the increased pace and tempo of the examination, culminating in suddenly throwing at the witness a question he never expected to be asked in that manner.

§13.3 SLOWING DOWN THE TEMPO

A technique in contrast to speeding up the tempo is to slow it down and leave great pauses between the asking of questions. Thus, when a witness concludes his answer, simply look at the witness without asking an additional question. It has been repeatedly confirmed that witnesses under such circumstances will simply keep talking and add to their previous answer. The witness draws the conclusion that his answer is incomplete or unsatisfactory and rushes to make it better by adding additional facts or explanations. The witness will often keep talking until the moment that the lawyer asks the next question. The things that come out of a witness' mouth are remarkable when he keeps adding to the previous answer. Very few witnesses have the restraint to give the answer that they intend to give and then remain silent. Of course, this is only done under the circumstances where the addendum is not harmful and the witness is supplying additional material that can be challenged and attacked.

Even within a single case, a cross-examiner should not treat all witnesses the same. Not every witness is there to be battered nor should every witness be treated with obsequiousness. It is variety, again, which can convey to the jury that a lawyer is not a mindless thug but really only bears down on a witness when the witness deserves it and is seemingly telling less than the truth. Thus, on occasion, cross-examination should be conducted with extreme courtesy and with respect so as to indicate a good faith mistake or simply elicit one or two facts which will be woven into a greater point on summation. If, on occasion, some witness can be handled in this manner, then for the singular witness who is hammered at, it will appear that the witness deserves it rather than that this simply being the cross-examiner's heavy-handed style. In other words, the approach and manner have to be modified to fit the circumstances.

Setting Up the Witness 14

§14.1 TIME TO SET UP CONTROL OF WITNESS

The best time to set about controlling the witness is at the outset of testimony before there are any clear paths drawn that the witness feels obliged to resist. If the witness is set up properly, it is an umbrella that governs the entire examination and creates an intellectual fence.

Control must be established at the outset of testimony since that is the moment when the witness sizes you up in terms of what he is dealing with and what kind of liberties can be taken. It is an early objective to show the witness that no liberties can be taken, that you are fully prepared and that the easiest way out of what promises to be a tense confrontation is by not resisting. The first few moments of cross-examination work not so much on the testimony of the witness but rather upon his will.

§14.2 TECHNIQUES

The techniques for setting up a witness are universal since they do not depend upon the facts and circumstances of a particular case. If a witness can be shown to have an obvious or inherent bias, it diminishes the weight that will be accorded to that testimony. It would also cause the witness to be inhibited in giving his subsequent answers so as to avoid the appearance of giving credence to the earlier demonstrated bias.

It is also the moment when you impose the rules of the courtroom upon the witness and convey to him that the rules are different than those of the work place, the laboratory, his home or any other places he normally frequents. Thus, as later demonstrated, merely pointing out to a witness the significance of the oath conveys to the witness that, in the courtroom, "talk is not cheap" and a heavy price can be paid for getting caught speaking falsely.

Do not be put off by the fact that the early points made in setting up a witness are obvious. They are obvious to you as a practicing lawyer who has seen a broad spectrum of witnesses and who has formed certain time tested beliefs. It would also be obvious to the jurors but only if it is brought to their attention. However, they may overlook the obvious unless you point it out.

§14.3 THE SKIRMISH

At the commencement of cross-examination, the witness measures his interrogator to estimate what he can expect. An assessment is made by the witness at that time, consciously or unconsciously, as to how careful he has to be or what liberties can be taken with the examining attorney.

Heavy artillery should never be used at the outset of cross-examination so that the balance of cross-examination becomes an anti-climax.

Worse yet, if the attack fails and the lawyer has to retreat, it is then the witness who is in control while the lawyer is then on the defensive from that point forward.

Despite eagerness and thinking that he possesses dynamite that will destroy the witness, the lawyer should resist going immediately for the jugular. It is the rarest of points that can be made without laying a foundation, closing the escape hatches and creating a perspective.

Cross-examination should always build to a climax. Many times, if a strong point is made in the middle of the examination, it is wise to conclude the questioning even at the expense of not asking certain questions that were anticipated to be productive.

However, a brief skirmish at the outset of cross-examination can serve to make a witness more cautious and not take liberties. The issue should not be one of great significance but simply to demonstrate to the witness that, if he gets into a quarrel or quibbles with you, there may be an iron fist in the velvet glove.

Reproduced at greater length later on is the examination of two expert witnesses who offered the opinion that the defendant suffered from battered wife syndrome to a charge of homicide. The examination of the first expert commenced as follows:

> Q: The battered wife syndrome is really a phrase that has gotten coined more or less by the works of Lenore Walker, I believe, who wrote the book "Battered Women."
> A: Right.
> Q: And most of what has been done with battered wife or battered woman syndrome has kind of followed her work, is that correct?
> A: A lot of it. She was one of the originators anyway. Other people have picked up on it.

This was one of the methods by which Lynn Crooks, the prosecuting attorney, conveyed to the witness that he had researched the subject and had a working familiarity with it. Making the point quickly, he moved on to the skirmish.

> Q: Actually, the concept should perhaps be more appropriately be battered spouse syndrome, isn't that correct?
> A: No.
> Q: There are males that suffer from similar types of mental syndrome, are there not?
> A: If you're asking if there are a percentage of men who are battered, there is five percent of men who are battered and ninety-five percent women.
> Q: Going to get to that.
> A: It started with women not with men.
> Q: The general concept of a battered person and the concept you talked about percentage wise fits more women than it does men but it actually works both ways.
> A: It could be applied, I guess, to men, I don't know. She hasn't done that study. I guess I would have to wait and see if they did a study and came up with the same results.

The issue was unimportant, but the witness chose to resist the irrelevant extended application of the syndrome theory. Without fireworks or the overt appearance of a battle, the witness was challenged and forced to admit that it could apply equally to men but that a study simply had not been done yet; however, there was no basis for the strong negative previously given. From that point on, the witness was far more cautious and inhibited from getting into a disagreement with his questioner.

§14.4 "YES" OR "NO" ANSWERS

The cross-examiner will always feel better to the extent that he can restrict the witness' answers to "yes" or "no." That means that all of the flavor and points sought to be made by the cross-examiner can come from the question rather than the answer. The answer will add nothing that the lawyer does not want added nor detract from any part of the question which was asked for a reason. The best opportunity to set up a witness for those responses is to ask at the outset of the examination the following questions:

Q: Doctor, my name is John Smith, attorney for John Doe, and it is my job to ask you certain questions about your testimony. You understand that, don't you?

A: Yes.

Q: The jury and I have a problem in that none of us have your background or experience, do you understand that?

A: Yes.

Q: You can appreciate that we would not be familiar with many of the terms that you might normally use, isn't that right?

A: Yes.

Q: The reason you are being permitted to testify is that your area is one that the Court recognizes that a jury needs your assistance in order to arrive at a conclusion, do you understand that?

A: Yes.

Q: If I ask you a question that you feel cannot be answered yes or no would you tell me?

A: Yes.

Q: If you do so, I will attempt to rephrase the question so that it can be answered yes or no, do you understand that?

A: Yes.

Q: After it is corrected, will you then agree to answer yes or no wherever possible?
A: Yes.
Q: Doctor X, you have now answered a series of questions yes or no, that wasn't so difficult was it?

The obvious implication of this is that, if the witness can be constrained to answer "yes" or "no," then the witness essentially is being controlled by the cross-examiner and has been set up to do precisely that. At the same time, every time that the witness tries to deviate from a "yes" or "no" answer the cross-examiner can point out that the witness is not keeping to his bargain under the definition and ground rules set up at the outset and is prepared to confuse the jury by rendering non responsive testimony. That give and take takes on greater significance with the jury than the testimony itself. All too often, when in the course of cross-examination a lawyer tries to restrict a witness to a "yes" or "no" answer, it appears that the lawyer is trying to suppress testimony and impress the witness. However, if the witness is properly set up, it will appear that the witness is not keeping to his bargain when he has already demonstrated that he can do so when he wants to.

§14.5 THE OATH

Reminding the witness that he is under oath midstream in cross-examination has little or no effect; and, oftentimes, an objection to such a statement by a cross-examining attorney will be sustained. However, at the outset of an examination, it is appropriate and permissible to test a witness' recognition of the oath and what it means. If the subject of the oath is undertaken at the outset of cross-examination, it should not be limited to a reminder that the witness is under oath but, in fact, can set up before any other testimony is given that the witness is a frequent violator of the oath.

Q: Mr. X, when you took the stand in this case, the first answer you uttered in this courtroom was "yes" in response to an oath that the clerk read to you?
A: That's right.

Q: You swore to tell the truth, is that right?
A: Yes, I did.
Q: And you are aware that the penalty for failing to tell the truth after taking an oath is perjury?
A: I understand that.
Q: And that perjury is a crime?
A: Yes.
Q: Now, you have frequently committed perjury outside this courtroom have you not?
A: No.

This is setting up a basis for diminishing the witness' testimony whether the answer is "yes" or "no." If the witness answers "yes," then the point is made. If the witness answers "no," it is subject to attack as to whether or not the witness has previously made a false statement after taking an oath.

This attack can be launched as a collateral attack outside of the issues in the case but solely on the issue of whether or not the witness has lied under oath.

Q: Do you recall making an application for a mortgage loan in the amount of $375,000 to the Federal National Bank in August of 1987?
A: I applied for a mortgage.
Q: And did you fill out an application?
A: Yes.
Q: And did you sign that application?
A: Yes.
Q: Do you recall what was printed on that application immediately above your signature?
A: I don't recall.
Q: [handing the witness the application] Does that refresh your recollection as to what appeared above your signature?
A: I see it there.
Q: And, in fact, it says that the information that you provided on that form, to which you affixed your signature, was true under the penalties of perjury, do you see that?
A: That's what it says.
Q: Now take a look at the amount you declared as your annual income, do you see that?

A: Yes.
Q: And you stated that your annual income was $175,000 per year, do you see that?
A: Yes.
Q: In fact, you only made $78,000 that year, isn't that correct?
A: Possibly, I didn't think it mattered.
Q: So, that $175,000 is a lie, is it not?
A: It's not accurate.
Q: That figure was stated upon a document where you swore to tell the truth and understood that the penalty for failing to tell that truth would be perjury, isn't that true?
A: You could look at it that way.

An effective application of the above technique was utilized with success by Frederick Hafetz, Esq., a talented and prominent defense attorney who was formerly Chief of the Criminal Division of the United States Attorney's Office for the Southern District of New York. The main government witness testifying against Hafetz' client was cross-examined, in part, as follows:

Q: Mr. X, when you took the stand in this case you took an oath?
A: Yes.
Q: You raised your hand on a Bible?
A: Yes.
Q: You swore to tell the truth, right, sir?
A: Yes I did.
Q: And one of the Commandments of the Bible is thou shalt not bear false witness, am I correct sir?
A: Correct.
Q: You would not want to violate that Commandment?
A: I did not violate it.
Q: Back in 1978 when you participated in the murder of Louis Y were you aware that the same Bible upon which you swore an oath had the commandment that thou shalt not murder?
A: Yes.
Q: Were you aware at that time that the Bible, the same Bible on which you took an oath here just about a month ago that thou shalt not murder, were you aware of that, sir?
A: Thou shalt not kill.

Q: And you were willing to do so, not withstanding that Commandment in the Bible which you swore here a month ago?
A: I violated it.
Q: Would you not agree that the taking of a life is a much more serious offense than perjury?
A: I would say that that is a serious offense.
Q: Taking a life?
A: The most serious offense that you could commit.
Q: And you, sir, could have committed that most serious offense that a human being could possibly commit at least six times. Am I right sir?
A: Yes.
Q: That meant you did not take the Commandment seriously, am I correct Mr. X? The Commandment that thou shalt not murder?
A: I violated it.
Q: And you want us to believe that you would not violate the Commandment that you should not bear false witness, in other words, perjury, is that correct?

§14.6 DUTY OR OBLIGATION

Another method of controlling subsequent testimony is to point out at the outset that a witness has a certain duty or obligation which you can point out in subsequent questioning was not strictly adhered to. Thus, in cross-examining the defendant in a libel case, the publisher of the newspaper in which an allegedly libelous story appeared was cross-examined at the outset as follows:

Q: Mr. X, how many issues of your newspaper are sold to the public on a daily basis?
A: 520,000.
Q: I take it you are aware that any mention of a person in your newspaper can dramatically affect their life?
A: Well, it depends on the context in which it is mentioned.
Q: I take it you are aware that, if in a news story you said something terrible about a person, that that person would be seriously affected by the story?
A: Yes.

Q: And that bad statement would reach 520,000 people, not counting the people that they told it to after they read it.
A: I presume so.
Q: And you are aware that this power that your newspaper has can seriously affect the lives of people about who you write?
A: Yes.
Q: You agree, don't you, that you have a duty to be fair?
A: Yes.
Q: And you recognize that you have a duty not to make false statements about people, isn't that true?
A: Yes.
Q: And you are further aware that you have to investigate every bad statement fully in order to make sure that you're not being unfair?
A: Yes.
Q: And not making a false statement against someone?
A: Yes.
Q: And before you ruin somebody's reputation you know you have to conduct pretty extensive investigation, isn't that true?
A: We try not to make mistakes.
Q: And if a mistake is made, do you agree that the person making the mistake is the one that should pay for it?
A: What are you getting at?
Q: Don't worry about what I am getting at. Can we agree that the person who makes the mistake is the one that should pay for it?
A: Yes.
Q: And you don't think that the mistake should be paid for by the person who was hurt who didn't make the mistake?
A: If that is the case, I would agree.
Q: Now, let us return to my original question. In order to avoid making a mistake don't you have a duty to conduct a thorough and extensive investigation?
A: Yes.
Q: Or that if you made a mistake, and the defendant's reputation was ruined, and you didn't conduct a fair, thorough and complete investigation, you acknowledge that you should pay for it?
A: [pause]

§14.7 PARTISANSHIP

All witnesses try to appear fair even when it is obvious that their sympathies are with one side or the other. A witness tries to convey to the jury that he has nothing to hide, certainly with regard to any matters that are at issue in the instant trial. That impression can be modified by the following exchange:

Q: Mr. X, have we ever met before?
A: No.
Q: Have we ever spoken before?
A: No.
Q: Have you ever spoken to the plaintiff before?
A: Yes.
Q: Have you ever spoken to the defendant's lawyer before?
A: Yes.
Q: Do you recall receiving a letter from me asking to interview you?
A: Yes.
Q: And you refused to speak to me did you not?
A: I wouldn't see you.
Q: Did you have something to hide?
A: Of course not.
Q: Nevertheless, you withheld from me and my client information which you freely gave to the other side, isn't that true?
A: I did speak to them.

§14.8 BIAS

Setting up and establishing the witness' bias is bringing out anything that puts the jury on notice that for any reason the witness is not objective nor was he brought to the courtroom to be objective. Showing that a witness is biased devalues any testimony that such a witness ultimately renders. With regard to an expert witness, variations of the following cross-examination can be utilized in virtually every instance:

Q: When did you first make contact with the plaintiff?

Q: Did he or his lawyer call you or did you call them?

Q: At the time that you first made contact with the plaintiff, were you advised of the existence of this lawsuit?

Q: Were you advised of the plaintiff's position in the lawsuit?

Q: Were you advised of the issues upon which you were requested to give testimony or render an opinion?

Q: Did you understand which position would be favorable to the plaintiff?

Q: And you understood all this before you rendered a report or formulated your conclusion?

Q: After all, you had to do an investigation and possibly some research before you rendered such opinion and conclusion.

Q: And while you were doing investigation and research, you understood which conclusion or opinion if arrived at would be favorable to the plaintiff?

Q: And at the time of the initial contact, was any compensation discussed?

Q: What were the terms of that compensation?

Q: You understood did you not that the compensation you would receive would be greater if you actually would be called to testify at this trial, did you not?

Q: And you further understood, did you not, that you would not be called to testify at this trial if the opinion you rendered did not favor the plaintiff?

Q: So, while you were doing your research, investigation and preparing your report, you knew what opinion or testimony the plaintiff hoped for?

Q: You further knew that you would not receive the higher compensation unless your findings were favorable to the plaintiff, isn't that true?

Q: And you arrived at that favorable conclusion, did you not?

Q: And you are aware that had you testified to any other conclusion, it would damage the interests of the person who was paying you?

You will note that no answers are included in the above examination since the witness has no choice except to acknowledge the obvious. The only acceptable answer to all of those questions is in the affirmative since no jury would accept the proposition that a person conducted an investigation and prepared a report without knowing what the issues were and whether or not the responses would favor one side or the other.

Leading to Summation 15

§15.1 INTRODUCTION

While it is reputed that all roads lead to Rome, it is a fact that everything in a trial should lead to summation. Earlier, it was described that a technique that has stood the test of time was to prepare the summation as the first act of case preparation. Everything favorable to your client brought out in the course of the trial should be woven into and highlighted in summation and, everything unfavorable, touched upon and minimized.

The most dramatic building block in the edifice that becomes summation is cross-examination. Anything of value that was obtained upon cross-examination can be exploited with far greater effect than any other testimony or document introduced into a case. Whether testimony or a document, that which is extracted on cross-examination can be exploited to a far greater degree, simply because it was obtained from the other side in the course of confrontation.

A document introduced upon cross-examination was either withheld by the other side or not offered in the hopes that the other side would not know about it. Therefore, it takes on greater significance and far more meaning than the words of its contents. The same is true of testimony in that that which is extracted under pressure has a far greater impact than the smooth delivery upon direct examination that was obviously rehearsed.

§15.2 TAKE NOTHING FOR GRANTED

Regardless of how effective cross-examination may be, its true significance may be lost upon the judge or jury if it is not highlighted and exploited upon in summation.

In this book, an effort was made to select graphic cross-examinations simply because they are graphic and self-contained so as to better make the point. However, for the most part, cross-examinations consist of a series of subtleties utilizing some degree of finesse in order to get the answer from the witness without putting the witness on stonewalling guard. It is unlikely that the jury will appreciate what has been extracted from the witness if you do not explain it upon summation.

The dramatic cross-examination that leads to immediate resolution of the matter on trial is rare. Rather, cross-examination seeks to raise questions about certain points in the testimony that you will strive to answer on summation.

It is an opportunity to tell the jury what you accomplished and completely exploit and widen whatever gains that you believe were accomplished.

Further explanation is required to persuade the jury of the full amount of damage that was done to the opposing case by such testimony or such document obtained upon cross-examination.

In effect, it is an opportunity to critique your own performance and the significance of what has been accomplished. It is the opportunity to be your own spin doctor.

No less important is the need to explain to the court, when sitting as trier of the fact, the significance of the cross-examination. Many lawyers overlook this necessity in the belief that the judge is a professional, presiding over a number of cases and, therefore, is in the best position to evaluate what has transpired in the trial taking place before him. While this may be generally true, it should not be taken for granted; and, therefore, in an excess of caution, the court should have the benefit of your explanation.

I learned this lesson early as a young prosecutor. I was presenting a case before a judge in which the testimony involved a complainant who testified that he got into an altercation with the defendant, who pulled a razor from his pocket and slit the throat of the complainant. A subsequent witness testified that he had observed the fact and, in retelling his observations, stated that he saw the defendant take a shiny metallic object from his pocket and saw the defendant's arm take a swipe across the area of the defendant's neck. He continued by testifying that he noticed a thin red line on the complainant's neck, then a drop of blood, followed by the neck appearing to open up and then a gusher of blood.

The trial took place several months after the incident, during which time the complainant had had significant surgery, including plastic surgery to attempt to correct the scar left by the incident.

The judge presiding over the trial was one of the finest in the criminal justice system in New York. Given the graphic nature of the testimony and the high intelligence and competence of the court, I felt that nothing else needed to be said in my closing statement about the severity of the injury and the obvious intention to kill the complainant.

Shortly after the conclusion of testimony, the court found the defendant guilty on a minor count of assault. Unconsciously, I registered my surprise whereupon I was summoned into the court's chambers. The court proceeded to excoriate me for giving a public indication that I thought that the court's verdict was in error and that I had held the court up to second guessing. I apologized to for the public display but, nevertheless, indicated that I was amazed at the verdict given the nature and depth of the injury to the complainant. The court then said, "what do you mean, he only had a scratch."

I indicated that I thought a cut throat with blood gushing was something more than a scratch. The court persistently stated that the independent witness had only said that he noticed a thin red line across the complainant's throat. I persisted in suggesting that the court had missed the balance of the statement which included the "gusher." The court stenographer was sent for and the testimony reread although the trial was over, simply to establish the point that was the subject of the discussion. When the stenographer read the significant portion of the testimony, the judge reddened and candidly stated that he had missed that.

The discussion concluded by the judge's apologizing for having missed it but still insisted that he had properly excoriated me for having a public reaction regardless of the verdict. I agreed with him.

Thus, having gone through a trial before one of the brightest and the best and having enough blood to substantiate a conviction of attempted homicide, I thereafter never took it for granted that the judge was an omnipotent sponge who would not only be aware and recall every word of testimony, but would also know exactly what was going through my head as I asked specific questions.

Over 30 years, the lesson has repeatedly been reinforced. Recently, in representing a plaintiff, I brought an application to disqualify the attorneys for the opponent on the grounds that they had undertaken to represent a witness which I had listed in a pre-trial order and whom I had under subpoena. The essence of my objection was that I was now supposed to call this witness and would be blindsided by the opposing attorneys' cross-examining their own client.

The court directed that a hearing be held to establish the circumstances of the representation and whether or not there was a conflict of interest in such representation. The controversial witness had completed testimony which seemed to suggest that the representation by the trial counsel for the opposing side was something that she was aware was significant.

At the outset of cross-examination, I asked whether or not this witness had reviewed her testimony with the trial counsel for the opposing side who were the subject of the motion. The witness acknowledged that she had so reviewed her testimony for this very hearing. At that point, the court interjected that, if it were to ask my client the same question, it was sure that my client would also say that I had reviewed with him his testimony. The court made further remarks to the effect that, since there was no jury present, I was wasting time by resorting to that old saw on cross-examination.

However, I pointed out to the court that, if my client were being called to the stand to testify as to whether or not I had engaged in unethical conduct in the face of an obvious conflict, I would be the last person in the world to prepare him for his testimony and, in fact, there would be little likelihood that I would have been seen in that witness' presence under any circumstances. The court grudgingly acknowledged that I was now making the point that attorneys alleged to have committed an ethical breach may well have demonstrated a continuing insensitivity to the appearance of impropriety by preparing the testimony of a witness who might be offering testimony adverse to the attorneys themselves.

Judges perform an overwhelming task under the most trying of conditions. As a result, like all other human beings, they tend to pigeonhole and categorize large masses of material. It is, therefore, not unlikely that a judge's perceptions are formed in the first few minutes or upon hearing the first few words of testimony since they need a survival mechanism for reducing large amounts of matter to quickly grasped concepts.

Under the circumstances, whether it be judge or jury, make the cross-examination as explicit as possible but, under all circumstances, explain fully what you believe has been accomplished upon cross-examination in summation.

This is particularly true when the area of cross-examination requires subtlety and finesse rather than bombast and aggression. Often, the most successful piece of cross-examination is when an admission is sought from the witness or where you are seeking to elicit from the witness agreement with you as to certain aspects of the testimony.

Most often, this will occur when a witness is offering an explanation which you recognize has an evolution that is harmful to the witness. It would be error to attack the witness and point out that the testimony when carried forward is absurd but rather by appearing to be cooperative and courteous and accepting of the explanation, the absurdity is better left to summation, rather than giving the witness a chance to make corrections in his testimony as it goes along.

An example also occurred in the same hearing during which the issue of disqualification of the opponent's attorney was at issue. The same witness who was testifying with regard to the representation by the defendant's counsel was also faced with the claim that her "attorneys" had denied access to her to the plaintiff who had such witness listed on their witness list and who had the woman under subpoena. She was aware that, if it were the attorneys who denied access to the other side, her attorneys would face difficulty and so she tried to soften the harsh reality. Thus, on cross-examination, the following took place:

Q: Can we agree that you became aware that the plaintiffs were trying to contact you during the week of June 15, 1993?

A: Yes.

Q: And during that entire time you refused to take their phone calls or messages?

A: Well that was because I was very busy and I was looking forward to a vacation the following week. It is very difficult for me, being in business, and having all of these matters that I had to deal with, to take time out to speak to them at that point.

Q: I can fully understand your situation. In other words, you weren't objecting to talking to the plaintiffs or their attorneys, only that that particular moment in time was inconvenient to you, right?

A: That's right.

Q: So that in fact if they had chosen a more convenient time you would have been more than happy to cooperate with them, isn't that so?

A: Yes.

Q: Now I understand, it really wasn't a matter of your refusing to talk to them, it was simply a matter of doing so under convenient circumstances?

A: Yes.

In this particular instance, in the week in which the witness had refused to meet with the plaintiffs, her attorneys had sent a letter to plaintiffs' counsel stating that they represented the witness and that the plaintiffs should make no further attempts to contact the witness. Significantly, since they indicated that the witness was now represented by them, the plaintiffs' attorneys similarly could make no efforts to contact the witness. Given the contents of the letter, complete access to the witness had been denied.

The area of cross-examination was conducted in an atmosphere of full understanding and consideration for the business problems of the witness. The cross-examination lasted a bit longer and sympathetic concern was shown for the difficulties of the business situation and drew out the willingness of the witness to be cooperative. It was the witness' belief that, by this testimony, it was shown that the plaintiffs had not been denied access to the witness. The tenor of the examination would seem to confirm the total acceptability of the explanation.

However, given the fact that the attorneys had written the letter as indicated, thus cutting off complete access, the cross-examination developed that it was not the witness who was refusing to see the plaintiffs or their counsel but rather it was the attorneys for the conflicting interests who had effectively dropped the curtain on any access to that witness. As an apparent throwaway at the end of the cross-examination, I asked the witness if she was aware of a letter which her "attorneys" had written to me and made a vague reference to the letter instructing me to advise my clients to attempt no further contact. Now relaxed, the witness indicated that she saw it within the last two days, the letter having been written some eight days earlier.

Again, the point to be made upon summation later, rather than quarreling with a witness who was interested in helping her "attorneys," was that the letter was written by the attorneys and that it was their decision to influence the access to the witness by cutting off complete access without getting clearance or prior approval from the witness.

Although I believed that the point was absolutely clear, I nevertheless insured that the court understood the nature of that testimony and all its implications.

§15.3 THE EXPLANATION IS BETTER COMING FROM YOU

One of the best methods of controlling the witness is to attempt to foreclose a witness from explaining an answer with which you are satisfied for any reason. Any explanation offered by the witness will be a prepared explanation that will take away any effect that the earlier answer may have had. It is not really a case of not permitting the witness to testify fully since the fullness of testimony is really an event by which the rehearsed lines are gratuitously inserted. If the other side feels that the explanation has merit, they are free to bring it out on redirect. Oftentimes, however, the opposing side does not know what you have in mind with a particular question and answer and so does not return to a particular point on redirect and no explanation is offered.

The explanation is provided on your summation when, at that time, you explain the significance and ramifications of such question and answer.

By way of example, a simple question may be asked upon cross-examination as to whether or not an appraisal report was prepared. The witness answers yes and the cross-examiner moved on, apparently a matter of little significance. With another witness, a blank appraisal form was casually introduced as a trivial detail.

However, in a recent case, the issue was whether or not the defendants had defrauded the Federal Home Loan Mortgage Corporation (''FHLMC'') by submitting false rent rolls in that the rents which were listed on such applications were non-existent or inflated. Subsequent to the time of the submission of the report, the lending agency contended that they checked and found that in fact a percentage of the apartments for which rents were listed were vacant and in other cases were substantially lower than the reported rent. It was the contention of the government that fraud had been committed. The government proceeded upon the theory that a potential borrower must report only actual rents of occupied apartments.

The appraisal report to which the simple question made reference was upon a form prepared by Freddie Mac and authorized by it to be utilized in the submission of applications. On the report, there was an entire section devoted to ''comparable'' rents; and, the appraisers had put in rentals per square foot for comparable apartments in the area.

There were three such appraisal reports using the same form for each loan application. One was prepared by the borrower, a second by the mortgage agent for Freddie Mac and a third by Freddie Mac itself. All contained upon the form the similar area requesting information as to comparable apartments.

On summation, it was a different story. The jury now had the appraisal reports before them and could see the area wherein ''comparable'' appraisals were made and listened to the following on summation:

> Let's now look at these appraisal reports. The Government contends that my clients have committed fraud because some of the rents which they listed and scheduled in their application were false. It is their contention that a substantial number of apartments in these buildings were empty and therefore no rents could conceivably exist. In other cases they contend that there were tenants occupying the apartments but who were paying a lower rental. In other words, it is their position and their entire case depends on whether or not they require ''actual'' rentals or whether they require something else such as projections or forecasts.
>
> Let's talk about projections. A projection looks to the future and something that it is anticipated will happen on a future date. Now, if Freddie Mac requires only actual rents then of course the making of a projection might constitute some

impropriety. So which is it, have they really requested projections or forecasts or do they require actuals?

Well, if they require only actual rents, why would they have an appraisal report that asks for comparable rents. Compared to what? In other words, if there is a specific person living in an apartment, paying a specific rent, then that's what should be put down and nothing else. There would be no need for comparables under any circumstances.

Why, then, request comparables? Obviously, because an apartment may be vacant and there is a determination trying to be made as to what rent can be anticipated from that apartment assuming that it is properly fixed up and presented to the marketplace in good condition. So, in other words, the minute you see the word comparable you know that what is requested is that the lender should tell Freddie Mac what rent he believes will be able to be obtained for that apartment, and maybe they require three appraisal reports to confirm that belief, by consulting three crystal balls, including their own.

If you look at apartments in the area and the average rent for the sake of argument is $8 per square foot for residential apartments, and this vacant apartment in the building has 200 square feet, then the annual rent for that apartment will be $1,600 a year divided by twelve and you've got the monthly rent. Now, you take a look at the loan applications and you will see that that's how the rents that were projected were determined.

So, in your deliberations when you look at the appraisal reports which are the heart of the matter, every time you see the word comparable, you know it has to mean something other than actual. And if the requirement is for something else beside actual rents, then there is no case. They asked for and received a reasonable projection of the future.

We all know that had to be right. You've heard the Government over and over again tell you how many vacant apartments there were in these various buildings and therefore it was a bald faced fraud. Well, that's really got to be a case of hiding an elephant in a telephone booth. After all, the property is inspected not only by the agent for Freddie Mac but by Freddie Mac itself. How did they miss all those vacant apartments? The answer is clear, there must be something in the system that permits projections and estimates being made of rents for vacant apartments once they are rehabilitated. So, now you not only have the common sense answer that if you see the word comparable it can't mean actual rent, you also have the confirmation of that plain sense by knowing that you can't hide an elephant in a telephone booth.

§15.4 A MATTER OF INSTINCT

During the course of the trial, it is frequently an option as to whether to cross-examine upon a point or to save it for summation, by just asking the question and making sure that the desired fact or discrepancy is admitted into evidence. Under different circumstances, either approach might be appropriate; but, generally, the foolproof one is where you get to make the explanation upon summation, rather than relying on extracting it grudgingly from an adverse witness or permitting the witness to offer a reconciliation.

§15.5 PLOWSHARES INTO SWORDS

By utilizing the restraint of withholding the explanation until summation rather than attempting to restrain a witness from giving an explanation you do not like, there is an opportunity for converting the strongest piece of evidence against you into the greatest of strengths for your client.

In a recent trial in which it was alleged that a defendant had deceived another by investing in property for his own use rather than offering it to the other person. The most damning evidence, blown up to billboard size by the prosecution, was a letter sent by the defendant stating that he had segregated a portion of the property for investment by a person other than the complainant. The government offered the letter as incontrovertible proof that the defendant had deceived his client and withheld from him the opportunities to which he was entitled.

The letter and its implication were not attacked on cross-examination and the prosecuting attorney believed that the evidence was so overwhelming that there could be no challenge and that explained the defense attorney's lack of cross-examination.

However, as an example of what can be done, the lighting was rearranged and now the evidence which is supposed to be the strongest evidence of misdealing can become proof of innocence.

> Let's go to this billboard over here. I assume its next stop is going to be Times Square because its certainly big enough and the Government has made sure that you're not going to miss one word of its contents. It is their claim that this letter proves that the defendant did the dastardly act of which he has been accused and that he intended to deceive and defraud Mr. Jones.
>
> Well, I'd like to ask you to consider with me if that letter isn't absolute proof of my client's innocence. Listen to the story the Government has told. My client is a shrewd sophisticated businessman, of high intelligence, who nobody has ever suggested is a fool. He has engaged in a subterfuge of deception and bad dealing behind Mr. Jones' back. My client is out to and intends to deceive Mr. Jones. He is going to withhold from him the critical information that this property is available to him, but he is not going to let him know that.
>
> So, what does my client do, this deceiver, this person who intends to clandestinely deceive and defraud? Why, he writes a letter that can be blown up as big as a billboard that anybody in the world can see. A letter that even before the Government chose to turn it into this work of contemporary art of vast size, could be read by anyone. Who knows into whose hands it would fall and to whose eyes it would become known. Why he composed a confession to be circulated to places which had no limit and he launched it.
>
> Now, I ask you, if my client thought he was doing something wrong, and if he thought he was deceiving Mr. Jones, would he write such a letter. The answer is obviously no. The last thing he would do is write such a letter. Remember, nobody ever said my client was a fool or anything other than intelligent

and a sophisticated businessman. The writing of such a letter, which is available to be blown up before you, is a clear indication that he entered into this transaction in the firm belief that what he was doing was entirely appropriate, open and straightforward. In other words, it was a business decision which he felt he was entitled to make and he didn't care who in the world knew it.

Ladies and gentlemen, I submit to you every time you look at that letter, you will not see proof of my client's guilt, but you will see unavoidable evidence of my client's innocence and the total lack of intent to deceive, act in a clandestine manner, or hide his activities from anybody.

No matter what you may think of this transaction, it is clear that there was no intent to deceive.

§15.6 INCONSISTENCY AND THE PASSAGE OF TIME

All reports, memoranda or notes made at or about the time of the event are likely to differ materially from the version that is given by an adverse witness at trial. At the time that the notes or memos are made, the person making such report does not anticipate being a witness; or, if they recognize the possibility of future litigation, they don't know what the issues will be at the time the matter arrives at the trial stage. As a result, the note or memo will normally contain some information which when measured against the issues at trial will contain serious discrepancies. The question then becomes how far to pursue the discrepancy on cross-examination and possibly have the witness explain the discrepancy away or simply ignore the discrepancy on cross-examination but exploit it upon summation.

Contemporaneous notes and memos are usually made in good faith at some point in the litigation path. However, as the trial date approaches, the issues become clearer and the sides become more clearly drawn. At that point, the witness' testimony is massaged, recollections are woven in and out as well as failures of recollection, and then funnelled through trial preparation. The foregoing massage often results in testimony that is materially different than the earlier note, memo or report. Again, the most effective use of that discrepancy may be made when you offer the explanation or its significance upon summation rather than engage in a battle with a witness who will tend to trivialize it while you intend to maximize it.

On summation, an attorney gets to utilize one of the greatest weapons in trial advocacy, i.e., the analogy. The analogy is so effective because it conjures up a visual image which incorporates all the technicalities and details in otherwise incomprehensible or controversial testimony. It is effective because it hits a responsive chord since it is always expressed in terms of common experience and understanding in terms of its graphic content.

Most recently, there has been the great controversy as to whether or not the new trade agreement with Mexico would or would not cause a loss of employment in the United States. Advocates for both sides presented statistics, projections, beliefs and more statistics. Those who indicated that they believed that employment would be lost in the United States pointed to various tariff regulations and comparable labor rates as well as numerous other technical considerations. However, it was Ross Perot who made the most graphic and eloquent of arguments against the agreement by referring to the "great sucking sound of jobs going South" if the new agreements were put in place as envisioned. The picture was worth a thousand words.

The same is true in the courtroom. It is only upon summation that one gets a chance to take the testimony that has been offered and make an analogy which can summarize the testimony more graphically than all of the intellectual and technical arguments that could be offered. This is particularly true with regard to facts obtained upon cross-examination which at the time do not appear to have great significance. However, when put in the context of an analogy, they take on significant meaning.

Quite often in trials, particularly one involving public officials, the answer is always given to the effect that "that is the system" or "that is the way things are done." The case usually involves somebody who has acted in a manner inconsistent with the way things are usually done or outside of the carefully prescribed rules, more often technical than practical; and, such deviation is used to demonstrate intent. Cross-examining such a witness will only elicit answers that that is the system that has been in place for forty years or something approximating that, its being commonly understood by all people that deal with the system and that your client should have known that he was acting in a deviant manner outside of the system when he engaged in some particular act of conduct which is the subject matter of the trial. In such instances, I like to tell the following story.

> Let me tell you about this fellow who had an unusual hobby. His hobby was religious ritual. He travelled the world far and wide studying various rituals. He went everywhere from synagogues to churches to tribal villages. In each case he studied the rituals that were utilized by the local population in the practice of their religions.
>
> On one such trip, he found himself in a small church in Greece. He observed the service which was beautiful in its pageantry but he noticed something he had never seen before. From time to time during the service various persons were called up to the pulpit which was on a slightly elevated stage. As each person was called to the pulpit they ascended the steps, took precisely six steps, bowed low from the waist, straightened up and then proceeded to the pulpit.
>
> Never having seen that particular ritual of the low bow he turned to the person sitting next to him and asked that person if he could explain what was that ritual and what was its origin. The person answered that he had only been coming to this particular church for ten years and they had been doing it ever since he had come so that he really did not know the origin of that particular practice.
>
> However, he was directed to an elderly person sitting in the front and advised that the man had been a member of this church virtually from its inception and that if anybody would know, he would.
>
> At the conclusion of the service, the student of ritual approached the elderly man and inquired if he knew the essence of the ritual which had been observed. The elderly man said, "Oh, you mean where they go up the steps, take a few steps, bow from the waist and then keep going?" Upon receiving an

affirmative response, the elderly man said, ''Oh, there used to be a chandelier hanging there.''

In other words, just because something is always done does not mean it has to be done.

§15.7 THE TESTIMONY OF THE MISSING WITNESS

Cross-examination can also be utilized to create the ''missing witness.'' That appears for the first time on summation. As each witness is produced by the other side who was present at a significant event, they may be simply asked, ''and was John Phillips also present?'' In an earlier chapter, this technique is described as setting up a witness who it is anticipated will subsequently appear. However, at this juncture, there is reason to believe that John Phillips will not be called by the other side; and, it is important to identify Mr. Phillips as a person who may have significant information. After repeatedly asking, ''and was John Phillips present?'' upon summation when he has not appeared, the summation becomes, ''where was John Phillips?'' and ''how is it that the opposition did not produce John Phillips?''

On summation, it becomes obvious that Mr. Phillips did not appear because he did not have the answers.

Expert Testimony 16

§16.1 INTRODUCTION

Today, there are virtually no limitations on scientific or technical theories or processes that may be offered as evidence at trial. Once a subject is acknowledged to be "specialized" or beyond the ordinary experience of laymen, it can be introduced at trial through experts who are permitted to give opinions and, often, ultimate conclusions on the issue. What has classically been regarded as science is now only a small portion of the totality of specialized subjects that are admitted into evidence through "experts" whose qualifications are marginal.

§16.2 SCOPE OF EXPERT TESTIMONY

Such testimony has routinely become an element in most significant cases. Custody battles often are swearing contests between psychiatrists, psychologists, sociologists and child care professionals. Environmental cases involve the testimony of toxologists, immunologists, biologists and doctors. Product liability can include everything from complex engineering testimony to statisticians. Medical testimony involves a myriad of new techniques for identifying and diagnosing illness and new surgical procedures of questionable general acceptance.

In criminal cases, it is highly likely that testimony will revolve around DNA fingerprinting, radar readings, ballistic reports, document analysis and even expert police testimony "decoding" what otherwise might appear to be obscure conversations recorded by electronic surveillance equipment. With regard to the same surveillance equipment, either audio or visual, whether tapes have been tampered with or edited or whether the recorded voice is that of the actual person or a computer recreation is frequently an issue.

In financial areas, accountants, forensic accountants, financial experts and economists project financial figures and offer assessments and appraisals. It is expert testimony that is utilized to establish the similarities between artistic works, books or musical compositions. Experts have also surfaced to give opinions on the reliability of eyewitness testimony.

Cross-examining an expert witness has its own advantages and pitfalls, separate and distinct from the examining of an adverse fact witness. However, given today's litigation menu, it is imperative to understand and be prepared for cross-examining an expert witness.

The medium by which such contemporary testimony or evidence is introduced in a trial is through an expert witness who is permitted to give his opinion in areas believed to be beyond the knowledge and experience of laymen so that his assistance is required in reaching a determination.

More often than not, such testimony consists of marshalled information massaged into statistical data which then constitutes the support for the witness' theory or conclusion. The data is organized in a manner that permits experts to make projections and conclusions from it. On cross-examination, it is vital to recognize the presence of statistical interpretation disguised as fact. This serves to dispel the mystique from what appears to be an overwhelmingly complex subject. By doing so, the task of developing effective cross-examination is less awesome.

Initially intimidating is that experts often come armed with charts, graphs and diagrams in the belief that "one picture is worth a thousand words." Being only a picture of words, if the preparer of the chart, the words or the statistical marshalling or interpretation is compromised, the chart is also compromised and stands only as a reminder of the witness' disingenuousness or error.

With any fact witness, the identification of the witness and the subject matter of the testimony that may be offered is determined by events, i.e., an eyewitness, a treating physician, a custodian of records or the parties to a contract. However, when it comes to expert witnesses, they are invariably people who have had nothing to do with the actual events under consideration but are carefully selected at the discretion of one or the other party to the litigation. This obvious circumstance that accounts for an expert's presence at a trial should be exploited by a collateral attack at the outset of an expert's cross-examination.

§16.3 DISCOVERY

While discovery is often overdone, it is absolutely critical when it comes to expert witnesses. There is no lawyer existent who can tackle an expert witness on his home ground and control that witness to the point of prevailing. It is critical to know the questions to ask and the documents to request on discovery. If at all possible, formulate the questions in discovery with the assistance of an expert retained by your client.

However, it is not always available to the attorney to have the assistance of such an expert in the earlier stages of litigation. Under the circumstances, the questions in discovery must be devised using a universal template so as to draw from the opposing expert all that he has to say on the matter, all of the processes utilized and all of the underlying work that went into the formulation of this witness' ultimate testimony.

Under those circumstances, the transcript of the examination before trial and the documents obtained can later be shown to an expert who can critique same and point out the vulnerabilities and gaps that the witness has demonstrated. That critique then becomes the basis of cross-examination at the time of trial. Two simple universal questions that can be followed up will effectively produce the result sought. One is simply to request and obtain any document, study or report upon which the witness relied and, the other, all work papers or reports which the witness prepared.

As with any witness, a prime purpose in discovery is to pin down the witness' testimony. It is more critical in the case of experts since they have more to draw upon to surprise you or buttress their opinion. However, if you pin the witness down, the cross-examiner gets to attack a stationary, rather than moving, target.

§16.4 DON'T CROSS-EXAMINE ON EXAMINATIONS BEFORE TRIAL . . . EXCEPT

Discovery is not cross-examination. The object is to gather information not discredit it. The practical reason for observing the rule is that, if a weakness is found in the witness' testimony, there is no point in making your awareness known so that the witness can correct it by the time of trial.

As with all rules, this one has two major exceptions.

It may be possible to so thoroughly discredit testimony or documents so as to negate any issue of fact and make possible the obtaining of summary judgment. However, such attack in pre-trial depositions should only be the result of careful assessment of the likelihood of summary judgment rather than a matter of routine. Otherwise, the lawyer simply gives away his position and ultimately prejudices his client.

The second exception should only be undertaken by the actual trial attorney rather than someone questioning on discovery only.

Cross-examination in discovery may be conducted in order to give the witness a vision of what he can anticipate in the courtroom. The witness learns that there is a probability that he or his testimony will not happily survive a courtroom confrontation. Simply being exposed to the trial attorney's style and method of questioning may give the witness pause.

It may be another means of setting up the witness thus negatively influencing the witness' certitude and confidence.

§16.5 FINANCING EXPERT TESTIMONY

A well-financed litigant can produce more and better qualified experts. A less-well financed litigant may be severely restricted, if not completely precluded from producing any meaningful expert testimony. In fact, many potential legitimate litigants are precluded from ever seeking redress for wrongs simply by knowing that the testimony involved will require extensive expert testimony which the other side has; but the ill-financed litigant cannot match.

Equalizing the dilemma is the cross-examination of the other side's experts. Obviously, the lack of funds to obtain experts, of necessity, places certain restrictions on cross-examination of the other side's experts. It is often the expert hired by your client that gives you the information necessary to understand the field, as well as to locate and identify the flaws in the testimony of the other side's experts. What can be done if such experts cannot be afforded?

One compromise that can be made is to locate an expert who is extremely knowledgeable but who will not be called to testify. The cost for a series of conferences in his office will be a great deal less while the insights obtained by the lawyer can be invaluable. The expert can suggest reading as well as other learned treatises on the subject from which the lawyer can obtain a sufficient understanding of the area.

The purpose is to develop a method of cross-examination which reduces the odds and takes away the greatest strength of the well financed litigating party, i.e., having a team of experts standing in the wings ready to testify. In fact, destroying the other side's expert is better than producing a number of experts of your own which only turns the trial into a swearing contest of conflicting opinions earning only a resultant "plague on both houses."

Courts vary from area to area with regard to their approach to the acceptance of expert testimony. At the threshold level, all courts pay lip service to the general concept that a specific technique or body of thought must achieve a level of general acceptability in order to be a proper area upon which an expert may offer his opinion. In reality, as soon as "enough" information generates some statistical tracking in excess of totally random results, statistical evaluation becomes the basis of general acceptance.

The two schools of thought are sharply divided. Recognizing the explosion of expert testimony that the revision of the Federal Rules of Evidence unleashed, one body of thought advocates that the Judge should carefully screen a proposed expert's qualifications before permitting the witness to offer confusing opinions to the jury. This has been referred to as the "gatehouse" approach.

The countervailing approach is to liberally permit "experts" to testify and rely on the adversarial system, particularly cross-examination, to determine the weight to be given to such testimony and reveal the marginal qualifications of the expert.

Dow v. Merrel-Dow may one day give rise to cases placing a greater onus on judges to screen experts qualifications but it will have little effect on a lawyer's responsibilities on cross-examination.

Should it be decided that careful filtration of experts by the court is appropriate, then cross-examination in *in limine* hearings will be required in order to induce the court to exclude the testimony.

As in earlier subjects, keep in mind the total environment in order to accurately assess what it will take to create the ultimate effect desired. Keep in mind that whether it is a jury or a Judge sitting as trier of the fact they are both laymen. It is for a judge to determine in the first instance whether or not an expert is qualified to testify. Yet, rarely does a judge have a full understanding of the subject matter by which to assess the expert's qualifications. Judges rely on whether or not the expert has been accepted elsewhere or has some experience, even if modestly so. More often than not, the court will cautiously admit the testimony stating that the trier of fact is to assess the weight to be given such testimony.

As to any witness who successfully negotiates the entry test, cross-examination remains the principal weapon to induce the jury to accord little or no weight to the testimony.

§16.6 MASTERING THE SUBJECT MATTER

A lawyer must master the subject matter about which the expert testifies. Included in such command is not only the limited subject of the questions intended to be asked but all the possible areas into which the witness may roam or throw at the questioner. It is not enough to master the questions but rather the subject matter sufficient to deal with the answers likely or anticipated to be received.

A significant disadvantage is that there is no way that any lawyer can master all subject matters with anything approaching the knowledge of the witness or to have access to experts presenting conflicting opinions from which to fashion a consensus. It is possible, however, to develop a general technique or procedure to be followed in most cases in the preparation and execution of cross-examination which, if the message cannot be completely destroyed, at least the messenger can be seriously wounded.

Cross-examiners should start with the recognition that anything that confuses him will confuse the jury or a judge sitting as finder of the fact. Do not be misled by your own ability to master or comprehend the subject after repeated sessions complete with a myriad of questions to your own expert and such additional research as you deem appropriate. It is imperative to spot the fact that, on the first blush, the testimony of the opponent's expert comes across as confusing or obfuscating. Remember that the object is to keep it simple.

§16.7 KEEP YOUR OWN CASE AND CROSS-EXAMINATION SIMPLE

Cross-examination should not reconcile the opposing testimony so as to iron out the rough spots for the jury. All too often, attorneys conducting such cross-examination proudly attempt to demonstrate their understanding and reconcile inconsistences or blanks in the witness' testimony. At best, it is resurrecting a straw horse in the belief that it can be subsequently knocked down. On the contrary, if the expert's testimony is confusing and without a clear conclusion, leave it that way, asking only enough questions to enhance the awareness of confusion. Remember always that it is the cross-examiner's first line of attack to exploit internal and external inconsistencies in the testimony being questioned.

Another mandate for simplicity is that the expert's opinion is given undue weight particularly if the jury is drowned in credentials that overshadow the actual testimony. Often, the meal does not live up to the menu.

Some years ago, I represented a man accused of trafficking in furs that had been stolen in interstate commerce. The furs in question were mink pelts and had allegedly been stolen from a ranch in Ohio where the minks were raised. Mink pelts have no unique markings except those which are stamped by the rancher, and these were unmarked. One of the theories of the defense was that not even the mother of a mink who has not seen her living offspring for several months could identify her offspring, let alone its pelt.

The government had difficulty in proving that the pelts which had been seized in Chicago were actually the ones which had been stolen in Ohio. The prosecutor was struggling to devise a theory which would establish the requisite identity.

He decided to solve the problem by contending that the processing of the pelts in this case was unusual. In the processing of mink pelts, it is common to stretch them on boards and to staple the pelt to the board.

The seizure of the pelts was from the defendant's offices in Chicago. During the raid, a stapler was seized. At the trial, the government produced an expert from the Federal Bureau of Investigation who went on for approximately fifteen minutes with a litany of credentials and particular examples of famous ballistic studies that he had performed.

The next onslaught came when the witness described the tests that he had performed and the equipment and machinery utilized in such tests. It was quite clear that we were about to be presented with the state of the art of scientific ballistic exploration and utilization of modern equipment, capable of not only testing but also proving beyond any doubt the existence of the atom bomb and its methodology.

After an endless stream of credentials and testing processes, the witness was finally asked if he formed an opinion. The witness stated:

> The tests proved conclusively that staples removed from some of the pelts seized from the defendant were of the same manufacture as the stapler taken from the office of the defendant.

After such a dramatic build up, it took a moment to realize that the connection was so weak that it was subject to being stricken in its entirety as having no probative value while being unduly inflammatory.

However, under the current rules of evidence that anything that makes an occurrence more or less probable is admissible, I was required to cross-examine in contrast to moving to strike as irrelevant.

Q: Does this manufacturer distribute its products nationally?
A: Yes.
Q: Is it a large manufacturer?
A: I think they are the biggest.
Q: Are both staplers and staples likely to be found in every State in the union?
A: I would assume so.
Q: How many staplers do you estimate this company manufactures in each year?
A: I don't know exactly.
Q: Would you say at least one hundred thousand?
A: Most likely.

Q: And staples, how about those?
A: Probably millions.
Q: How many offices in the United States do you estimate have staplers of that manufacturer, as we speak?
A: I couldn't begin to guess.
Q: Maybe even your office?
A: Maybe.
Q: Based on possession of the stapler alone, you wouldn't suggest they are all suspects, would you?
A: I never said that; I only testified as to my findings.

The above is a simplistic example of what all too often happens with the testimony of experts. The impressive recitation of qualifications and testing processes completely drowns out the fact that the opinion that he is rendering may be faulty in that there is an impermissible leap to a conclusion with the conclusion missing the mark.

It must always be remembered, however, that, if experts giving opinions were always right, then no human being would ever lose a dollar betting on a football game or a horse.

§16.8 KNOW THE ANSWER

Having failed in making the identification through his own expert, the prosecutor sought to do it through the cross-examination of one of my experts. The expert had been employed by the Hudson Bay Fur company for 40 years. It was he who testified that identification of unmarked furs was impossible.

The prosecutor brought out that, in stretching mink pelts upon boards and hanging them, it was customary to pin the tail and hang the board with the tail at the top. The prosecutor, pursuing his theory of unique processing, sought to show on cross-examination that, unlike every other rancher, the one in this case mounted them by pinning the head and hanging the pelts accordingly.

Thus, he asked:

Q: It is customary to pin the tails of the pelts to the board and hang up the board with the tail up and the head down, isn't that true?
A: Usually.

Q: As to these pelts, do you notice two small holes in the area of the head?
A: Yes.
Q: And doesn't that indicate that these pelts were stapled by the head instead of the tail when mounted?
A: Those are nostrils, you idiot.

In other words, never ask a witness a question unless you know the answer or you win whichever way the witness answers.

§16.9 AIMING BEYOND TOTAL DESTRUCTION

It is important to keep in mind that the total destruction of an expert is not necessarily the only acceptable outcome in cross-examination. Remember that you have an expert of your own who will be testifying at some point or who has previously testified who can help shoulder the burden. Thus, one of the goals of cross-examination is to establish the superiority of your own expert or the greater common sense appealability of the opinions of your expert. This greater appealability may occur through the manner in which the testimony is given or the ability and ease of breaking down hypertechnical subjects to everyday phraseology or simplicity. Thus, your cross-examination may have as its only aim the enhancing of your expert's testimony. As with other witnesses, it may be sufficient to merely elicit a response unremarkable on its face that can be expanded upon in summation or demolished by subsequent witnesses. In those instances, it is good practice to be repetitious in the questioning so as to indelibly make the point for easy recall when it is subsequently addressed.

It is effective just to get an expert to waiver. Responses such as "that requires more study" or some qualification of the opinion may seriously compromise the testimony.

Eliciting several points of agreement can similarly prove productive. That can illustrate that it is only in the quantum leap to a conclusion in which the opposing expert differs from your client's position. If you can marshal the points of agreement so that they flow into your conclusion, you will prevail.

The entire object of cross-examination may only be to create a discrepancy with other experts called by the opposition. While coordinated testimony on direct examination is the rule, it is not necessarily the case on cross-examination. Different witnesses respond differently, and it is rare that two or more experts will respond to questions identically. This is particularly true if the same question is worded differently on cross-examination in each case. Remember, all witnesses respond to the adjective or modifier.

Harsh economic reality causes an expert witness to pull his punches and qualify much of his testimony to avoid the professional embarrassment of a demonstrable refutation. The softening of such testimony is all that the cross-examiner may seek to accomplish, thus neutralizing its effect. Each time that an expert testifies, he puts his professional reputation and standing on the line. If an expert is successfully cross-examined, there is a transcript available for circulation, certain to be utilized in any subsequent appearances by such witness. It is not uncommon for experts who have been demolished upon cross-examination to discover that their phone suddenly stops ringing.

§16.10 ADVANTAGE—CROSS-EXAMINER

The expert has the advantage of knowledge and, by reaching into that bag of knowledge can, if permitted to do so, distract, confuse and otherwise evade any trap set in cross-examination.

In selecting the jury, regardless of how brief that process is, the lawyer develops a sense of the people and their backgrounds. He knows that the juror in jeans and a sweatshirt is a financial analyst and the well-dressed distinguished looking individual is a currently unemployed dog trainer. He knows his natural advantages.

A further advantage that the attorney has is that he gets to develop and choose the theme, sequence and pace of cross-examination. The attorney picks the point from which to launch the attack and the target at which it will be directed. The lawyer also gets to rearrange the focus so as to enhance certain aspects of the testimony and downplay others.

Thus, lengthy testimony of an expert witness may, when considered in its entirety, be highly effective; but, if it contains one or two points of vulnerability, the entire testimony can be brought down. The expert only prevails if his entire testimony stands up. Cross-examination of an expert is an excellent area in which to always keep in mind that a chain is only as strong as its weakest link.

Another advantage to the cross-examining attorney is that before the expert gets to render his message the attorney gets the chance to kill the messenger or, at the very least, minimize the significance of the message as emanating from a dubious source.

Scientific Testimony 17

§17.1 INTRODUCTION

At its cutting edge, science is comprised mostly of experiments and theories yet to be proven. The theories are routinely light years away from the limited factual underpinning from which they spring. It is almost exclusively issues at or near the cutting edge that find their way into the courtroom. When a significant scientific issue is litigated, it is axiomatic that there are many unanswered questions existing in the laboratory.

The area is one in which there are few answers, only decisions. Consequently, many of the significant decisions are being made by laymen in courtrooms rather than scientists.

Nothing is beyond the expanded conceptual mentality that the last forty years have brought about, especially among laymen. What would have been dismissed as the hallucinatory ruminations of Jules Verne or Buck Rogers are today accepted without question. The predictions or projections and theories that flow from any set of facts are rarely objected as absurd.

At the intersection of law and science, there exists a quandary as to whether or not a vast portion of the testimony being admitted into evidence in trials is valid scientific or technical testimony permitting opinions and conclusions by experts or junk science. Suffice it to say, the nature of the testimony confronting a cross-examiner has dramatically changed within past years.

Judges and juries alike are baffled by the distinction between true science and pseudo-science. In the course of a trial when scientific opinion is offered, it is rarely excluded if it springs from some nominal facts previously placed in evidence or upon the representation that some facts will subsequently be offered.

Inflammatory evidence, hearsay and other evidence previously inadmissible upon a number of grounds can now be accepted into evidence as the underlying basis for an expert's scientific or other opinion on the statement of the witness that, in some manner, it was taken into consideration in arriving at the conclusion to which he testified.

While the debate has reached the United States Supreme Court (*Daubert v. Merrel Dow* (92-102)) and has resulted in more stringent guidelines than those evolving after the revisions of the Federal Rules of Evidence, the expanded nature of the subject matter will inhibit any meaningful restriction on the nature of testimony offered. Such revised decisional guidelines will, however, chart areas of cross-examination.

Compounding the difficulty is that the advances of true science in the last generation are so mind boggling and unpredictable that junk science thrives because its fiction is no stranger or beyond credulity than the real thing.

The floodgates opened by the revisions of the Federal Rules of Evidence are not limited to the Federal Courts. Invariably, state courts, when presented with the comprehensive and coherent marshalling of the Federal Rules are not anxious to give deviate rulings or rulings which would be inconsistent with such a learned work. To the extent that state rules seem to be in conflict with the Federal Rules, judges commonly interpret the state rules to arrive at a position roughly, if not precisely, consistent with the Federal Rules.

Rule 702 of the Federal Rules in describing permissible "scientific" testimony by experts, states:

> If scientific, technical, or other specialized knowledge will assist the trier of a fact to understand the evidence or to determine a fact in issue, a witness qualified as an expert by knowledge, skill, experience, training, or education, may testify thereto in the form of an opinion or otherwise.

For the first time, highly speculative evidence was defined as that which could be either scientific, technical or "other specialized knowledge," a concept which realistically lacks discernible boundaries.

The only litmus test is that it assists the trier of the fact to understand the evidence or to determine a fact in issue. Axiomatically, a concept without limitation.

An expert is qualified either by knowledge, skill, experience, training or education. In other words, virtually anything. Significantly, the Rules do not require any combination of the foregoing traits or balancing test. The Rules are written in the conjunctive.

Virtually anyone can qualify as an expert. It requires no special insights to recognize that a person may be trained but utterly incompetent, or educated and equally incompetent. There are persons with 30 years experience and others with one year experience 30 times. Skill and knowledge are valid and, were that always required along with experience and training as a means of arriving at a judgment, greater validity would exist.

When the words "specialized knowledge" are added, the concept of wisdom becomes illusory. Specialized knowledge literally means that a person may know a little more about a particular subject than the average person. In the dynamics of an actual trial, it is difficult, if not impossible, to disqualify an expert given the ground rules for his acceptance or the subject upon which he might opine.

In the courtroom, it is certain that a proliferation of pseudo-science has come crowding through that opening, often obscuring true science. If it isn't actually science, it is, nevertheless, admissible as specialized knowledge. If the testimony being rendered is not emanating from an historically recognized expert, it is likely to be a person who can make a semblance of showing some experience, training or education. The liberality as to the substance of testimony to be delivered by the persons who can qualify as experts renders the entire area illusory.

Our judicial process depends upon the adversarial system, particularly cross-examination, to be the watchdog against abuses likely to occur under this vague criteria. However, the cross-examination safeguard is made more challenging as Rule 703, in describing the basis of opinion testimony by experts, states:

> The facts or data in a particular case upon which an expert bases an opinion or inference may be those perceived by or

> made known to the expert at or before the hearing. If of a type reasonably relied upon by experts in the particular field in forming opinions or inferences the facts or data need not be admissible in evidence.

Essentially, there is no time limitation when an expert may choose to consider something and which may be sprung upon a cross-examiner for the first time at trial. Moreover, it is a land mine since probing for the basis of an opinion may elicit damaging testimony or evidence otherwise admissible and without advance warning.

What experts can reasonably rely upon in arriving at an opinion is a debate without answer. The most proficient medical experts in the world consider tribal customs in remote parts of the world in trying to explain a discrepancy in the incidence of disease. Home remedies are not discounted in the world of medical science, which science often does not have a clue as to why they work, only that there seem to be statistical indications that they do. To this day, no one can clearly explain why aspirin works, only that it does in a number of instances.

A cross-examiner may at any moment be faced with a witness qualified only as possessing some "specialized knowledge," who is free to reach out at will and incorporate something that is claimed to have been considered in order to suit or fortify the opinion that is currently being offered.

Rule 704 permits, with the exception of a person's mental state, an expert to testify as to an ultimate issue. Given the preceding two rules, it appears that, if any restrictions manage to limit expert or scientific testimony, the witness is now permitted to do what was historically prohibited as invading the province of the jury.

Rule 705 assures that the proliferation of "anything goes" is not undermined. It states:

> The expert may testify in terms of opinion or inference and give reasons therefore without prior disclosure of the underlying facts or data, unless the Court requires otherwise. The expert may in any event be required to disclose the underlying facts or data on cross-examination.

Consequently, unless a court rules otherwise, which may or may not be problematical, the witness is not required to disclose the basis of his opinion or inference until he is cross-examined on the subject and given the opportunity to ambush the cross-examiner with an answer that is incapable of being resolved at that moment, thus creating an impression that can never be expelled.

If cross-examination is an antidote to abuses or testimony of marginal validity, then to fulfill its purpose techniques must be developed that can be generally applied in order to effectively deal with the broad range of subjects and the endless variety of prophets. Nitpicking a particular subject or witness will not suffice as it plays only to the witness' advantage. Neither is it tactically sound to focus on the witnesses conclusion. Rather, the sound practice is to focus on and attack the method or process by which the conclusion was reached.

§17.2 OPENING THE DOOR

The recurring nightmare for a lawyer conducting cross-examination is to open the door to otherwise inadmissible or inflammatory evidence. The Federal Rules appear to institutionalize the likelihood that the bad dream will become reality since they permit previously unidentified facts or hearsay otherwise inadmissible, inflammatory or surprising to find their way into evidence because they formed one of the elements taken into consideration in arriving at the opinion or theory being rendered.

To rebut or erode such testimony requires questioning that achieves the desired result on the spot when the questioner is confronted with the testimony for the first time. There is no time to reflect or research.

It now becomes apparent why the collateral attack on the expert is so vital, either to prevent the testimony altogether or, more likely, to diminish any weight that may be attributed to it, no matter what is opined. It also serves to inhibit the witness.

Failing that, the cross-examiner may well be left without the ability to stem the resulting hemorrhage since, having asked the question on cross-examination, the door is opened through which charges a tide of damaging testimony.

These were difficulties that the cross-examiners of yesteryear did not have to deal with to the extent that is prevalent today. There was a tighter screen that restricted such testimony and diminished the weight of what survived.

§17.3 *FRYE* AND CROSS-EXAMINATION

While "technical" and "specialized" still enjoy unfettered latitude, "scientific" has been slightly reined in by the recent United States supreme court decision in *Daubert v. Merril Dow, supra.* Judges are now obliged to screen the proferred evidence to make sure scientific conventions are followed in producing the result or conclusion. In other words, scrutinize the process.

It still remains a subjective process that will vary from court to court. The cross examination technique suggested here remains particularly viable as both judges and juries can understand missteps, errors and omissions.

Before addressing the process, *Frye v. United States* 293 F.1013 (D.C. Cir., 1923) must be revisited. No matter what revisions occur in the law, it still provides a common sense basis for challenging "scientific" evidence.

The earlier approach by the courts regarding scientific testimony was that there was safety in numbers. There was an insistence that there be a measurable consensus recognizing a subject as a "science" before evidence was accepted and opinion testimony permitted.

Prior to the codification of the Federal Rules of Evidence, the threshold was keynoted in *Frye*. Frye sought to establish his innocence to a charge of homicide by offering polygraph evidence which supported his contention.

In rejecting the proffered evidence, the court stated that lie detectors had "not yet gained such standing and scientific recognition among physiological and psychological authorities as would justify the Courts in admitting expert testimony deduced from the discovery, development and experiments thus far made."

The *Frye* rule as it is known utilized a "general acceptance" test for the admissibility of novel scientific evidence in stating:

> Just when a scientific principle or discovery crosses the line between the experimental and demonstrable stages is difficult to define. Somewhere in this twilight zone the evidential force of the principle must be recognized, and while courts will go a long way in admitting expert testimony deduced from a well-recognized scientific principle or discovery, the thing from

> which the deduction is made must be sufficiently established to have gained general acceptance in the particular field in which it belongs.

Realistically, the courts will never wholly abandon that standard. Thus, *Frye* is still illuminating for developing cross-examination that will minimize the weight to be accorded to scientific testimony.

Dissecting *Frye* provides the skeleton form for a significant portion of the cross-examination of an expert offering scientific testimony.

1. Is it a well recognized scientific principle?
2. Is the deduction that is made sufficiently established?
3. Is there general acceptance of that deduction? and
4. In the particular field in which it is offered.

Each of the above elements is a quagmire. What is the accurate definition of "well-recognized," "sufficiently established," "general acceptance," as well as an accurate definition of the particular field?

However, for purposes of this analysis, it is not important to arrive at accurate definitions of those concepts but only to recognize that they are vulnerable to attack. Because of the nature of the definition and the ensuing debate as to interpretation, a court will permit close questioning in order to permit the jury to assess such weight as is appropriate.

The court room is not insulated from dubious science and a substantial area of cross-examination should be designed to demonstrate that the testimony offered is little better than that, even if well meaning.

§17.4 PROCESS

The key to negating or minimizing the weight to be given to scientific testimony is by collateral attack and by questioning the process by which the conclusion or opinion is reached.

In analyzing the various processes or underlying basis for the fact or opinion, quite often the opinion is dependent on the performance of certain tests performed by the witness or others. In questioning such tests, the cross-examiner should look to:

1. Was there a protocol established prior to the test and was it explicitly followed;
2. Was there a low error rate or one that demonstrates that any results obtained were inconclusive;
3. Was proper care used in the methods by which the test was performed;
4. Were any equipment or chemicals used that were not functioning properly or that were chemically unstable;
5. Is there a similarity to other tests which would indicate that the results testified to are aberrational; and
6. What controls were present to confirm the validity of the test.
7. Will similar methods produce the same or substantially similar result.

Each of the above provides leads for cross-examination. If the error rate is anything other than minimal, it can be analogized through questions to the instant trial to show that this is one of the instances in which an error has occurred.

Any deviation from standards with regard to the performance of tests in the particular case invalidates the result of the test and thereby the opinion that follows.

Any absence of care with which the technique is utilized, even if acceptable, would invalidate the testimony offered. Whether or not they are acceptable in the first instance should not be overlooked.

Similarity to other tests can cut both ways. If it is similar to other tests which have a high degree of reliability, then focus should be made on any aspect which is dissimilar to avoid being overwhelmed by the excellent results obtained in such similar tests. Conversely, if the similarity is to other tests where high error rates resulted the similarity should be brought out by the cross-examiner.

Fail safe characteristics should be checked on a one-sided basis since a cross-examiner will only be concerned with the absence of fail safe characteristics in order to invalidate the testimony which he is seeking to compromise.

If the results are primarily determined statistically, cross-examination would focus upon the degree or percentage of change that would be effected by any modification in the statistical universe.

§17.5 LACK OF FIRST HAND KNOWLEDGE

As to the substance of the testimony, an expert rarely has first hand knowledge of all of the facts or other basis on which his conclusions or opinions are based. The expert accountant may not have done the bookkeeping or posting of entries himself. A scientist may not have performed the underlying research but bases his opinions and conclusions upon the research of others as well as literature generated by others. The engineering expert relies upon tests performed by others.

A predominant strategy of cross-examination is to identify through questioning each of the underlying basis upon which the testimony is based in discovery and then, at trial, attack any of those underlying basis that are vulnerable. Thus, if any of the underlying research was inadequate or poorly performed, it should be challenged. If an underlying investigation was incomplete or inadequate, there should be questions to demonstrate that fact with the resulting negative effect upon the conclusion.

§17.6 WHAT IS LEFT OUT

There is virtually no research, investigation or testing that can completely withstand the "second guessing" cross-examination.

There always exist tests that were not performed, leads that were not followed or hypothesis that were not checked. Each missing link should be explored.

For example, in medical malpractice cases involving erroneous diagnosis and treatment, there are a myriad of tests available to be performed which may or may not make sense to conduct dependent upon the particular situation and the doctor's judgment. Bringing out their existence suggests that had they been performed the unfortunate result could have been avoided. It is highly effective in the courtroom to point out anything that the expert could have done but did not, or that others could have done but did not, which might conceivably have altered his findings. Care should be taken to avoid the appearance of nitpicking for the sake of quibbling. Such questioning should always be the prelude to interrogation demonstrating the possibility that, if the missing element had been included, it would have changed the result or caused the expressed opinion to be reconsidered.

§17.7 LEAPING TO CONCLUSIONS

A vital area of focus in cross-examination is the nature and extent of the gap between the factual foundation or test result and the opinion or conclusion being offered. It is here that the testimony is the most vulnerable.

Judge Jack Weinstein of the United States District Court for the Eastern District of New York, a highly-regarded activist jurist, is probably the most enlightened jurist in dealing with complex scientific testimony as offered by expert witnesses. He is also superb at managing widespread and far-ranging unmanageable cases of which the "Agent Orange" litigation is a classic example.

Interestingly, Judge Weinstein approved the settlement of class claims but granted summary judgment against plaintiffs who chose to "opt out" primarily because he believed there was inadequate evidence of causation. Judge Weinstein, on his own, reviewed most of the available literature on the health effects of low level dioxin exposure and concluded, in the face of contrary expert testimony, that adequate proof was lacking.

Judge Weinstein gave greater weight to epidemiologic studies and concluded they were the only useful studies having any bearing on causation. He further concluded that such studies did not provide adequate support for the plaintiffs' claim of causation.

In arriving at these conclusions based upon his research, which went far beyond what was submitted to him by the parties, he found that the experts' reasoning was flawed in that as to one expert his finding contained an assumption which invalidated the conclusion. The expert's testimony essentially indicated that the plaintiffs in fact suffered from a variety of medical problems and that animals and humans exposed to extensive dosages of the toxic substance, *i.e.*, dioxin, have suffered from related difficulties. The expert then assumed that nothing else caused the plaintiffs' illnesses; and, therefore, they were caused by dioxin.

Judge Weinstein logically concluded the validity of the bridging assumption was questionable thereby making the ultimate conclusion lacking in any weight.

§17.8 EXPLOIT THE VARIABLES

Just as omitted steps, acts or tests are a focal point of scientific testimony, so, too, is anything in the process that is a variable or an assumption. Cross-examination should demonstrate that if a different available option or approach were selected the conclusion or opinion would vary accordingly.

A hypothetical example is a lawsuit arising out of a plane crash. The plaintiff's theory of liability is that a given airplane possessed a part which in testing indicated that after a certain number of miles it developed certain stress defects and lost all or a part of its function. That loss of function is claimed as the cause of the crash.

Questions on cross-examination develop that the particular airplane was serviced under a maintenance program that reduced the stress levels below that which was the foundation of the laboratory test. The plane had been in service which placed different stress factors on it in that it operated in different weather zones and was subject to different climatic effects. The same airplane had different manufacturers producing component parts other than the one tested which had different properties and had not been tested. Each individual plane's prior history, which may have telegraphed trouble, is distinguishable from the events in the laboratory which led to the final loss of function. As always, there may have been the existence of human error.

Depending on the answers to those questions, the original opinion is fragile, at best.

Both positive and negative variables should be identified and exploited. A witness offering scientific or technical opinion does not have first hand knowledge. Even a doctor or scientist who has first hand knowledge having treated the patient or analyzed the specific event must usually rely on other studies, statistical probabilities or consensus opinions in arriving at his viewpoint.

The ultimate question on scientific direct testimony generally concludes with the question:

> Can you state with reasonable (medical, scientific, engineering, accounting, etc.) certainty that X caused Y.

If, on cross-examination, you have introduced a number of variables that existed in the instant case that were not taken into account or that did not exist but were built in as a building block of the expert's conclusion, then the certainty of the witness is demonstrably unreasonable and his opinion lacks credibility.

§17.9 THE SCIENTIFIC OPEN END

Today, scientific testimony is not limited to what springs from the laboratory but includes anything from which a pattern emerges that can serve as a statistical overlay to a particular case. There is no purpose in attempting to enumerate the myriad number of cases in which "scientific," "technical" or "specialized" testimony can arise since the list is virtually without limitation. It is restricted only by the imagination of the attorney preparing a particular case on any subject, civil or criminal.

By way of illustration, a number of years ago I was a member of a defense team representing a prominent attorney charged with failing to file Federal income taxes for a period of five years. There was no questioning the fact that the returns had not been filed. The defense adopted a version of the insanity defense.

Secretaries and partners of the defendant were placed on the stand to testify that the lawyer's desk was always an absolute mess. Further, he was sloppy in his billing practices and inefficient in the expenditure of his time. He frequently appeared at the office with socks that were mismatched and, on occasion, a mismatch between his pants and jacket. The factual underpinning was that but for his apparently autistic ability to function as an effective attorney he led a disoriented and incredibly sloppy existence.

This foundation was followed by the testimony of two psychiatrists who testified that their observations indicated a clinical anal complex. The failure to file the income tax returns had nothing to do with attempting to avoid tax collections. Rather, it was the result of his clinically identified pathology that characterized virtually his entire existence and was responsible for the failure to file. It was another symptom of his disoriented, unorganized methods of dealing with responsibility. While the first psychiatrist was testifying, the trial judge turned to his law assistant and, in a whisper that could be heard throughout the courtroom, said "Damn, this is the first time I ever heard that bad toilet training was a defense to tax evasion."

The jury did not convict, demonstrating that only the imagination limits the "scientific" issues that can be introduced into any trial.

§17.10 THE JURY INSISTS ON PATTERNS AND ORDERLY SEQUENCE

The acceptance of scientific testimony is enhanced not only by its delivery by a credentialed expert but also because it offers the solace of reconciling otherwise random events into an orderly and, therefore, comforting theory.

Most people accept that a past sequence of events will determine the next event. It is much like the mathematical progression that one finds on intelligence or college entrance exams. There, such questions appear as:

What is the next number?

and then gives:

Five, nine, fourteen, twenty, twenty-seven.

The correct answer is thirty-five, arrived at by noting that the gap between the first and second number is three, between the third and fourth, four, and between the fourth and fifth, five, and so on until it is apparent that the gap between twenty-seven and the next number should be eight, totalling thirty-five. That approach and conditioned mentality surface in the courtroom in scientific, technical or specialized opinion. Based on a series of preceding events, testimony which projects the next likely event which is the essence of the lawsuit is appealing.

The general public is unwilling to accept that life in its various elements is random. The prospect is too frightening. Comfort only exists emotionally and intellectually when there is a discernible pattern and regularity.

The demand for such order is so great that it is satisfied by theories.

The phenomenon is analogously described by Thomas Friedman in "From Beirut to Jerusalem" wherein he tells of the constant civil wars among a number of factions in Beirut resulting in widespread killing and destruction of property that by any rational measurement was mindless and random. No resident of that city knew if they left their house in the morning that they would not walk into a fire fight or be gunned down by a stray bullet. Leaving the house contained no guarantee that the house or their apartment would exist at the time they arrived home. On other occasions, many people would simply disappear never to be seen or heard from again. Friedman reports:

> In an attempt to make the anxiety this produced more controllable, the Lebanese would simply invent explanations for the unnatural phenomena happening around them; they would impose an order on the chaos. Their explanations for why someone was killed or why a certain battle broke out were usually the most implausible, wild-eyed conspiracy theories one could imagine.
>
> * * *
>
> Similar ''rational'' explanations were also employed to explain why the other guy got killed and you didn't. I rarely heard any Beiruti admit that the violence around him was totally capricious and that the only thing that kept him alive was callous fate—which was the truth. Instead, I would hear people say about a neighbor who got killed by an errant shell, ''Well, you know, he lived on the wrong side of the street. It is much more exposed over there than on our side.'' Or they would say, ''Well, you know, he lived next to a PLO neighborhood,'' or, ''He shouldn't have gone out driving fifteen minutes after the cease-fire started; he should have waited twenty minutes—everyone knows that.'' In order to continue functioning, Beirutis always had to find some way to differentiate themselves from the victim and to insist that there was a logical explanation for why each person died, which, if noted, would save them from a similar fate. Without such rationalizations no one would have left his home.

The above insight reveals that, in order to survive, people demand a reason or a logic that has nothing to recommend it but the need to impose order in order to achieve comfort. Were anything further needed to establish the point, simply note how many inexplicable tragedies, when there is no potential defendant, are logically accepted as "God's will."

This phenomenon of human nature accounts for the success and acceptance of many of the "scientific" theories that are accepted by juries. A plaintiff or defendant who can evolve an "orderly" theory that does not offend such need will achieve credibility in a courtroom.

Cross-examination should be structured to demonstrate that the opposing theory is not orderly, just simplistic, and to substitute in its place a theory that is at least, if not more, orderly but which places the jury outside of the sphere of risk. If the jury feels threatened by the risk, they will gravitate to the plaintiff. If an orderly theory can be imposed that places them outside of the risk, the compulsion to accept that approach can be overwhelming.

Recently in the media, a story appeared concerning a lawsuit proclaiming the theory that the frequent use of a portable cellular telephone accounted for a particular plaintiff's developing brain cancer. Although no proof of any significance exists with regard to such theory, it took advantage of sequential logic to get from cause to effect. The unproven but simplistic sequential order appears to be:

1. Microwaves have been found to be a carcinogenic;
2. Cellular telephones depend on microwaves for their transmission;
3. The instrument is held near the head;
4. Microwaves are near the head;
5. The brain is in the head and brain cancer developed; and
6. The cellular telephone utilizing microwaves is the source of the problem.

Although neither scientific tests nor scientific chain of logic have ever substantiated such theory, the public did not dismiss the theory out of hand and the theory became a major media event. Daubert v. Merrel Dow will not do away with such lawsuits as each of the elements is essentially established. It is the marshalling of the sequence that produces the theory.

Cross-examination should demonstrate that the proposed theory was illogical and survived only by ignoring detail. The lack of logic should be able to appeal not only to the scientist in the laboratory, the mathematician or the doctor who deals with the situation every day. Such persons have the ability to dismiss the subject out of hand based upon background and experience. The cross-examination should appeal to the layman who, like all of us, needs the comfort of believing that there is a reason for everything and that his own future will be governed by that orderly or logical sequence and not aberrational events.

Upon trial, to dispel the theory that cellular telephones cause brain cancer, the cross-examiner must demonstrate that telephones are basically safe or that the circumstances of the particular case are different and do not have universal application to all of the people using such telephones. Upon questioning, a probe should be made of distinctions, details and questions still untested and unanswered while focusing on the quantum leaps that disguise fatal gaps in the theory. Understand that human reaction and customize it to a particular case and you have the essence of cross-examination of scientific testimony.

In fashioning a cross-examination of the witness in the above case who theorizes the cause and effect, the lawyer should be prepared to challenge the witness after considering the following details:

1. What studies exist as to the cause and effect of microwaves and cancer;
2. Is there a consensus as to what dosage level is believed to cause cancer;
3. Is there a consensus as to the time period over which exposure must take place;
4. Do cellular phones emit microwaves;
5. If so, at what measurable level;
6. If microwaves are emitted, what level would reach the head and penetrate the body when the phone is held to the ear;
7. If the microwaves are emitted and do penetrate the body, what period of time would be required to arrive at the dosage levels believed to cause cancer;

8. Did the person always use the same hand in using the phone so as to demonstrate lower dosage at any potential exposure site on the head or body;
9. Have any controlled tests ever been performed as to the relationship between cellular telephone microwave emissions and human cancer;
10. What is the statistical evidence of brain cancer among all persons in the same demographic category as the plaintiff;
11. What is the utilization rate of handheld cellular telephones in that same demographic category;
12. Obtain all phone bills of the plaintiff so as to ascertain if there is even a mathematical possibility that the usage (emission level x frequency of use) could ever reach the dosage levels believed to cause brain cancer;
13. What is the plaintiff's medical history;
14. What is the plaintiff's family's medical history; and
15. What are the instruments that measured the microwave emissions in the case.

There are infinitely more details that could be listed. However, in working one's way through the above list the information elicited there would provide the basis for further cross-examination.

The theme of such cross-examination would be to demonstrate:

1. That any microwaves that are emitted are of such low dosage that it would take an individual three lifetimes of twelve hour a day usage to arrive at a dosage level that might cause cancer and the telephone bills establish (aside from common sense) that no such usage occurred;
2. That would only be true if the plaintiff only held the phone to the right side of the head for the three lifetimes of twelve hour a day usage;
3. No known test has ever established this cause and effect between cellular phones and cancer;

4. The incidence of brain cancer in persons in the same demographic grouping is no higher than among non-users of cellular phones;
5. The plaintiff's personal or family history put him in a higher than average risk category; and
6. It is alright to use a cellular phone and you don't have to worry if you are near someone using one.

The jury will prefer your theory as it makes their lives much simpler and they can take advantage of a modern convenience if they choose to.

§17.11 IMPRESSIONS

Scientific data, qualified experts and jargon notwithstanding, impressions or the perception of truth still rule the courtroom. In today's crowded courtrooms, it is almost axiomatic.

When addressing the court or providing a short summary of the case to the judge during a conference, both sides race to speak so as to give the first impression of the case. Each lawyer knows that, if the court's radar locks on a particular vision of the case, there is considerable difficulty in ever changing the court's direction.

The same is true of juries who are subjected to a broader range of impressions to which a court may be indifferent.

Juries evaluate lawyers as to who seems more sincere or knowledgeable, which of the parties seems to be telling the truth and which version of the conflicting presentations are they more comfortable with in terms of their own experience.

Successful cross-examination does not exclusively appeal to the mind but rather to the person, the soul or the fear of the trier of the fact. The likelihood of hitting a responsive chord in those areas is far greater than appealing solely to the intellect since, however bright, a judge or jury simply has not dealt with this subject previously and lacks the background or experience for fully appreciating the technical differences. As with all cross-examination, the critical issue has to be brought down to gut level.

While it is true that jurors possibly may be able to discern the difference between a chronological sequence of events and cause and effect, the likelihood of error is simply too great as even experienced persons of extensive background have an overwhelming compulsion to perform the same statistical exercise.

The discipline of science and technicality requires that an inordinate amount of time be spent and a significant number of situations be evaluated in order to prove or disprove the theory. This is unlike the courtroom where a single or limited number of events result in a conclusion that may or may not be accurate but depend on the impression of the moment. Returning to the laboratory and applying the disciplines of science as the protective guard against legal imagination and the expanded and liberal Rules of Evidence as well as the liberal interpretation of those rules is not a viable option. The only answer to deal with such situation is in the place where the impression was born, in the courtroom and in the testing crucible of cross-examination.

That courtroom impressions prevail over even conclusive laboratory proven science is demonstrated in the case of Charles Chaplin. Chaplin, defending against a complaint brought against him alleging paternity of a child born out of wedlock, was found by a jury to be the father despite the introduction of evidence that based on his blood type he could not have fathered that child. However, Chaplin had slept with the mother and a child was subsequently born. The cause and effect syndrome prevailed and science lost.

Upon the appeal, which affirmed the jury's judgment, one judge dissented arguing:

> But modern science brought new aids and new scientific means and instrumentalities have revised the judicial guessing game of the past into an institution approaching accuracy in portraying the truth as to actual fact. If the Courts do not utilize these unimpeachable methods for acquiring accurate knowledge of pertinent facts they will neglect the employment of available, potent agencies which serve to avoid miscarriages of justice[1]

---

1. *Barry v. Chaplin,* 169 P.2d at 453.

Although recognizing the problem that science in fact might possess pertinent facts which will avoid miscarriages of justice, there is no assurance that the science will objectively emerge in the courtroom. That gap has yet to be solved, although cross-examination can narrow or widen the gap.

All strategies, while seeking to avoid the worst result, do not necessarily have as their goal the maximum possibility. The goal is to achieve the optimum result that can realistically be obtained under the circumstances.

In the courtroom, particularly with complex scientific testimony, the optimum result may be creating a good impression.

Statistics 18

§18.1 INTRODUCTION

In the age of the computer, the findings and opinions of experts regarding scientific, technical or specialized knowledge, more often than not, is dependent upon statistics. It is the statistical correlation that establishes the cause and effect between smoking and cancer, exposure to a toxic substance and the existence of disease developed years later, as well as transactions versus price discrepancies in antitrust cases. Statistical patterns are routinely accepted to establish the cause and effect of a number of events.

Statistics may also be used to demonstrate a lack of causation by showing that the statistical incidence of a particular event or illness is within a "normal" statistical range absent the claimed cause that is the focus of the trial.

The danger is that, in utilizing statistics, the outcome will vary, dependent on the selection of criteria that is included or excluded in arriving at the statistical conclusion.

§18.2 CONFIRMATION OF STATISTICS

The essence of cross-examining any witness who utilizes statistics to make his point or confirm his opinion is to attack the selection of facts or figures that go into the determination of the statistical universe.

In the recent presidential election, polls were taken frequently on a week-to-week and, subsequently, on a day-to-day basis. It was noted that significant differences in results were obtained dependent on any change of criteria by the poll taker. At the outset of the election campaign all persons were polled as to their presidential choice. When the criteria was changed to registered voters, the statistical margin between the candidates varied substantially. When the poll takers revised their questions to party registrants, the results varied again. On the final weekend, when poll takers restricted their questions to persons likely to vote, what appeared to be a runaway suddenly appeared to be a dead heat in that any gap was within the statistical margin of error.

§18.3 TOXIC TORT CASES

Cross-examination primarily consists of questions eliciting the resultant variety of conclusions as a result of any variation in the statistical universe.

For purposes of illustration, the toxic tort provides the clearest examples. Toxic substances and the effect that exposure to that substance may have upon persons, which effect is not recognized for many many years, is generally dependent upon statistics.

Returning to the "Agent Orange" case, the testimony of a second expert was rejected by the court because the expert's findings contained no showing that the incidence of the illness in question was greater in the plaintiffs than would be found in the general population.

Judge Weinstein in refining his approach also took into consideration the general scientific techniques that were utilized by some of the experts which had been accepted by a sufficient number of courts to allow judicial notice of the techniques' general acceptance. The court's conclusions were not based directly on the defects in the experts' reasoning but also upon adherence to Rule 703 of the Federal Rules of Evidence which permitted expert reliance on otherwise inadmissible facts or data "of a type reasonably relied upon by experts in the particular field in forming opinions or inferences upon the subject." The court also balanced probative value against the danger of unfair prejudice, confusion or misleading a finder of fact. Judge Weinstein further noted that the experts relied on questionnaire checklists for their information about the plaintiffs and upon certain animal studies regarding the health effects of dioxins, yet had ignored other available epidemiologic information of which the court was aware.

In this instance, the court was actually the cross-examiner and asked precisely the same questions of himself on the evidence submitted to him that a knowledgeable cross-examiner would ask of the witness on the stand. Judge Weinstein, as finder of the fact in that instance, then reached a conclusion much the same as if the process had played out before a jury.

Consequently, it appeared that highly complex and sophisticated testimony by a highly regarded expert was flawed based upon an assumption that was required to build a bridge between basic fact and ultimate conclusion. The plaintiffs had the burden of demonstrating that the results attributable to a particular toxin exceeded statistical evidence of illness in the general population, which burden they did not statistically meet.

Juries are not as trained or astute in analysis as Judge Weinstein nor do they have his background or experience with the particular issue. If a jury were to come to the same correct result, it would only be if the lawyer, during cross-examination, exposed the flaws in the experts' testimony by a series of repetitive leading questions that focused on the statistical similarity of disease between the general population and the toxin.

§18.4 ANTITRUST CASES

Antitrust cases are so complex and multifaceted that they are particularly susceptible of being proven or disproven by statistics, with the computer and a statistician being virtually the only witnesses. I was retained as trial counsel in an antitrust suit against Iowa Beef processors alleging that they had entered into a price fixing scheme in violation of the Robinson Patman Act. The specification was that they favored a single customer, Waldbaums, with lower prices, contrasted to a competitor, Bohack, who they required to pay higher prices.

It is virtually impossible to prove a price fixing case absent the use of statistics. There is rarely an audio or visual overheard wherein a group is sitting around a table deciding to give special consideration to a particular customer. Nor is there likely to be a witness who has knowledge of all the circumstances necessary to support a case.

The problem was compounded in that this commodity, **i.e.**, meat, is extremely volatile. The prices are quoted in "pink sheets" quite similar to stock quotations. The prices can vary several times a day occasioned by sudden changes in supply and demand, particular cuts of the same kind of meat, volumes purchased, shipping arrangements, dates the orders were placed, dates the orders were shipped, as well as special, but legal, promotions.

Witnesses were difficult to come by. No one at either Iowa Beef or Waldbaums would acknowledge the existence of any price fixing. To compound the problem, Bohack did not have the information regarding other sales to prove its case. Even obtaining records of all sales would virtually not have been effective given the voluminous nature of the essential transactions. The personnel and expense necessary to review the records and make comparisons would be out of the question. Bohack had previously gone into bankruptcy alleging that one of the causes of its bankruptcy was that it was the victim of a price fixing scheme which placed it at a competitive disadvantage.

It was determined early in the case that the only conceivable method for establishing the claim was by utilization of a computer and the development of a statistical basis for the claim of price fixing. The sales records of Iowa Beef were subpoenaed for the four years preceding the institution of the litigation, which sales information included sales to all other purchasers, sales to Bohack and sales to Waldbaums. Some 300,000 transactions were fed into the computer, sales to Waldbaums on one side and Bohack on the other, with sales to other purchasers as a third category as a control. The quest was for a perfect match of a sale made to Waldbaums or someone other than Bohack which was identical in all aspects to the sale made to Bohack. Of the 300,000 transactions, the computer identified 600 perfect matches or "hits."

Absent the computer, it would have taken an indefinite number of individuals an indefinite number of years to assimilate this information and develop with absolute accuracy the number of "hits." The computer did it in minutes after the information was "punched" in.

Of the 600 "hits," 594 of the transactions favored Waldbaums in that Waldbaums obtained the product at a price cheaper than the one accorded to Bohack.

With computer printouts in hand, a statistical expert then testified that the probability of 594 transactions falling in favor of Waldbaums in contrast to 6 for Bohack was beyond any statistical likelihood of random circumstances. Such an absolute disproportion testified the statistical expert could only be the result of a deliberate scheme or plan which deliberately accomplished that result. The jury decided that Iowa Beef had fixed prices by favoring Waldbaums and discriminating against Bohack.

The attorneys for Iowa Beef appropriately hammered away at the process by which the printouts were generated and the "hits" established. They cross-examined as to the number of hours and number of persons who had punched in the information. They attempted to show that the slightest deviation with regard to any particular entry was enough to discredit that transaction from being a perfect match. They questioned whether the computer programmers had been furnished with all of the transactions or whether or not there had been any selectivity involved. They even questioned whether the computer persons read the invoices correctly and understood the entries contained on them.

Their efforts failed with regard to negating the existence of a price fixing scheme, primarily because the jury in all likelihood believed that even if 90 of the "hits" were discredited and the results were 500 to 100 the point was still made.

Cross-examination as to whether the price fixing had caused Bohack's financial difficulty was different. There, the attorneys cross-examined Bohack on every financial transaction over a substantial period of years. They attacked Bohack's form of merchandising as well as the fact that Bohack had not modernized or kept pace with new developments in marketing meat. They pointed to acquisitions that Bohack had made that constituted a financial drain on the company. They attacked the competence of the executives running Bohack and questioned every transaction or policy with which it had ever been associated. They questioned store locations and the demographic makeup of consumers surrounding those locations contrasted to the demographic makeup of Waldbaums' customers. They interrogated on variations in debt service and fluctuating interest rates on such debt. Their theme on cross-examination regarding causation was that Bohack's troubles would have been caused absent a price fixing scheme. Graphically, statistical evidence clearly established liability while a different use of statistics was used to advantage on the issues of causation and damage.

Once again, it was confirmed that cross-examination of opinion testimony, scientific or otherwise, is the process by which the conclusion is reached. Regardless of the complexity of the subject, breaking the process down to each of its elements and questioning accordingly can expose the vulnerability of the most intimidating matter.

The Collateral Attack 19

As its name implies, a collateral attack seeks to demolish testimony by means other than a direct challenge to the contents of the testimony itself. This is often done by questioning the qualifications of the witness, impugning his credibility generally or provoking him into an unflattering position.

§19.1 KILLING THE MESSENGER

On cross-examination, the interrogator gets two opportunities to negate the testimony of an expert. Initially, there is, at the outset and continuing throughout the testimony, the opportunity to kill the messenger. The second is to compromise the message.

Once an expert is permitted to testify, his opinion may be so speculative that it can only be thwarted by the most comprehensive examination judged by persons who are themselves knowledgeable and sophisticated in that particular area. Since simplicity is the key, such comprehensive examination may, at worst, confuse the jury or, at best, put them to sleep.

§19.2 OVERALL IMPRESSION

More than any other witness, an expert will be judged by his demeanor, appearance and the impression he creates. A jury is less able to evaluate the content but are more familiar with sizing up people.

People have high expectations of knowledgeable individuals and the failure to meet those expectations will have a greater negative impact than would be the case of someone from whom less was expected.

Traits that would tend to present an expert in a favorable light start with the appearance of fairness.

Does the witness testify in a simple, non-technical fashion as contrasted to jargon that tends to confuse or seems to mislead or obfuscate?

Personality and appearance play a part so that the witness looks like he knows what he is talking about.

Is the witness a professional witness or does he appear to be an infrequent visitor to courtrooms?

Cross-examination seeks to dispel any of the above good impressions.

Rather than fair, the witness is shown to be an indiscriminate hired gun whose testimony is for sale to anyone willing to meet the price.

The studied and thoughtful answers on direct testimony give way to strident and stubborn on cross-examination. An attack on the ego of the witness often provokes a Jekyll and Hyde transformation in response to the confrontation.

On cross-examination, experts often seek to avoid the challenge by retreating behind jargon and unfocused stringing together of technical dissembling.

Last, but by no means least, by showing that the witness spends more time testifying than practicing the expert is weakened in the eyes of the jury.

§19.3 QUALIFICATIONS

Attacking the qualifications of an expert to the extent of successfully excluding his testimony is recognizably unlikely. Notwithstanding any change in the nature of admissible scientific testimony, an expert under the current rules of evidence given a few years experience, attendance at an accredited college or professional training program and no known criminal record for practicing witchcraft is generally all that is required to have a court opt to recognize an expert.

However, in the course of cross-examination regarding qualifications, an attorney gets the opportunity to test the expertise of the witness.

Under the guise of testing that expertise, questions are permitted on a wider range of subjects than may be encompassed within the confines of direct testimony, the facts of the particular case or information relied upon by the expert in forming his opinion.

While certain learned treatises would be inadmissible during cross-examination in chief as not being germane to the particular issue or not utilized by the expert, they are permissible in testing the knowledge and expertise of the witness regarding the field in which he purports to be qualified.

This is also an area in which the attorney gets to exercise selectivity as to questions and subject matter for which the witness has not been prepared. In that circumstance, the witness' answers may vary materially in tone, content, and confidence level which may serve to indicate that the witness is not particularly knowledgeable or qualified in the field generally, only in the limited area in which he has been prepared and for which he has been paid. Should the witness survive the attack on qualifications, the residual effect of such questioning may seriously compromise subsequent testimony and detract from the weight such opinion or conclusion may otherwise be given. The transcript of the hearing on qualifications is a useful tool in cross-examining the expert if held separately from the testimony in chief.

In such preliminary examination attacking the qualifications of the witness, the cross-examiner also gets an opportunity to demonstrate the complexity of the subject matter to the jury. A series of questions which are appropriate at this time would likely begin with:

> Are you familiar with the theory of . . .?
>
> Have you heard of . . .?
>
> Have you had experience with . . .?

While it is true that a number of such questions could easily be incorporated into cross-examination itself, an exclusionary ruling is not unusual. It is, however, a fair area of questioning on the issue of qualification to see if the witness is truly qualified in the area which he suggests. Such discussion of the various aspects of the field using terms that at that point contain no explanation as to their meaning for the jury, can serve to demonstrate to the jury how unbelievably complex the area is and how limited is their knowledge of the subject. This, in and of itself, will present to the jury a self-recognition that this witness' testimony, simply on his say so, is beyond their ability. This is a ground for their discounting the testimony.

In conducting such early questioning, the lawyer himself should not fear appearing confused since the jury might identify with the lawyer and conclude that the subject is beyond the understanding of laymen.

The Federal Rules indicate that a witness may qualify as an expert if in the conjunctive he possesses knowledge, skill, experience, training or education.

Each of the foregoing is subject to question. Is the skill demonstrated or only claimed? Has the expert published and, if so, has there been any peer acclaim for his work?

The same holds true for knowledge. What independent confirmation of that knowledge exists other than the witness' pretensions?

Questioning experience often demonstrates a lack of substantial experience as contrasted to an only extended passage of time in the same vocation. It is a question as to whether the expert has thirty years experience or one year experience thirty times.

Was training and education obtained from a recognized and accredited source as contrasted to on the job training from an unknown quantity or some limited courses?

It is surprising what is revealed when the labels are punctured and reality emerges. However, even though the witness overcomes the challenge to qualifications, the substance of his testimony can be materially weakened.

§19.4 BIAS

Another area of examination that collaterally undermines any testimony rendered, expert or otherwise, is demonstrating that the witness is biased. All experts are biased either because it is the means by which the witness obtains substantial income or because he has a sincere affection for his own opinions. The classic method of demonstrating bias at the outset is to ask questions sufficient to suggest that the witness' opinion is for sale. This may be accomplished by bringing out the frequency with which the witness testifies, if that is the case. If not, there are a series of questions designed to establish that the opposing party only recruits experts who agree with his position.

A series of rhetorical questions along the following lines conveys the sought after impression in virtually every case. The line of questioning would proceed as follows:

Q: When did you first make contact with the plaintiff?

Q: Did he or his lawyer call you or did you call them?

Q: At the time that you first made contact with the plaintiff were you advised of the existence of this lawsuit?

Q: Were you advised of the plaintiff's position in the lawsuit?

Q: Were you advised of the issue upon which you were requested to give testimony or render an opinion?

Q: Did you understand which position would be favorable to the plaintiff?

Q: And you understood all this before you rendered a report or formulated your conclusion?

Q: After all, you had to do an investigation and possibly some research before you rendered such opinion or conclusion?

Q: And while you were doing investigation or research you understood which conclusion or opinion if arrived at would be favorable to the plaintiff?

Q: And at the time of initial contact was any compensation discussed?

Q: What were the terms of that compensation?

Q: You understood, did you not, that that compensation would not be forthcoming if the opinion you rendered did not favor the plaintiff?

Q: So, while you were doing your research, investigation and preparing your report, you knew what opinion or testimony the plaintiff hoped for and you knew that you would not receive compensation, even for your appearance here today, in the maximum amount unless your findings were consistent with that favorable position?

Q: And you arrived at that favorable conclusion, did you not?

Q: You are aware that to testify to any other conclusion will damage the interests of the person who is paying you?

Such questions consisting of nothing more than the obvious dispel the impression of impartiality or objectivity. If the witness answers "no" to any of the above questions, the jury simply will not accord such witness any credence. How could the witness presume to testify or conduct any investigation if he does not understand what the issues are? The witness would also have to be deaf, dumb and blind not to understand what would be favorable to the party hiring him or detrimental. By pointing out the apparent coincidence of knowing in advance what opinion or testimony was sought with all or part of the compensation to be received dependent on arriving at that conclusion is sufficient to convey the impression intended. There may be dozens of professionals who, after being solicited rendered adverse opinions, but they are not the ones that appear in court.

More subtle forms of bias can also be brought out other than that the witness is a hired gun. Ironically, an expert is not normally described as an interested witness when the judge charges the jury. In reality, an expert witness is one of the most interested parties. Every expert witness has a vested interest in his own opinion. The professional rewards and financial benefits that can flow from having his opinion influence a judge or jury frequently leads to professional recognition and future employment. A large number of such witnesses benefit simply by a court recognizing them as experts, a fact which they promptly add to their professional resume. That vested interest is sufficient to generate a substantial bias on the part of the witness and leads to a determination to resist all challenges to that opinion. The witness strenuously resists any effort to show the opinion to be erroneous, poorly developed or otherwise ineffectual. For an expert witness there is no easy out in the face of a challenge such as "possibly I was mistaken." The minute the stand is taken, the expert witness puts his professional soul on the line. Compromise the testimony or the opinion and you compromise the expert and his professional standing. Moreover, when an expert starts to back down, he knows he is "biting the hand that feeds him." It is that very self-interest which provides the most effective tactic on cross-examination by causing such witness to retreat graciously by qualifying the opinion, rather than risking professional embarrassment. In this regard, the expert is more vulnerable than the normal fact witness, other than a party, as he believes his future may depend on it, separate and distinct from the particular case.

§19.5 ASSUMPTIONS

There is invariably some portion of an expert's testimony which is dependent upon assumptions, either those made by the expert himself or assumptions made by others supplying the underlying information upon which the expert relies. Assumptions always provide the opportunity for effective cross-examination as they go to the heart of the speculation known as opinion. If any of the underlying assumptions are modified the ultimate opinion or conclusion offered by the witness would change.

The key is to identify the assumptions which are often disguised as facts. In order to accomplish this, the lawyer must have a comprehensive knowledge of the subject matter being discussed. For example, in sophisticated accounting or economic testimony, an expert witness may testify that the proper rate of capitalization is five percent. Given the context in which the rate is used, the lawyer knows that the witness, to be accurate, should say "assuming a capitalization rate of five percent" since such rates frequently change based on activity in the market place. Upon recognition, a series of questions designed to demonstrate that the proper rate might actually be three percent or six percent is not difficult to develop.

Consequently, the one assumption that an attorney should make is that virtually all expert opinion is dependent upon assumptions. If there were no need for assumptions or "educated guesses" requiring the judgment, experience and training of an expert, then there is no need for the expert, only a calculator to calculate or a ruler to measure.

I recently defended a group of doctors against a former colleague who was suing for the value of his share of the practice after being terminated. The plaintiff called an accountant economist who came to court with charts, diagrams and formulas allegedly to demonstrate the market value of the practice. He offered formulas based on projected earnings as an element of a capitalization formula and, alternatively, another possible method of valuation dependent upon return on investment. Both methods appeared to demonstrate that the practice was worth far more than reality indicated. Each of my clients would have been glad to sell his interest for fifty percent less.

The witness described his exhaustive investigation into the history of the practice for the preceding five years from which he gathered documented information upon which he based his testimony.

Upon completion of this impressive display of diligence and multicolored charts, I asked a series of preliminary questions:

Q: Is it fair to say that all of your formulas, theories and conclusions are based upon the assumption that things would continue as they existed for the past five years?
A: Yes, that was my frame of reference.
Q: Are you aware that as of January 1 of last year certain reimbursement rates for Medicare and Medicaid were revised?
A: I knew that there were some revisions but I am not completely familiar with their nature.
Q: Are you aware that certain reimbursement rates were reduced?
A: No.
Q: Have you ever made a computation as to what the income of the practice would be if precisely the same number of patients receiving the precise treatment received was rendered next year as contrasted to last year in terms of Medicare or Medicaid reimbursement?
A: I never made that computation, it is possible.
Q: Are you prepared to quarrel with the suggestion that because of the reduction in reimbursement rates and redefining of reimbursable treatment, the practice would not receive the same gross income?
A: I never made that computation, it's possible.
Q: Did you include the value of the building in which the practice is housed as part of your computation as to the value of this practice?
A: Yes.
Q: I notice that your values for the practice as a whole including the real estate are rather high. How did you assess the value of the building?
A: Market value.
Q: Are you aware of recent developments in the real estate market, particularly loss of value in the last year?
A: Yes.
Q: Tell us if you took that into account.
A: I reduced the value by five percent in recognition of present declining values.

Q: Five percent from what value?
A: From 1987 value.
Q: Isn't that four years ago?
A: Yes.
Q: What happened between 1987 and 1988, did you make that particular computation?
A: No.
Q: 1988 and 1989?
A: No.
Q: 1989 and 1990?
A: No.
Q: Do you know whether or not the value of this type of building declined in the years between 1987 and 1988?
A: I'm not sure.
Q: Would your lack of certainty extend to the years between 1988 and 1989?
A: Possibly.
Q: Isn't it a fact that when you assumed the proper reduction of five percent from the year 1989, you may have missed intervening reductions between 1987 and 1988 and 1988 and 1989, isn't that so?
A: Possibly.
Q: Did this medical practice have a contract with a hospital for the referral of patients?
A: Yes.
Q: When does that contract expire?
A: Three months from now.
Q: Can you testify under oath that it will be renewed?
A: No.
Q: You assumed it would be renewed?
A: Yes.
Q: Even if renewed, do you know if it would be renewed at the same rate of compensation or possibly less?
A: No.
Q: You assumed it would be renewed at the same or a greater rate, did you not?
A: Yes.

It became apparent throughout that virtually every aspect of his testimony regarding value was premised upon an underlying assumption which may or may not have been accurate. While it is true that the assumptions made and their acceptance by the jury may well depend on the expertise and impression of the witness, it is vital to show the testimony for what it is. No assumption is etched in the same concrete as the expert's firmly stated conclusion.

The cross-examination in that case continued. The witness was asked to make other assumptions which may or may not have had equal validity. It was rapidly demonstrated that if one or more of the assumptions upon which the expert based his opinion was different or modified, his opinion would, of necessity, be different. If he quarreled with that inevitable result, credibility, was lost.

§19.6 CHARTS AND DIAGRAMS IN REVERSE

An effective technique is to hoist the expert by his own petard and make a chart or diagram of his testimony while cross-examining.

Each time that the expert is forced to acknowledge the possibility or likelihood that one or more of his assumptions may have variables the modification is noted on the chart. The jury will clearly visualize that each variation leads to a different bottom line or conclusion.

The chart can then be offered into evidence and the jury takes a picture of the witness' impeachment into the jury room.

§19.7 GARBAGE IN—GARBAGE OUT

The expert shares with the computer the vulnerability that the information that comes out is only as good as the information that goes in.

It is important to show that the study or investigation performed by the expert or that of an individual upon whose work the witness relies was not adequate or complete or that the information provided to the witness by the attorney preparing him was inadequate, incomplete or slanted.

A line of questioning that elicits testimony that would lay the groundwork for such attack is:

Q: Were you told . . .?
Q: Did you see . . .?
Q: Had you heard . . .?
Q: What was the source of that information . . .?

If the witness answers ''no'' to such questions, then the follow-up questions would seek to elicit if he had been told something else that would cause him to vary his opinion, all the while blending into the question the suggestion that the information was deliberately withheld or biased in its presentation. This is accomplished by phrasing the question:

Q: As to the information that your client failed to provide you with, now that you are aware of it, would that cause you to reconsider your opinion?

If the witness answers ''no'' to a series of such questions, the witness will simply appear stubborn or determined to earn his fee at the cost of truth. Notice that the witness is not asked if he would change his opinion, only reconsider it. ''No'' is an unacceptable answer to the jury. To fail to reconsider any additional information impeaches the witness' credibility.

Should the witness answer ''yes'' to having been provided with the information you list, check if the item was provided to the witness in a slanted or distorted form. If you can point out the distortion, you have invalidated the witness' opinion and shown his client in an unfavorable light by his attempt to manipulate the expert's testimony inappropriately.

§19.8 CONFLICT AMONG EXPERTS

Another method of attacking an expert witness is to show that his opinions are in conflict with those of other experts. This area will be difficult upon cross-examination since it is difficult to establish a proper foundation being laid to permit the opinion of some non-witness expert who may not have had all of the facts being used to confront the current witness, absent the witness stating that he relied on some portion of the other person's work. An effort should be made in discovery to ascertain if there are any experts who have been consulted by the party but who have been rejected because their opinions did not conform to the desired result. However, keep this tactic in mind on the *voir dire* regarding qualifications where it may be more likely that a foundation can be laid to show that this witness is out of step with his profession generally, as well as out of step with other experts whom the opposing party consulted.

If the other side produces more than one expert, then any discrepancies or disparities between the two witnesses can be used to good advantage in cross-examination. Any deviation can be made to appear as a conflict or disagreement as between experts. The jury will begin to understand that the subject matter of the opinion is not an exact science, otherwise both experts should testify similarly.

Of course, were two witnesses to testify identically a cross-examiner would make much of that symmetry and point out that it could only be the result of rehearsed and prepared testimony rather than the result of independently ordained truths which everyone knows and believes will always vary.

§19.9 EXPERT TRUMP

In any case where the credentials of your expert clearly overshadow those of the opposition, inquire on cross-examination as to whether or not the witness is familiar with the work of your expert as well as his standing in the professional community. The witness is virtually forced to give your expert a reference.

While there is some risk, it is negligible if your expert's credentials are strong enough. Professional politics alone may elicit the desired answer as well as the unwillingness to appear churlish in the face of recognized accomplishment.

Should the witness deride your expert or even damn with faint praise, his own credibility will be suspect when your expert takes the stand and recites his background.

§19.10 PRIOR INCONSISTENT STATEMENTS

An expert witness is particularly susceptible to being impeached by a prior inconsistent statement. Because of the likelihood of writing or lecturing, experts leave a greater trail of previously held positions or opinions than is the case with other individuals. If the expert is truly one of stature, there should exist substantial writings of one form or another. Experts have a tendency to write articles if for no other reason than to promote recognition of their expertise or their profession requires publication as a mandate for recognition or advancement. Of course, if there are no articles or prior writings, that fact should be used to demonstrate that the expert is hardly one at all and should be accorded little weight.

If writings exist, it is highly unlikely that some inconsistency cannot be found in such writings. A prior lecture or article was not designed or written with a particular case in mind. There likely exists a discrepancy either in the premises upon which the earlier article was written, the facts which were being reconciled into a theory or conclusion, or the issue considered to be of prime significance in the area.

As with lay witnesses, it is important to keep in mind that a prior inconsistent statement is not simply one which directly contradicts the testimony being offered in the courtroom. A prior inconsistent statement or article is one which includes more than the witness testifies to, or less, by silence, or simply differs in form from the presentation being made. In other words, any deviation from the presentation and content offered in the courtroom upon proper questioning is considered to be a prior inconsistent statement and serve the impeaching purpose of such statement.

It is not enough to simply confront the witness with a prior inconsistent statement. The questioning must be set up and all escape hatches closed; otherwise, the witness will simply explain the discrepancy and the jury may accept it whether or not it makes sense. The best method of closing an escape hatch is to anticipate all of the possible answers which a witness may offer to wriggle out of an inconsistency and exclude them in early questioning before the critical portion of the examination is reached. If the witness does not follow this feint and adds qualifications so as to build in a number of escape hatches, the testimony has been successfully cross-examined.

A preferred technique is to question the witness based upon his own prior discrepancy or contradictory statement without identifying it as such. The prior inconsistent statement is masked as an attack by the cross-examiner which the witness reflexively resists. It is only after the witness rebuts the attack showing a lack of validity and significance that the witness and the jury are now advised that it is the witness' own statement made on a prior occasion.

Once again, every rule has its exceptions. Often, you will find a prior writing that appears to be contradictory. But, your own research or knowledge leads you to understand the nature of the discrepancy and its reasonable reconciliation. In those cases, rather than setting the witness up with the discrepancy and making it appear as a challenge simply confront the witness with the discrepancy head on. The witness may offer the reconciliation but the appearance of direct contradiction will make a point with the jury if it is only to show that this expert changes his opinions or views from time to time or place to place.

Cross-Examination of the Medical Expert 20

§20.1 THEORIES AND ASSUMPTIONS

Five doctors practiced together in a professional corporation in which each owned twenty percent of the shares of stock of the corporation. A dispute arose; and, as a consequence, one of the doctors wished to leave the practice and be bought out. When the four others would not agree to his demands, he commenced an action for dissolution of the entire corporation. Pursuant to §1120 of the Business Corporation Law, the majority shareholders had a right to elect to buy out the shares of the suing doctor. The matter came on for trial; and, as a significant portion of his case, the plaintiff produced an expert for purposes of assessing the value of the shares of the professional corporation in support of his demand for $780,000.

The expert, a certified public accountant who claimed to have extensive expertise in business valuation, offered several different theories, complete with charts and diagrams, as to why a twenty percent interest in the corporation was worth what the plaintiff claimed.

Of the several theories, only two had any validity in terms of being generally accepted formulas by which evaluations are arrived at. Although market value was attempted as a theory, it soon became apparent that there was no ready market value for a minority interest in a highly personal professional partnership. The two theories that survived even the early rounds were capitalization of income and a not too distant cousin called the investment theory.

Capitalization of income as presented by the expert depended upon ascertaining the actual profits of the professional corporation and then determining a multiple of those earnings to arrive at a capital value.

There were an extensive number of variables that were required for anyone to make an appraisal utilizing this theory. There were a number of assumptions which had to be made in order to arrive at a figure designated as profit if that number was going to be different than the one shown on the recent financial statements of the corporation.

The selection of the multiple was also a matter of assumption and variation based upon an estimate of the stability of the practice, risk factors and the ability to project future income.

The investment theory, as it was presented, appeared on the surface to be somewhat different, mainly because the expert produced a different set of charts and diagrams. In effect, it was conceptually similar to the capitalization theory in that the theory depended upon determining what amount of profit would be available for distribution to the various partners over and above the amount of salary and benefits they would receive as employees. When the amount of additional profit available for distribution was determined, the calculation would have to be made in accordance with current returns being realized upon investments; *i.e.*, what is the amount of money that would be required to be invested in order to realize that return.

Thus, as to both theories, there had to be a determination of projected income of the practice and the profit that would be realized by the practice after expenses, which included compensation to the doctors and taxes.

It was the position of the four defendants that, given certain regulatory and business conditions, it was impossible to project profits in any meaningful manner and that the only fair method of valuation was book value which calculated any excess of assets over liabilities.

§20.2 COLLATERAL ATTACK

The cross-examination of defendant's expert commenced with a collateral attack upon his expertise.

Q: Mr. Andolfo, you indicated that you had a background in evaluation of businesses including medical practices; is that correct?
A: Yes.
Q: You actually practice or do you just consult or advise?
A: I don't know what you mean.
Q: Well, do you actually have clients to whom you give specific advice as to whether or not they should buy or not buy a particular business?
A: Yes, I have.
Q: And do you specifically have or represent any clients with regard to the purchase of medical practices?
A: I did.
Q: Do you now?
A: As of now, I do not have those under my direct control.
Q: When was the last time you had a client in the medical field under your direct control?
A: About four years ago.
Q: When was the last time you actually advised a living breathing client who was going to part with a real dollar as to the value of a medical practice?
A: Approximately four years ago.
Q: And what kind of practice was that?
A: That happened to be chiropractic practice?
Q: And, just out of curiosity, are chiropractors reimbursed under Medicaid or Medicare?
A: I do not believe they are.
Q: To your knowledge, is there any distinction in either the fee schedules or the way the doctors get paid if they are under Medicare or under Medicaid versus not being subject to the regulations of those plans?
A: Well, there's numerous fee arrangement schedules that depend on the individual and the type of plans; HMO plans, Blue Cross, Blue Shield and there's numerous arrangements depending on who they are contracting with.
Q: The question was Medicare and Medicaid and chiropractors. Is there a difference when one is restricted under the particular regulations of Medicare and Medicaid and practices which are not restricted by those particular regulations?

A: I would have to assume there is a difference.
Q: Do you suggest sir that you consider yourself to be an expert on health care reimbursement, particularly Medicaid and Medicare reimbursement?
A: No.
Q: Are you aware of the percentage of income derived by this practice as a result of being reimbursed by Medicaid or Medicare?
A: I know that most of it comes from Medicaid or Medicare, but I didn't break it down exactly.
Q: But it is most of it is it not?
A: Yes.
Q: Would you then tell us sir how you can presume to evaluate the income of a medical practice that it subject to health care reimbursement principles about which you do not regard yourself as an expert?
A: Well I . . .
Q: Never mind; you've really already answered that question. Let's go on to something else.

The examination continued pressing home this point of vulnerability in the expert's qualifications or expertise.

Q: Now, Mr. Andolfo, you've acknowledged to us that you're not an expert in health care reimbursement under Medicare and Medicaid is that correct?
A: By your definition of an expert, you're correct.
Q: Well, wasn't that your answer and didn't you decide that you were not an expert?
A: I've already answered that.
Q: Well, if I asked you to compute exactly how radiology fees are computed, or reimbursed by Medicaid or Medicare, could you do that?
A: I can't do it anymore. I did it about fifteen years ago, but I can't do it anymore.
Q: Do you think the principles and the reimbursement schedules are the same as they were fifteen years ago?
A: Of course not.
Q: Isn't it true that your theories which try to predict the future depend on what happened in the past?

A: Yes, we try to evaluate what took place historically and then project that forward to arrive at an assessment.
Q: Do you have to take into account new and different things which might occur in the future which didn't occur in the past in arriving at some sort of meaningful evaluation?
A: I would think that you would have to.
Q: Well, do you know what legislation is presently pending which could materially effect both the rate of reimbursement and the gross receipts of doctors, particularly radiologists, under health care reimbursement principles of Medicare and Medicaid?
A: I only know very generally that there has been a lot of discussion and some proposed legislation.
Q: Can you predict what legislation if any will occur tomorrow?
A: No.
Q: Do you know what legislation or revision of rules has taken place in the last three years which have an effect on the income of physicians?
A: Well again.
Q: Can you or can't you?
A: Even if I could, it would be too speculative for me to put myself in the mind of the State Legislature.
Q: I'm asking you Medicare and Medicaid; has there been any revision in the governing rules in the last three years?
A: I'm sure there have been.
Q: Do you know the effect on doctors' income of those revisions?
A: I don't know exactly.
Q: Can you tell us if a doctor's practice remained exactly the same as to the number of patients treated and exactly the same as to the medical mix of treatment rendered to those patients, has the doctor's income increased or decreased as a result of revisions in the reimbursement principles of Medicare and Medicaid?
A: I don't know exactly, but I imagine it would have been reduced.
Q: By how much?
A: I'm not certain.
Q: Well, Mr. Andolfo, if you don't know what effect and to what extent a doctor's income is effected by Medicare and Medicaid revisions over the past three years, and you can't predict what

new revisions or changes in the law there will be in the next several years, then any prediction you might chose to make about future earnings of doctors has to be pretty speculative, isn't that true?

A: Somewhat.

Q: Well, if you're going to predict the future which you don't know based upon a past that you admit you also don't know, it doesn't make for a pretty reliable prediction does it. Let's move on.

The last question, in reality or statement, is optional. It is the kind of maneuver that is often left for summation rather than the mini-summation in the form of the statement that is quickly withdrawn. In any event, the thought encapsulated in that statement would be expanded upon at length in the course of summation with the short underlining taking place during the examination when the point is graphically clear to the jury.

The next series of questions is also a form of collateral attack in that it is attacking the process by which the conclusions were made and the gaps that existed in the expert's experience and, consequently, the validity of any conclusion reached.

The collateral attack can also be interwoven with the attack upon a specific part of the theory or conclusion. In the case we have been reviewing, the conclusion or the expert's valuation was reflected in a number which constituted the bottom line of a series of numbers which he had entered above the line. Therefore, any number above the line that was subject to attack or vulnerable in any way should be the subject of cross-examination since any variation would cause a variation in the bottom line, if not wipe it out altogether.

The basic approach of the expert was to establish a value of the practice by first determining what the "real profit" of the practice was and then multiplying it by a factor or number which he determined was appropriate based upon his experience. The actual balance sheet of the practice showed a very slight profit of $27,000 remaining after salaries and expenses. For the expert to testify as to any substantial value of the practice, that modest profit had to be greatly increased so that, when it was multiplied by a number, it would equal a total practice value of several hundreds of thousands of dollars.

One of the methods by which the bottom line could be inflated was to knock out as many expenses as possible, either claiming them to be unnecessary or in excess of what they ought to be. Every time that a dollar of expense was knocked out that dollar fell to the bottom line and increased the profit. This is precisely what takes place in the actual operation of the business. Hold income stable and reduce expenses thereby increasing expenses.

Cross-examination continued challenging any expense that was disallowed.

Q: What profit does the balance sheet actually prepared by the accountants for the practice show?
A: $27,500.
Q: And it is your contention that the real profit is $450,000, is that correct?
A: Yes.
Q: And you arrived at your determination as to the real profit by disallowing certain expenses that the practice actually had disbursed?
A: Yes.
Q: Just so there is no confusion, the money claimed to be expended by the practice was actually expended was it not?
A: Yes.
Q: And it's your position that they shouldn't have spent the money; or, if they did, they shouldn't have spent as much?
A: Yes.
Q: In other words, we should substitute their business judgment who are actually engaged in the practice on a day to day basis, with your business judgment as to what's appropriate, who have never spent a day in the actual practice. Isn't that what you're really saying?
A: I'm not saying it that way.
Q: Whether you say it that way or not, isn't that the real bottom line?
A: I'm suggesting what I think is appropriate.
Q: If you were a doctor and actually engaged in that particular practice every single day, you might think differently as to what is appropriate, isn't that true?

A: I might.
Q: Now you have given us a schedule that you created that shows a number of expenses that you felt were unnecessary or inflated and could be eliminated, isn't that right?
A: Yes.
Q: And it was your judgment that led to the selection of items to be eliminated altogether and your judgment what portion to eliminate of those that were not to be eliminated altogether, correct?
A: Yes.
Q: Do we agree that in order to arrive at the profit you project depends on every one of your disallowances surviving intact?
A: Obviously.
Q: Mr. Andolfo, would you please select the disallowance that you are most comfortable with in defending and tell me which one it is.
A: Auto expense, they're all driving Mercedes.

The question to the expert to pick the number that he is most comfortable in defending is a challenge with little or no risk. As soon as the witness answers the question, he telegraphs to the jury that he does not feel as strongly about all of the disallowances as he does about that one. If you can successfully challenge and demolish the first one that he has selected, there is no need to pursue the rest as they will all fall as dominoes.

If the witness survives the attack on the number first selected, the damage to the cross-examiner is very slight since that was the strongest. However, you also know that the witness does not feel as strongly about a number of the others and greater success can be anticipated, particularly since the next number to be attacked will be of the cross-examiner's selection.

Any possible risk was already previously minimized in the series of questions which indicated that the witness was substituting his business judgment for the people on the scene. It has already been pointed out that he was not a doctor nor was he engaged in that particular practice. Through his distant viewpoint regarding appropriateness, the purpose of testifying has probably negated any weight that would be attributed to his testimony. All that is required is simply to make the point by picking a number or two and showing that the expert is really being presumptuous.

The point is reiterated regarding the invalidity of the entire exercise as a means of insuring that no matter what the expert testifies to the testimony would be meaningless. Such cross-examination took place as follows:

Q: Now the party that you represent is a twenty percent stockholder—is that correct?
A: Yes.
Q: Based upon your knowledge of corporations, does a minority shareholder have the right to impose his will on the majority?
A: He can discuss it.
Q: And after discussion the majority stockholders thank him for his thoughts and then out vote him, is he in a position to impose his will on the majority?
A: No.
Q: So that in fact if the party himself were to disagree with how much money was spent and on what, he wouldn't be in a position to do anything about it since he would be outvoted?
A: Yes.
Q: And those are the practical and legal facts of life, are they not?
A: Apparently.
Q: And will you please tell us how you get to do what your client who actually owns the stock has no right to do?
A: I don't understand your question.
Q: Your client owns twenty percent of the stock. He can't change the way the majority spends money, what they spend it on, and how much they spend. The balance sheet shows what they actually spent. Your client has no right to change that or force them to do otherwise. So, sir, tell us by what right you have to come in to this courtroom, and project a profit, by dictating how these doctors should spend their money and in what amount, when neither you nor your client have the ability to make that happen.
A: I'm only giving my opinion.
Q: But in real life, reality as to how the money is spent is decided by the majority stockholders, isn't that true?

A: Yes.

For all intents and purposes, the cross-examination could have concluded at that point. Clearly, nothing that the witness had to say as to specifics would have very much meaning. However, since there might have been a residue of emotional impact regarding the image of everybody driving around in Mercedes while the plaintiff was getting nothing for his interest, the cross-examination continued.

Q: With regard to the auto expense how much did you disallow?
A: $86,000.
Q: That's virtually the entire auto expense.
A: I felt that given the fact that their offices were in the hospital, they really didn't need a car.
Q: How about when they went to another hospital?
A: They would need a car.
Q: Didn't they have a private office outside the hospital?
A: Yes.
Q: How about getting from their office to the hospital?
A: They would need a car.
Q: So you really don't know how much they need a car or how much they don't, isn't that true?
A: I never broke it down.
Q: Basically you disallowed the amount that you did because the cars were all Mercedes Benz is that true?
A: Yes.
Q: What car do you think they should have driven?
A: I don't understand.
Q: Are you suggesting that they should have no car?
A: Of course not.
Q: So what car would you find acceptable, a Cadillac, a Pontiac, Buick, Honda Civic, Volkswagen, what?
A: I can't answer that.
Q: Well, instead of a Mercedes Benz, they all had Buicks, would you object?
A: No, but Mercedes is far more expensive than a Buick.
Q: How about a Volvo? There have been a lot of ads on television on how safe they are.
A: That's also an expensive car.

Q: But if they are particularly safe, isn't that a sound basis for selection regardless of price?
A: I see what you're driving at.
Q: Just answer the question. Is it a valid buying choice to select a car for its safety features, even if it's more expensive?
A: Yes.
Q: How much is a top of the line Volvo?
A: Why top of the line?
Q: You're not suggesting that you have the right to select the features of a car that they are entitled to buy are you?
A: No.
Q: So how much is a top of the line Volvo, with all features?
A: I don't know.
Q: Do you know the price difference between such a Volvo and the models of Mercedes that the doctors are driving?
A: No.
Q: The cars are leased, are they not?
A: I believe so.
Q: So maybe the difference is nothing depending on the price of the car and the leasing terms on that amount on an annual basis, isn't that true?
A: So why did you ask me about the price of the cars if they're leased? Is it one of the major elements on how much you pay per month on an auto lease the price of the car that is being leased?
Q: Yes, so that if the car were less expensive the monthly payments would be less, would you say so?
A: Yes.
Q: Are you sure about that? Suppose a less expensive car is leased for two years and a far more expensive car is leased for five years. Would there be a difference in the monthly payments on an annual basis?
A: Maybe not.
Q: So, let us see where we have come to. It is a valid and binding choice to buy a more expensive car based upon safety features, correct?
A: Yes.
Q: And you would agree a Mercedes Benz has more safety features than some less expensive cars?

A: Yes.
Q: And you further agree that a less expensive car could cost the same on an annual basis if it is a shorter lease as contrasted to a longer lease for the more expensive car?
A: It could be.
Q: What were the terms of the leases on the Mercedes driven by the doctors?
A: I did not check that.
Q: Whats the monthly charge for leasing a Buick Century?
A: I don't know.
Q: And you certainly wouldn't know the difference between leasing a Buick Century for two years or a Mercedes Benz for five years?
A: No.

The balance of the cross-examination attacked a few of the other numbers but utilizing the same method. The questions consisted of pointing out things that the witness never considered or did not check or that what might have sounded significant at first blush was more form than substance when viewed from a different position.

As the mathematics in the particular case worked out, obtaining a variation on almost any of the categories which the expert used would tend to wipe out the mythical profit and restore the profit to no greater a number than was actually shown on the balance sheet.

It was also part of the case that the twenty percent shareholder was obliged to pay $36,000 for his shares which he had not done. Any recovery that he might make in this case would be reduced by $36,000 representing that purchase price. Thus, the final questions on cross-examination of the expert after attacking the various numbers was:

Q: Can we agree, Mr. Andolfo, if for any reason the jury were to prefer my hypothetical basis to yours or the actual balance sheet to your hypothetical, the plaintiff would be entitled to no recovery in this case, isn't that correct?
A: Under your hypothetical and according to the balance sheet, he would not be entitled to any recovery.
Q: So the answer is yes?
A: Yes.

§20.3 APPLICATION OF METHODOLOGY

The methodology of this cross-examination can be applied with regard to most expert witnesses, save for those which are forensic in nature or have some other hands on foundation for their testimony.

In the first instance, the witness' background and expertise, whatever it is, is compared to the instant case which can demonstrate that the expertise is not at all fours with the issue in the case as you take pains to define it.

The next aspect is to identify variables and press home the point that they are actually judgment calls dressed up as facts or numbers. The questioning then becomes whether the judgment of the expert is predominant over the judgment of another witness or over the persons who made judgments actually on the scene.

Anything that is left out or not fully considered is the subject of questioning. The effect that something left out might have is the basis for another question. Concessions from the witness that certain considerations might have influenced his opinion are dramatically important; and, of course, once the witness has been compromised successfully, a series of questions which seem to suggest that the witness has some nerve coming into court and trying to pull the wool over the eyes of the jury is appropriate.

Of course, if a witness is really circumspect and not given to overstatement or erudite arrogance, the approach would be somewhat different. In such a circumstance, cross-examination would seek to develop simply "possibilities" which an honorable witness would be obliged to acknowledge. Similarly, such a witness will always acknowledge that some bit of additional information, were it to exist and, if known by him, might have had an influence upon his ultimate opinion.

The Expert In Criminal Prosecutions 21

§21.1 PREPARATION AND EXECUTION

Many of the experts called by the prosecution in criminal cases are different only in name from experts likely to be found in civil cases. A doctor testifying regarding DNA fingerprinting is another scientist to be examined on the process by which he arrived at his findings and any open questions in the development of the field of such identification. Forensic accountants, psychiatrists and physicians, as well as the broad range of law enforcement technicians, are simply applying the same technology and principles to different facts.

The preparation of cross-examination of such experts is substantially similar to that in any case in which a testimonial opinion is sought to be compromised or impeached.

However, there exists an ever widening acceptance of expert opinion that is exclusive to criminal cases which present special problems in the preparation and execution of cross-examination. Experts are now permitted to decipher otherwise obscure taped conversations or give their opinion that otherwise equivocal actions constitute criminal conduct.

§21.2 *U.S. V. YOUNG*

The problem was well defined by Judge John Newman of the Second Circuit Court of Appeals in *U.S. v. Young*, 745 F.2d 733 (2nd Cir., 1984):

> JOHN O. NEWMAN, Circuit Judge, concurring:
>
> I concur in Judge Pratt's comprehensive opinion, but write separately to express a caution concerning expert opinion offered to establish that ambiguous conduct constitutes criminal activity. My concern is prompted by the "Flash Inn Incident," which comprises three of the predicate acts the jury was permitted to rely upon in finding Myers guilty of a "continuing criminal enterprise" offense. 21 U.S.C. §848 (1982). A telephone call was made from Myers' home at 9:34 p.m. on January 14, 1983, to arrange a meeting with a man at the Flash Inn. Shortly thereafter Myers and another man drove to the inn and waited. Within a half hour, another car arrived with two men: the driver of the second car spoke with the occupants of Myers' car. All four then entered the inn. Myers' companion entered with a light-colored handbag and exited two minutes later with a dark-colored handbag, which he placed in the trunk of the second car. Myers left two minutes later in this car. Detective Magaletti was permitted to testify that in his opinion a sale of drugs had occurred. The episode raises two distinct issues: (1) whether the expert testimony was admissible and (2) whether the evidence was sufficient to show the commission of predicate offenses.
>
> 1. Until this Court's decision last year in *United States v. Carson*, 702 F.2d 351 (2d Cir.), cert. denied , __ U.S. __, 103 S.Ct. 2456, 77 L.Ed.2d 1335 (1983), I would have had serious doubts that an observed set of circumstances constituted commission of a crime. The test for admissibility is whether the witness's "specialized knowledge will assist the trier of fact to understand the evidence or to determine a fact in issue." Fed.R.Evid. 702. I do not doubt that an experienced narcotics agent has the requisite knowledge to assist a jury by explaining

"the clandestine manner in which drugs are bought and sold." *United States v. Carson*, supra, 702 F.2d at 369. But I question whether an expert's opinion that the events he observes constitute a drug transaction provides very much, if any, assistance to a jury, beyond whatever inference is available to be drawn by the jury from all the evidence. Not too long ago we characterized as "highly unusual" an expert's opinion that observed events showed a defendant to be a "controller" of a gambling operation. *United States v. Sette*, 334 F.2d 267, 269 (3d Cir., 1964).

Even if admissible under Rule 702, opinion testimony is still subject to exclusion under Rule 403 "if its probative value is substantially outweighed by the danger of unfair prejudice." Whatever slight probative value arises from a narcotics expert's personal opinion that an observed transaction involved a sale of drugs must be carefully weighed against the distinct risk of prejudice. The "aura of special reliability and trustworthiness" surrounding expert testimony, which sought to caution its use, *United States v. Fosher*, 590 F.2d 381, 383 (1st Cir., 1979), *United States v. Amaral*, 458 F.2d 1148, 1152 (9th Cir., 1973), especially when offered by the prosecution in criminal cases, *United States v. Green*, 548 F.2d 1261, 1268 (6th Cir., 1977), poses a special risk in a case of this sort. That risk arises because the jury may infer that the agent's opinion about the criminal nature of the defendant's activity is based on knowledge of the defendant beyond the evidence at trial. The risk is increased when the opinion is given by "the very officers who were in charge of the investigation." *United States v. Sette*, supra, 334 F.2d at 269.

I recognize, however, that in *United States v. Carson*, supra , we upheld the admission of expert opinion under circumstances very similar to those in this case. Other circuits have also permitted an expert to give his opinion that a defendant's ambiguous conduct is criminal. *United States v. Fleishman*, 684 F.2d 1329, 1335-1336 (9th Cir.) (defendant's role as "lookout" in drug transaction), cert. denied , 459 U.S. 1044, 103 S.Ct. 464, 74 L.Ed.2d 614 (1982); *United States v. Scavo*,

593 F.2d 837, 840, 843-44 (8th Cir., 1979) (defendant's role in gambling operation); *United States v. Masson*, 582 F.2d 961, 963-64 (5th Cir., 1978) (same). In light of Carson and these other rulings, I cannot say it was error to admit the testimony of Detective Magaletti that Myers was selling narcotics at the Flash Inn on January 14. But the very breadth of the discretion accorded trial judges in admitting such an opinion under Rules 702 and 403 should cause them to give the matter more, rather than less, scrutiny. A trial judge should not routinely admit opinions of the sort at issue here and should weigh carefully the risk of prejudice.

2. Even though it was not error to admit Magaletti's opinion that Myers was selling drugs at the Flash Inn on January 14, the question remains whether the evidence concerning that episode sufficed to permit the jury to find beyond a reasonable doubt that a narcotics violation had occurred on that occasion. The hazard of permitting the opinion in evidence ought to make courts cautious in assessing the sufficiency of a case based heavily on such an opinion. If the observed actions of a defendant do not establish a prima facie case, I do not believe that an expert's opinion that his actions are criminal may carry the prosecution's proof above the requisite line. It is one thing to permit a jury to weigh that opinion in considering an otherwise adequate case; it is quite another matter to let that opinion salvage an insufficient case. In *United States v. Sette*, supra , we rejected the sufficiency of the prosecution's case that rested primarily on an expert's opinion that observed conduct was criminal. "We are cited to no case, and have found none, that remotely justifies this highly unusual method of establishing a prima facie case in a criminal prosecution of this type." Id. at 269. In *United States v. Carson*, supra, and the other cases allowing an expert to give an opinion concerning criminal conduct, the evidence, apart from the expert opinion, provided the jury with a substantial basis for finding guilt beyond a reasonable doubt.

If Freddie Myers had been on trial charged with the substantive offenses of possessing and distributing narcotics at the Flash

> Inn on January 14 and the evidence against him had consisted solely of the observable events of that evening, I would not consider the evidence sufficient to support a conviction on such charges. See *United States v. Suarez*, 487 F.2d 236, 238-40 (5th Cir., 1973) (suspicious contact with known narcotics dealer insufficient to support narcotics conviction), cert. denied , 415 U.S. 981, 94 S.Ct. 1572, 39 L.Ed.2d 878 (1974); cf. *United States v. Ceballos*, 654 F.2d 177, 184-186 (2d Cir., 1981) (suspicious contact with known narcotics dealer insufficient to establish probable cause to arrest). However, in determining whether Myers was dealing in drugs that evening, the jury was not limited to the evidence of the wiretapped phone call from his home and the ambiguous events observed at the scene. Strongly reinforcing the inference of a drug transaction was all of the evidence in the case, including the evidence tying Meyers to a heroin cutting mill and his vast amounts of cash. When a person already implicated by such evidence participates in a clandestine exchange of handbags, a jury may infer that he was exchanging drugs for money.
>
> For these reasons I agree that the Flash Inn evidence supports Myers' conviction on the criminal enterprise count and therefore concur in Judge Pratt's opinion. It also guides the lawyer to the substance of cross-examination when confronted with such testimony.

The above opinion is reproduced here in full because it demonstrates one of the most dramatic evolutions in the Rules of Evidence which thoroughly revises what is today required of a lawyer upon cross-examination.

§21.3 BASIS FOR OPINION

In a criminal case, the conviction of the defendant may be solely dependent upon the opinion of the investigatory or arresting officer. In this case, the investigation had been ongoing for ten months. All manner of external facts had been digested by the investigators. As in most cases unshakable mental sets had been developed through the investigators' own involvement and through numerous conferences with other agents. Deeply imbedded was the unwillingness to accept the possibility that so much time and effort was expended for nothing.

There is little doubt that even with the sincerest of intentions any opinion rendered in these circumstances would be biased and partisan.

§21.4 THE BADGE OF VIRTUE

An additional problem with expert testimony in a criminal case is that, like it or not, the prosecutor vouches for the credibility of the expert he calls. This is unlike the civil case in which a party who does not have a badge of virtue for protecting society of which the jurors are members, calls a witness. When the Government or the People call a witness, that witness is one of the juror's defenders. The more highly respected that a particular prosecutor's office is, the more there is produced a correlating vouching for the expert witness. Attacking such a witness, the cross-examiner is not only attacking the particular witness but the police, the prosecutor and the entire protective system that has called such a witness in order to establish the criminal liability beyond a reasonable doubt of a particular defendant.

§21.5 LIMITED DISCOVERY

Discovery in criminal cases, while expanding significantly through a series of constitutional hearings, liberalized bills of particulars and document production, has not yet adopted the examination before trial.

Even requiring that each witness be identified prior to trial does not comprehensively apprise a defendant of the substance of the witness' testimony. There certainly is no clear warning that an investigating law enforcement officer will don a second hat while testifying and become an expert offering opinions, particularly if he does not render a written report as to his "expert" opinion.

It is significant to note that the explosion of subject matter upon which experts could opine was permitted in civil cases only because discovery expanded in lock step to level the playing field. The same is not true in criminal cases where the stakes may be infinitely higher.

There the subject matter increased geometrically while discovery increased less than mathematically, usually on a decision by decision basis.

Cross-examination techniques have to be developed that are effective without a dependency on pre-trial discovery. Not surprisingly, the simple but analytic approach provides the key.

Following the pattern for successful cross-examination of experts, the effort is made to establish:

1. the contested evidence is opinion, not fact;
2. the witness offering the opinion is biased;
3. the opinion is faulty due to internal and external inconsistencies; and
4. the case depends on the opinion rather than the facts which may be subject to different interpretations under different "lighting conditions."

§21.6 OPINION NOT FACT

Juries have difficulty recognizing opinions disguised as facts, particularly when the subject is one with which they are unfamiliar. Just as the accountant testifying to capitalization rates is only testifying to his opinion, that will not be opinion to the jury unless it is made clear on cross-examination. The initial questioning should seek that distinction as its goal.

§21.7 BIAS

The impeachment of a witness is always advanced by demonstrating that the witness is biased.

An expert witness called by the government in a criminal prosecution regards himself as a member of the prosecution team. Under no circumstances will he be called unless he strongly supports the theory of the prosecution. His salary is paid from the same treasury that pays the prosecutor and he could not survive for any significant period of time with a history of testifying adverse to the prosecution. Simply stated, it is his job to make the prosecution's case.

When an expert testifies that equivocal conduct is criminal activity he is justifying his own conduct. The time and money that was spent in the investigation was not wasted and the arrest in which he participated, if not responsible for, was justified. Advancement may hinge on successful prosecutions that result from his efforts.

With some modification dependent on the facts of a particular case, the cross-examination should commence:

Q: Agent Jones, on what date were you assigned the investigation leading to the arrest of this defendant?
A: I forget the exact date but approximately eleven and one-half months ago.
Q: I take it that this investigation then became part of your official responsibilities?
A: Yes.
Q: For the past eleven and one-half months, how many other investigations were you actively engaged in?
A: There was one other that I was finishing up, but this was the primary one.
Q: I take it then that it was this investigation that consumed a greater part of your working day, and possibly some nights, for the past eleven months?
A: Yes.
Q: And I guess if I was your superior writing an evaluation report of your performance over the last eleven months, I guess I would have to judge your performance in this investigation, isn't that true?
A: Not necessarily.
Q: You mean I could write a report fairly evaluating your performance without considering the primary activity in which you were engaged for almost the past year?
A: That would have to be considered.
Q: And is it fair to say that your evaluation would not be hurt if your efforts for the past eleven months resulted in a successful prosecution, isn't that true?
A: I don't think it depends solely on that.

Q: But it doesn't hurt, does it?
A: No, it doesn't hurt.
Q: Now, the events about which you have offered your opinion were actually observed by you, were they not?
A: Yes.
Q: Were there any others who were present at the time you made your observations?
A: Yes.
Q: Who are they?
A: Agents Smith, Doe and Williams.
Q: And did you write up a report immediately upon making your observations?
A: Yes.
Q: And in that report you stated what you observed, isn't that true?
A: Yes.
Q: Agent Jones, you have that report in front of you do you not?
A: Yes.
Q: And in that report you state what you observed?
A: Yes.
Q: I heard it correctly that you stated that you observed the defendant entering the restaurant with an attache case and leaving with a different attache case?
A: Yes.
Q: Does it also state that you observed, before going into the restaurant, the defendant got out of a car that was driven by Richard Roe?
A: Yes.
Q: Did you hear any of the conversation which took place between the defendant and Richard Roe?
A: No.
Q: And when the defendant came out of the restaurant he got back into the car with Richard Roe, did he not?
A: Yes.
Q: Did you hear any of the conversation that took place with the defendant and Richard Roe after he got back into the car?
A: No.
Q: Did you ever see the contents of the attache case that the defendant carried into the restaurant?

A: No.
Q: Did you ever see the contents of the attache case that the defendant was carrying when he left the restaurant?
A: No.
Q: Did you observe the defendant while he was in the restaurant?
A: I did not, but Agent Williams did.
Q: Did you learn that the defendant spoke to someone in the restaurant?
A: Yes.
Q: Did you learn what the conversation was between the defendant and the person he met?
A: No.
Q: So that all you know is that the defendant went into the restaurant with an attache case, gave that attache case to someone, received one in exchange, and left?
A: Yes.
Q: And those are the specific facts that you set forth in your report?
A: I did.
Q: Did you ever hear the defendant at that time utter the word drugs?
A: I told you we did not hear any conversation.
Q: And you told us you did not hear any conversation in which the other person in the restaurant participated?
A: Yes.
Q: So you did not hear this other person utter the word drugs?
A: That's right.
Q: And in your report, Agent Jones, you were quite careful to put down precisely what you observed?
A: Yes.
Q: Just so we are clear, Agent Jones, what we have then is your opinion that what you saw was a drug transaction?
A: That's my opinion.
Q: That's your opinion?
A: Yes.
Q: Do you state that opinion in your report?
A: Not that way.
Q: I'm being very specific. Do you state in your report that it is your opinion that what you saw was a drug transaction?

A: No.
Q: So that your opinion was not in the report?
A: I said that.
Q: So that the opinion that you are giving in this courtroom is something you did not think belonged in your report?
A: I didn't say that.
Q: Well, if it belonged in your report, wouldn't you have included it?
A: If I thought it was necessary.
Q: Obviously you didn't think it was necessary?
A: No.
Q: In fact, your opinion might change, as opinions sometimes do?
A: Possibly.
Q: For all we know, you might have had a different opinion the night you made these observations, isn't that true?
A: I didn't.
Q: Since you didn't put it in your report, we have only your word that your opinion was the same that night as what you have testified to in this courtroom, yes?
A: Yes.
Q: But you really don't know for a fact what was in those attache cases, isn't that true?
A: Yes.
Q: And you really don't know for a fact what the people making the exchange were talking about, isn't that correct?
A: That's correct.
Q: So, the only thing we have that makes what you observed a drug transaction is your opinion, isn't that true?
A: That's my opinion.
Q: An opinion that you never put into your report, did you?
A: It was not in my report.
Q: Agent Jones, did there come a time when you learned that without your opinion there was no case against this defendant?
A: I don't know if that's true.
Q: Well, without your opinion isn't all we have here people exchanging attache cases?
A: Those are the facts.
Q: How long after you made these observations was the defendant arrested?

A: The next day.

Q: You have not testified to any observations or activities which occurred between the time of your observations and the time the defendant was arrested have you?

A: No.

Q: And you did not arrest the defendant prior to the time that you made the observations upon which you have offered your opinion, isn't that true?

A: Yes.

Q: In chronological sequence, there was no arrest of the defendant, you made observations that you didn't see drugs, hear drugs, or smell drugs, am I right so far?

A: Yes.

Q: And then you added your opinion to those observations and arrested the defendant?

A: That's the sequence.

§21.8 OPINION CONTAINS INTERNAL INCONSISTENCIES

As with any other opinion testimony, it can be effectively challenged by bringing out internal or external inconsistencies. An external inconsistency, more often than not, is demonstrated through another witness or document after the cross-examined witness is firmly pinned down to an unequivocal position. A reiterated example is a witness who states with certainty that a picnic took place under sunny skies and through a subsequent witness you established that on that date, at that time, it was pouring.

Internal inconsistencies are brought out in the direct confrontation of cross-examination.

In a recent case, Peter Schlam, formerly Chief of the Criminal Division in the Office of the United States Attorney for the Eastern District of New York, and now outstanding defense counsel was confronted with opinion testimony asserting criminal activity. In the following cross-examination, he demolished the testimony leading to the acquittal of his client on the count that was dependent on such opinion.

Q: Now yesterday, sir, you gave some testimony as an expert witness; is that correct?
A: That's correct.
Q: And I'm going to read you a question and an answer and ask you if this is the testimony you gave in that regard. Were you asked this question and did you give this answer, Agent Bonino:
"Question: Agent Bonino, as a result of your having participated in investigations related to so-called shylock loans, what, if anything, happens if those loans are not repaid?"
"Answer: Physical threats are initiated and ultimately if a loan is not repaid in the instances that I am familiar with, there has been physical beatings."
Did you give that answer to that question?
A: Yes, sir, I did.
Q: Okay. Now is it your position that the term shylock means the same thing in every conceivable case?
A: Yes, sir, it is.
Q: Okay. Now is it your position, sir, that every shylock loan is a loan such as that which you described in your testimony yesterday?
A: I don't know about every shylock loan. I'm talking about those loans which you asked me about.
Q: Wait a second, sir. Did you not say as an expert witness that shylock loans when they are not repaid result in physical threats and physical beatings? Did you say that or didn't you say that?
A: I said that.

* * *

Q: Is it your position, sir, that as far as you know shylock loans are characterized by the kinds of consequences that you testified to yesterday?
A: Those that I know of, yes.
Q: You know of this case; do you not?
A: Yes.
Q: Okay. And is it your testimony, sir, that with respect to the Ruggiano $25,000 loan there were as far as you know physical threats?

A: With respect to me?
Q: As far as you know with respect to that loan, were there physical threats with respect to you?
A: No.
Q: As far as you know with respect to you, were there physical beatings?
A: No.
Q: Now this loan as you testified this morning was not repaid; am I correct?
A: That's correct.
Q: And you further stated in your testimony that in your expert opinion based on your experience if a shylock loan is not repaid, a physical beating results; is that correct?
A: That's correct.
Q: Now with respect to this $25,000 loan, I want you to tell the ladies and gentlemen of the jury who received the physical beating in this case as a result of that loan not being repaid?
A: No one, to my knowledge.
Q: So, is it therefore fair to say that the experience on which you relied as an expert does not apply to this case, sir?
A: It does not apply to me.
Q: Does it apply to—are you saying that there's someone else who received a physical beating as a result of that loan not being repaid, sir?
A: No, sir.
Q: Is it fair to say that this testimony which you gave yesterday as an expert does not apply to this case?
A: It does not apply to me, Mr. Schlam.
Q: Agent Bonino, you have testified, sir, that there was no one in this case who received a physical beating even though there's no dispute that this loan was not repaid.
Is it therefore fair for me to say that this case is different from the other cases which you relied on in giving your testimony about shylock loans yesterday?
A: Of course, it is—-
Q: Okay.
A: —of course it is different, is my answer.
Q: Of course, it is different?

A: Right.
Q: And when you say that shylock loans if they are not repaid result in physical beatings, you were referring to a different kind of shylock loan from the one which the jury is considering in this case; am I correct, sir?
A: No, sir.
Q: And therefore not all shylock loans are correct—isn't it that not all shylock loans are different—are the same?
A: Would you restate it?
Q: And therefore, sir, is it fair to say that not all shylock loans are the same?
A: Well, of course, that's fair to say.
Q: Okay. So when somebody says shylock loan, I'm going to give you a shylock loan, that does not necessarily as you stated in your testimony yesterday, mean that the person who does not repay the loan will receive a physical beating; is that correct?
A: Not if he pays his loan.
Q: We're talking about if he doesn't pay his loan, sir, as was the case with the $25,000 Ruggiano loan.
If a person does not pay a shylock loan, isn't it fair to say that that person will not necessarily receive a beating?
A: It is fair to say he will not necessarily receive a beating.
Q: And in fact the truth of the matter in this case is that nobody received a beating; am I correct about that?
A: That's correct.
Q: And isn't it further fair to say, Mr. Bonino, that in a shylock loan—in not every shylock loan, nonpayment will result in the receipt by the individual of a physical threat; isn't that also fair to say?
A: Not in every shylock loan.
Q: Fine. And as far as you know in this case at least with respect to you, there was no physical threat received by you, despite the fact that you were late with your interest payments and with respect to the fact that the loan was not repaid on time; am I correct about that?
A: I think I have already answered that in the affirmative.

§21.9 TRANSFERENCE

Cross-examination techniques are transferable from case to case, breaking down the particular fact pattern to correctly determine the category into which the testimony falls.

A recent civil medical case in which I appeared produced the following cross-examination which is the same approach taken in the preceding cross-examination:

Q: Now, doctor, you testified that upon testing the patient showed elevated TSH levels, is that correct?
A: Yes.
Q: And from that, you determined that that was an abnormal reading?
A: Yes.
Q: And you concluded that the patient suffered from a hyperthyroid condition based upon the elevated TSH levels?
A: Yes.
Q: And that led to your conclusion that the patient had been misdiagnosed and was not receiving proper care?
A: That's correct.
Q: Is it a fact, doctor, that in diagnosing hyperthyroidism one would also look to the T3 and T4 levels?
A: Yes.
Q: And, in this case, the testing of the T3 and T4 levels showed them to be within a normal range?
A: Yes.
Q: Isn't it true doctor that with hyperthyroidism, while the TSH levels would be elevated, the T3 and T4 levels would test below normal range, isn't that true?
A: Quite often.
Q: Well, isn't it a fact that before you can confirm a diagnosis of a hyperthyroid condition you would find elevated TSH levels and decreased T3 and T4 levels?
A: Usually.
Q: But that's not the case here, is it?
A: The T3 and T4 levels were normal.

Q: In fact, doctor, are there not other recognized conditions which are characterized by elevated TSH levels and normal range T3 and T4 levels?
A: Yes.
Q: And further, doctor, is it not a fact that elevated TSH levels and decreased T3 and T4 levels are consistent with an aging pituitary gland?
A: Yes.

Cutting through the mystique, the above is simply another example of internal inconsistency where the known facts did not support the judgmental leap. This method of cross-examination is effective in any case where the testimony can be broken down to identify the gap between the facts and the opinion.

In civil cases, where there are examinations before trial, the identification of the gap can be made under more leisurely and reasoned circumstances. In criminal cases where that opportunity is lacking, the weakness has to be determined on the spot. It is there where instinct and experience triumph over intellect. As in many other things, repetition through experience produces a swifter reflex.

The Electronic Witness 22

§22.1 INTRODUCTION

The courtroom has not escaped the invasion of the electronic age. Cases can now be proved or disproved with the utilization of computers which can either simulate events when the details of the occurrence are fed in or reconcile vast amounts of data into statistical findings. There are also devices which test, others which measure and still others which assist in the making of a diagnosis or prognostication. Frequently encountered are those which produce audio or video recordings and which are used to buttress the testimony of a witness whose credibility might otherwise be negligible.

Audio versus visual presents different problems and the cross-examination when dealing with these devices will be materially different.

§22.2 VIDEO

Video, absent an audio soundtrack, may be the picture which is worth a thousand words; but, the words will materially differ. Visualizing actions from a distance is subject to infinite interpretation as to what is really transpiring. Thus, such recordings may serve to establish a person's presence at a particular location but do not necessarily establish what took place among the persons appearing on the tape.

The trial of the four police officers in California alleged to have beaten Rodney King whose actions were captured on an amateur video tape demonstrates the point. When the tape was run through without comment, it appeared that Mr. King had received an unmerciful beating for which there was no justification. At the first trial of the officers, the defense ran the film in slow motion, stopping it frequently, and offered an interpretation of what was taking place almost on a frame by frame basis. The slowing down of the action and the dissecting of the movements analytically led the jury to conclude that the defendants were not guilty save for one count against one of the officers upon which the jury could not agree. The theme in the first case was that the beating was not as bad as first appeared and was justified under the circumstances.

In the second trial, the theme changed. In that proceeding, all but one of the four defendants did not testify. On April 2, 1993, shortly after the defense rested, Michael P. Stone was quoted in the New York Times as stating:

> The general theme of this case is that they functioned out there as a team led by the sergeant. The sergeant stood up and said, "they did what I said. They were under my control."

At the trial, the prosecution called expert witnesses who testified that the beating administered exceeded permissible bounds and used various parts of the tape recording to demonstrate their point. Conversely, using the same tape, the defense produced experts who testified that it was completely within proper police procedure under the circumstances. In short, it became a question as to what was actually taking place. Cross-examination would necessarily focus upon a particular interpretation that is offered.

§22.3 AUDIO

Audio recording is another matter. Once the voices on the tape are identified, there is a greater likelihood and less confusion as to what is taking place. The lack of confusion is not complete since often expert witnesses are required to decode what otherwise seems to be obscure conversation. However, for the most part, successful cross-examination is required to focus on excluding the tape recording altogether with a collateral attack upon the chain of custody, technical aspects which indicate that the tape recording has been tampered with, and inaudibility.

Only after the collateral attack fails does cross-examination attack the internal and external inconsistencies of the contents of the tape. External inconsistencies would include other tape recordings which should exist since the opportunity, inclination, means and determination of producing a tape recording of everything which transpired in an instant case is present but no tape is produced.

§22.4 CHAIN OF CUSTODY

There are two cross-examinations which come into play when a tape recording is to be offered in evidence. The first is the collateral attack upon the process by which the tape was produced and the chain of custody running from production to the courthouse. A successful attack upon the chain of custody excludes the admission into evidence of the tape recording leading to the second cross-examination, that of the witness who is no longer fortified by such tape.

An example of the path that leads from the suppression of tape recordings based upon failure to properly exert custodial supervision over the tape recordings, to the successful cross-examination of the prime government witness, to the acquittal of three defendants was recounted in *Vicious Circles* by Jonathan Kwitney (1979):

> The government brought George Gamaldi to trial November 17, 1975. Gamaldi was the first of the three Hills' supermarket executives to fight, they were the three charged with taking the most money—Gamaldi $267,300, Blase Iovino $297,800, and Salvatore Coletta $306,174, all over four years. Even persons who were convinced that the three men did take kickbacks doubted that they could have pocketed such staggering amounts. They had asked for and received the right to separate trials. But the evidence against them was similar, and the Gamaldi case was regarded as a bellwether. It was the first courtroom test of the credibility of Moe Steinman, the man whose testimony was brought by the government at so high a

price. The case against Gamaldi rested principally on the testimony of Steinman and his brother Sol.

Nicholson and Montello had caught Gamaldi in some potentially incriminating conversations back when they were wiretapping Moe Steinman. But a federal judge refused to allow the tape into evidence, because Snitow, too soon out of law school, hadn't understood the proper procedures and failed to have the tape sealed in time by a state judge (early in the investigation, when Gamaldi was overheard, Snitow thought the sealing could wait until the particular wiretap order expired, where in fact it must occur within a few days). Nicholson had also made some interesting observations of Gamaldi meeting with Steinman and Aaron Freedman at Patrick's Pub, on Long Island. But the state and the strike force hadn't been cooperating, and the government, perhaps forgetful of what Nicholson knew, never called him to testify.

So the case was almost entirely up to the Steinmans. But were the Steinmans up to the case?

* * *

Goldman took Steinman through a merciless cross-examination. Steinman was pitifully unable or unwilling to be specific about his own financial history. He seemed to be hiding something when he talked about the deals he arranged for himself and Bodenstein. And he was even less specific about how much money he had given Gamaldi, Coletta, and Iovino, where he had given it to them and on what dates. "This was cash money kickbacks," Steinman said. "We have no record of the kickback money." He said the payments started at twelve or fourteen hundred dollars a month and "it was going up an average of about one thousand dollars a month."

Sol Steinman offered little improvement.

When they had finished, Goldman appealed to U.S. District Judge Henry Werker for a dismissal of all charges. Werker gave it to him. "What you are asking me to say in keeping this indictment alive," Werker told Prosecutor Jones, "is that I can expect that reasonable people will find beyond a reasonable doubt on your proof that in each of those years an average of twenty-three thousand dollars was paid monthly . . . and that Mr. Gamaldi got a third of each of these payments. I think this is too highly speculative and too highly ambiguous because there is no showing as to exactly when and where those payments were made in each of the years. It is a generalized statement. It's too vague in my opinion to be sufficient proof in law."

Thus ended Moe Steinman's only appcarancc as a witncss at a criminal trial of the men he "gave up" to win his own freedom. As a result of Judge Werker's decision, the government dropped its charges against Iovino and Coletta.

Without suggesting that the tapes were particularly damaging to the defendant, it is clear that the cross-examination of the Steinmans was materially different once the tapes were no longer a factor. Without more, the mere existence of tape recordings cloaks a witness with an aura of credibility where but for the existence of such recordings, no credibility would exist.

The only opportunity to test the Steinmans was on cross-examination. As Kwitney said:

So the case was almost entirely up to the Steinmans. But were the Steinmans up to the case?

§22.5 PROCESS

The second litmus test in determining the admissibility into evidence of electronic evidence is whether or not the proper procedures were followed in the obtaining of the evidence. This includes the obtaining of court orders and the execution of those orders in strict conformity with the authority granted by the. As to electronic evidence, the cases and the rules generated by them is often clear and graphically shows the path that cross-examination should take.

Joseph Macy, formerly an Assistant District Attorney in Nassau County, now in criminal defense, recently secured the acquittal of a defendant in that most difficult of cases, driving while intoxicated.

The defendant had been stopped at a roadblock and, upon suspicion of the arresting officer, was subjected to certain tests designed to establish intoxication.

Upon trial, in the course of a cross-examination which, on its face, was neither dramatic nor confrontational, he asked the following questions:

Q: By the way, how long a period had elapsed between the time that you first stopped Mr. Jones at the roadblock and the time the alco-sensor was administered?
A: I would say maybe five minutes.
Q: And I think you have testified to earlier that the time when you had encountered the vehicle initially was approximately 1:30?
A: That is correct.
Q: So the time you administered the alco-sensor and placed Mr. Jones under arrest was approximately 1:35?
A: Approximately.
Q: Did you record that in any manner?
A: In the arrest paperwork, I believe, yes.
Q: At that time that you arrested him?
A: Immediately at that time—-
Q: Yes.
A: -—I believe I recorded it in the memo book, just put the arrest time down.
Q: And that entry in your memo book would have been relatively contemporaneous with the administration of the alco-sensor?
A: I don't recall specifically if I made that right at that moment or if I had made it up at the 2-8.
Q: You mean up at the precinct?
A: Up at the IDTU testing place, yes, sir.
Q: Officer Ipsen, you noted that the time was 1:35, did you look at your watch at that time?
A: I believe so, yes, because we have to call it over a police radio into our base.
Q: So to call it in, you would have—?
A: You have to look at your time to know what time it is.
Q: That's how you know the time was 1:35 at that time?
A: Yes, sir.

* * *

Q: Now at some point you requested that Mr. Jones submit to a breathalyzer examination; is that correct?
A: That is correct.
Q: And do you recall what time that was?
A: I have to look at the arrest paperwork again. I think it's my recollection that it was at some point, possibly 3:30 in the morning or thereabouts.
Q: Do your documents reflect what time the examination took place?
A: They indicate 3:50 a.m.

That portion of the cross-examination led to the acquittal of the defendant as evidenced by the decision of the court, who wrote:

> V.T.L. section 1194(2)(a) provides, in substance, that any person who operates a motor vehicle in this state shall be deemed to have given consent to a breathalyzer test provided it is administered at the direction of a police officer within two hours after the person has been placed under arrest for driving under the influence of alcohol. The courts of this state have been divided as to whether the defendant's consent to be tested permits the introduction of the breathalyzer results even if the test is administered more than two hours after arrest. Compare *People v. Brol*, 81 A.D.2d 739 (4th Dep't 1981); *People v. Keane*, 76 A.D.2d 963 (3d Dep't 1980); *People v. Ali*, 151 Misc. 2d 742 (Crim. Ct. N.Y. County 1991); and *People v. Edwards*, N.Y.L.J., May 12, 1992, p. 26, col. 6 (Crim. Ct. N.Y. County) (all holding that test administered after two hours is inadmissible) with *People v. Abel*, 166 A.D.2d 841 (3d Dep't 1990), *People v. Mills*, 124 A.D.2d 600 (2d Dep't 1986); and *People v. Dillin*, N.Y.L.J., Oct 5, 1990, p. 23, col. 3 (Crim. Ct. N.Y. County) (holding that two hour rule does not apply when the test is administered with the defendant's consent).
>
> This court is persuaded by the line of cases holding that the defendant's consent to take a breathalyzer test does not relieve

> the state from its obligation to administer the test within two hours after arrest and it adopts the reasoning of these cases. Thus, since the test here was administered after the two hour period had expired, the People will be precluded from introducing the test results as evidence at trial.

§22.6 CONVERTING CASES TO CROSS-EXAMINATION

Current case law provides an excellent outline for cross-examination, leaving for the cross-examiner the selection of questions to establish the point that the cases suggest needs to be made. In other portions of the opinion dismissing the charges against the defendant in the driving while intoxicated case, the court wrote, in pertinent part:

> In evaluating the validity of a particular checkpoint, the court must ensure that it was "being maintained in accordance with a uniform procedure which afforded little discretion to operating personnel, and that adequate precautions as to safety, lighting and fair warning of the existence of the checkpoint were in operation." Scott, 63 N.Y.2d at 526; see also *People v. John* BB., 56 N.Y.2d 482 (1982) (upholding checkpoint in heavily burglarized area).
>
> * * *
>
> No testimony was elicited to establish that Officer Ipsen either had the authority to permit any vehicles to go through without stopping them or that he allowed anyone to avoid the checkpoint while he was stationed there.
>
> In his written summation, the defendant argues that the hearing record was deficient because the People failed to establish that a written plan existed governing the layout and operation of the roadblock. In *Scott*, the Court of Appeals noted that the existence of such a plan was one factor to be considered in determining whether the roadblock was being conducted in a neutral manner. It did not hold, however, that the prosecution must introduce evidence of a written plan in every case. Since

> the record here established that the checkpoint was operated in a nondiscriminatory way, the absence of any testimony about written guidelines is of minimal significance. See *People v. Egan*, Docket No. 92N047413 (Crim. Ct. N.Y. County Jan. 12, 1993). Furthermore, Officer Ipsen stated that there was a supervisor present at the checkpoint (Tr. 27). Although this would not necessarily substitute for written guidelines, the supervisor's presence provided an important mechanism to ensure that the officers operating the checkpoint did not act in a capricious manner.

That decision, as in the case of others, absolutely points an attorney to the cross-examination that should be conducted with regard to the procedures to be tested. The content of questions to pursue the point is a matter of instinct and experience.

As is obvious, the balance of Macy's cross-examination included a series of questions as to whether or not the roadblock was conducted in a neutral manner, whether a written plan existed, whether the entire procedure was "being maintained in accordance with the uniform procedure which afforded little discretion to operating personnel, and that adequate precautions as to safety, lighting and fair warning of the existence of the checkpoint were in operation."

The same principles can be put to use with regard to any technical evidence. Thus, the cases will recite the criteria for admissibility and the questions designed to test that criteria. Evidence is further challenged collaterally by questioning the operating condition of the equipment which produced the evidence, the accuracy of the results obtained and the chain of custody prior to arriving at the courthouse so as to insure the proper identity of the evidence and preclude tampering.

§22.7 TAMPERING

Tampering, whether deliberate or inadvertent, is a frequent occurrence in the obtaining and development of electronic evidence. Everyone is familiar with the missing eighteen minutes in the Watergate tapes, as well as familiarity with the current commercials showing actors appearing in scenes with persons who died twenty years ago. Splicing and image alteration are highly developed techniques with regard to film and voice alteration and unexplained gaps in tape recordings are a common occurrence.

The demonstration of the existence of such tampering requires a technical knowledge far beyond anything that was required of lawyers a generation ago, if for no other reason other than that the techniques of alteration and tampering have advanced so dramatically in recent years.

A recently concluded case in the United States District Court for the Southern District of New York graphically demonstrates what today's cross-examiner must be prepared to deal with.

The charge was conspiracy and mail fraud. One of the co-conspirators was the prime witness supported by a series of tape recordings. A government expert, as indicated in the following cross-examination, was being pressed by defense counsel as to whether or not the tapes had been altered:

Q: Is that your report?
A: This is my report.
Q: Now, in that report, which is your report of the examination of these two tapes and other tapes and that machine, you have a number of graphs and stuff; do you not?
A: Yes, sir.
Q: And that you told us about is like this heart monitoring thing and the oscilloscope?
A: Yes, sir.
Q: And it prints out a form, a graph. Is that right?
A: Yes, sir.
Q: And you have those graphs contained in your report. Is that right?
A: Yes.
Q: Before you testified, did you have an opportunity to take a look at these charts numbered 1 through 11?
A: Yes, sir. I assume that was the—that's the same group.
Q: It is?
A: Yes.
Q: And are they, in fact, an exact duplicate, just a copy of the graphs that you have in your report?
A: They appear to be; yes.

Q: Is there any question in your mind that they are?
A: I didn't look at every one and compare exactly. I would say they appear to be correct; yes.
Q: Well, would you take a look at them as we conduct the examination? If you find any difficulty, please tell me.
A: Sure.
Q: Is this the waveforms that you're talking about?
A: That is the one.
Q: Subsequently?
A: Yes, sir.
Q: You talk about looking at a start signature on the tape?
A: Yes, sir.
Q: And making a picture of it. Is that correct?
A: Yes; yes, sir.
Q: And that picture would be on your oscilloscope, which would be on your report, which would be the same as one of these charts. Is that right?
A: Yes.
Q: Now, I want to ask you questions just about tape number 6.
A: All right.
Q: Okay. So, let me direct your attention to that, if I may?
A: Surely.
Q: Did you look for a start signature on the tape?
A: Yes, sir.
Q: And there is none?
A: Not at the beginning.
Q: So, what that means is that the tape was placed in the record mode on a leader. Is that right?
A: That is correct.
Q: And the leader doesn't pick up these magnetic little particles, so it doesn't leave a signature?
A: That's correct.
Q: If the record button is pressed on the actual tape, it leaves a signature. Is that right?
A: Yes, sir.
Q: And that's what we're talking about, this fingerprint signature; right?
A: Yes, sir.

Q: So, as to number 6, we have no signature for the start?

* * *

Q: Did you locate what we're talking about, the stop signature that we want to take a look at?
A: Yes, sir. I think it's figure 4.
Q: That's just one. Did you do two stop signatures, one on the tape and one on the copy to compare them?
A: Wait a minute.

* * *

Q: One on the test tape and one on the exhibit tape. Do you have two pictures of stop signatures?
A: Yes, sir.
Q: One on the test tape and one on the exhibit tape that you can compare?
A: Yes, sir.
Q: What are those numbers?
A: Figure 4 is the final stop signature on the subject tape.
Q: Okay.
A: Figure 8 is the stop signature from the test tape.

* * *

Q: That's a stop at the end of the tape. Is that right?
A: No. That's a stop tape on the test tape. It's a specific point of— at the count of 143 on it, not at the end.
Q: So, what you do is you just put the test tape in, stop it anywhere, and take a picture of it?
A: Yes.
Q: It didn't matter where you stop, a stop is a stop?
A: Correct.
Q: Now, you've got a picture of the test tape; right?
A: Yes.
Q: And now, you take the exhibit tape, the one that's in evidence that we have here and you want to take a picture of that stop. Is that right?

A: Yes, sir.
Q: Now, the stop that you take a picture of, that is at the end of the tape. Is that correct?
A: No, it's at the end of the conversation.
Q: Correct. The end of the conversation. Is that right?
A: Yes; correct.
Q: There is, in fact, more than one stop on that tape. Is that correct?
A: Yes.
Q: So, but this picture that we're talking about, which is exhibit 6, your figure 8 is the one at the end of the conversation?
A: That is correct.
Q: Okay. So, here we have the picture of the stop at the end of the conversation; right?
A: Yes.
Q: That you have a picture of. And now you make a test tape and take a stop anywhere and you take a picture of that; right?
A: Yes.

* * *

Q: Okay. And what you do is you compare them; right?
A: Yes, sir.
Q: And you say, hey, these look almost identical; right?
A: That is correct.
Q: Okay. So, and by doing that, you say that the tape, the tape that you're examining, the exhibit tape was an original and not a copy?
A: That's correct.
Q: Okay. That's one way you can tell. At least, that gives you some information to form your opinion. Is that right?
A: Yes, sir.
Q: Now, when you're looking at this, I see on here, 12, 14, M.S.?
A: Yes.
Q: M.S. stands for milliseconds?
A: Yes, sir.
Q: I see these big lines up and down here, that I'm pointing here on 6 and the number is 525, 80 M.V., what are those numbers?

A: P-P.
Q: P-P, what are these? What does that stand for?
A: That stands for the amplitude or the height of this major lobe from minus, down at the bottom, to the plus side on the top? And it says its 4,475 millivolts, peak to peak.
Q: So, what you do basically, is you measure. Is that right?
A: Yes; that's correct.
Q: You measure the peaks?
A: Yes.
Q: And if they come out pretty close or identical, you know it's an indication that you're dealing with an original tape. Is that a fair statement?
A: So far as it goes, that's acceptable; yes, sir. There's more to it than that.
Q: Okay. I'm just—we're doing piece by piece. Have I said anything incorrect so far?
A: No, sir.
Q: All right. Now, did you take a picture of any other stop in the exhibit tape?
A: Yes. At the end of 4.9-second gap, there was also a stop signature.
Q: Because the tape was stopped at that point; right?
A: Yes.
Q: And that creates a signature. Is that right?
A: That's correct.
Q: And as you told us with the test tape,a stop is a stop is a stop; right?
A: One proviso, sir. That is, if you notice both of these exhibits stop signatures have been made when there was no conversation present on the tape.
Q: Right.
A: If you make a stop signature on top of or in the presence of audio that you're recording or on top of audio that pre-existed—-
Q: Yes.
A: There may be some differences from these, some.
Q: May or should be?
A: There may.
Q: May not be?

A: There may not be, but there may be. But, however, they will not be significant enough to preclude your recognizing them for what they are.
Q: But you may have some differences?
A: There may be.
Q: Now, did you take a picture of the stop at the end of the gap?
A: Yes, sir.
Q: What—what number would that be?
A: In fact, there were two take there, as you remember.
Q: That's right.
A: Oh. Could I direct you to 14, if that will help you?

* * *

Q: On your test tape, I want it on your test tape, the stop at the over-record on the test tape, did you take a picture of that?
A: Yes.

* * *

Q: Okay. Now, this is what, your test tape; right?
A: That's one of the stops on the test tape during one of the two over-record gaps that I made, and you notice now, for example, this signature naturally here is different from what we saw on either of the other two exhibits we just looked at. And it's because of the fact that there's pre-existing audio there.

One can clearly envision the endless hours that were required to be closeted with an expert just to be able to conduct such an examination. Unfortunately, it is not like riding a bicycle which, once learned, is never forgotten. By the time that an attorney's next case comes around in which a similar issue is present, three new devices will have come into use requiring a new education.

§22.8 CONTENT TO PURPOSE MISMATCH

Omissions on tape recordings consist not only of unexplained gaps but also of conversation which ought to appear, but doesn't, in an unbroken, unaltered conversation. Utilizing the step-by-step analysis of external and internal inconsistencies will frequently identify statements that should appear upon the tape recording that are curiously absent. The absence of such statements indicates that the conversation is being manipulated in a way the party offering the tape is not admitting. A failure to raise and address a particular subject may be the strongest evidence that an earlier claimed incident never happened or that the witness is giving a false version.

A review of tape recordings that provides excellent material for cross-examination is matching the content of the recording to the purpose for which the recording was made. A tape recording in a criminal case is commonly made to confirm the information provided by an informant or other person in difficulty who has agreed to become a government or state witness in exchange for leniency. It may also be made by an undercover agent who has a specific purpose in initiating the conversation.

An informant or prospective defendant will inevitably seek immunity or a reduced plea with accompanying lenient sentence as the price of his cooperation. Prior to obtaining this concession from the prosecution, the individual is required to make a "proffer" of the information in his possession in which the Government has an interest. Albeit incomplete, there is sufficient detail in the "proffer" to motivate the authorities to believe that the person does in fact have valid information and agreement is reached.

The agreement takes primarily one of two forms. Either the person will not be prosecuted under a grant of transactional or testimonial immunity or will be permitted to plead guilty to lesser charges which provide for a reduced maximum sentence. *Inter alia*, the agreement provides in substance that the prosecution will recommend a sentence below that maximum dependent on the value of the individual's cooperation.

The authorities recognize that going to trial solely on the unsubstantiated word of such an accomplice is likely to be fruitless. Required cooperation starts with the witness' willingness to attempt to engage the target of the information in taped conversations. These taped conversations may be either obtained in direct conversation through the use of a recording device secreted upon the body, telephonically or through eavesdropping devices.

Effective cross-examination can occur when the content of the secured conversation does not match the purpose for which the conversation was undertaken.

By way of illustration, John Doe, an employee finding himself in personal difficulty as a result of allegations made against him by his employer, Mr. Jones, for embezzlement of funds sought to extricate himself from his difficulties by offering the authorities information against Jones, who was a much bigger prize. The information consisted of alleged payoffs to public officials in the past, as well as two current projects in which payoffs were allegedly being made.

In return for this cooperation, the witness secured an agreement with the authorities whereby he would be permitted to plead to a single felony count carrying a maximum penalty of five years incarceration. But for the agreement, the charges that might have been brought against him provided for penalties totalling sixty years of incarceration.

Upon the trial, the witness testified in accordance with the story which he had told the authorities at the time he entered into the agreement with the government. He further testified that, in accordance with the cooperation agreement, he did undertake and secure taped conversations with Mr. Jones on several occasions. On cross-examination, first establishing bias, the witness was asked:

Q: There came a time when you learned that Mr. Jones made several criminal allegations against you, isn't that correct?
A: Yes.
Q: And you were further advised that he had delivered certain books and records to the Government supporting those allegations, true?
A: Yes.
Q: And you further learned that the Government intended to seek an indictment against you somewhere between eight and fourteen counts of mail fraud and larceny, right?
A: My attorney told me they were looking to indict me.
Q: And you sought to make a deal with the Government to try and get out of this situation, didn't you?
A: My attorney spoke to them.
Q: You tried to get full immunity from any prosecution, didn't you?

A: Yes.
Q: But the Government wouldn't give you complete immunity, would they?
A: No.
Q: But they did agree to let you plead guilty to a single count that would limit your jail exposure to five years. Without that deal you might have gotten sixty years, isn't that true?
A: I don't think I would have gotten sixty years.
Q: But you understood you could serve a lot longer than five years, right?
A: Yes.
Q: In fact, under the deal you made with the Government, five years is the maximum, true?
A: Yes.
Q: And if the Government tells the Court that your cooperation was really valuable, you might get less?
A: Possibly.
Q: In fact, if they really step up to the plate and take a hard swing for you, you might even get a suspended sentence, isn't that right?
A: I hope so, but they never promised me that.
Q: And as part of this cooperation that you hope makes them go to bat for you, you agreed to try and get Mr. Jones on tape?
A: That was part of the deal.
Q: And, in fact, you did get him on tape?
A: Yes.
Q: And particularly you made tape recordings on October 4, 9, 14, 21 and 25, 1990?
A: I don't know if those are the exact dates, but its something like that.
Q: In any event, you made tape recordings with Mr. Jones on five separate occasions, right?
A: Yes.
Q: And the purpose of making those tape recordings was to get information about payments made to public officials?
A: Yes.
Q: And in particular with regard to the Montrose job, the Blackburn job, and the Landowne job that is still going on?

A: Yes.
Q: And prior to making these tape recordings you had given the Government information about those jobs where alleged payoffs to public officials were involved?
A: I told them what happened.
Q: And you were asked to make tape recordings so that your story could be confirmed?
A: Partially.
Q: I assume the other part is so that you could get Mr. Jones to make incriminating statements?
A: Yes.
Q: And if you got Mr. Jones to make incriminating statements and your story was confirmed, your cooperation would be valuable, would it not?
A: That's not for me to judge.
Q: But in your mind you believed it would be valuable if you got incriminating statements that backed up your story?
A: I thought it would be.
Q: If it was valuable, there would be a greater likelihood that the Government would go to bat for you on sentence?
A: Yes.
Q: You didn't want the Government to believe that any information you had given them was false, did you?
A: It wasn't.
Q: Just answer the question. You didn't want the Government to believe the information you gave was false?
A: No.
Q: Because if they believed that the information you gave was false, that might have blown the whole immunity deal, isn't that right?
A: That's right.
Q: And even if the Government couldn't prove that what you said was absolutely false, you didn't want them to think you were just blowing smoke?
A: I wasn't.
Q: Once again, please answer the question, you didn't want the Government to think you were just blowing smoke?
A: No.

Q: Because if they thought that, any statement they made to the Court on your sentence might be pretty weak?
A: I guess so.
Q: So it was in your interest to get confirmation of the story that you had told the Government?
A: Yes.
Q: It would be in your interest to get Mr. Jones to incriminate himself in these conversations, true?
A: Yes.
Q: And it would be against your interest if anything popped up on these recordings which showed that the information you gave the Government was false?
A: That wouldn't help me.
Q: Or if you were blowing smoke?
A: If you say so.
Q: Well that wouldn't do you any good, would it?
A: No.
Q: So, let's be clear; if anything on the tape confirms your story, that's good, right?
A: Yes.
Q: But if anything comes up on the tape that shows you were lying or blowing smoke, that's bad, true?
A: It wouldn't help me.
Q: And might put your entire deal at risk?
A: It could.
Q: And the whole reason you were making these recordings was to get evidence about pay offs to public officials, yes?
A: Yes.
Q: And the period of time you were zeroing in on getting this information ran from October 1 to November 16, true?
A: That's true.
Q: And to try and accomplish what you and the Government wanted, you taped him on October 4, 9, 14, 21 and 25?
A: Again, I don't know the specific dates, but that sounds right.
Q: And, in fact, we know that Mr. Jones was in town at least until December 1, right?
A: I know it was some time in December.
Q: And while he was in town he was at the same address and had the same telephone number?

A: Yes.
Q: And there are no tape recordings after the 25th of October?
A: That's right.
Q: Although you could have made more recordings between the 25th of October and the 1st of December?
A: If necessary.
Q: Now, prior to your testimony in this courtroom, did you listen to the tape recordings that had been made?
A: Yes.
Q: And, to your knowledge, were transcripts made of the conversations as they appeared on those tapes?
A: Yes.
Q: And did you review the transcripts of those conversations?
A: Yes.
Q: Let me hand you what has been marked as Exhibits 32 through 37. I ask you, are those the transcripts of the conversations you had with Mr. Jones that you reviewed prior to testifying here today?
A: These are the transcripts.
Q: Now, sir, I ask you to go through each of those transcripts and tell this jury any place in those conversations where there is any mention of payment to public officials.
A: You want me to do it now?
Q: Right now.
A: [After five minutes] I don't see any.
Q: Take as long as you need.
A: I can't find any.
Q: Do you find any place about any payments to public officials in the past?
A: No.
Q: Do you find any place about an intention to pay a public official in the future?
A: No.
Q: Do you find a place where you even raise the subject about pay offs to public officials?
A: Not specifically.
Q: The whole idea of making those recordings was to talk about those very subjects, isn't that true?

A: Yes.
Q: But you never even brought it up?
A: It didn't seem appropriate.
Q: That's because you were discussing basketball, right?
A: We talked about basketball.
Q: And business in general, true?
A: We discussed that, too.
Q: And a trip you had just come back from to Cancun?
A: That too.
Q: But no payoffs to public officials, right?
A: I didn't see any.

The above cross-examination can be utilized with remarkable frequency as there is often a mismatch between the purpose for obtaining the recording and its contents. It is a universal cross-examination that can be used as a template when recording equipment inexplicably malfunctions at a particularly critical point in the conversation or where the responses do not jive with the leading conversation of the individual initiating the recording.

This technique is available when, as in this case, there is silence, but also when there is an inconsistent response, a malfunction or, again, as indicated in the above cross-examination, a period of time when it was possible to make tape recordings but no advantage was taken of the opportunity.

The import of some of the questions asked in the above cross-examination as to the availability of the target between October 25 and December 1 was exploited upon summation and pointed out that while the opportunity existed, no effort was made to obtain better tapes which dealt with the actual subject during that period. The implication was that the witness, if not the government, knew that any repeated attempts would be fruitless or that the government concluded but did not admit that their witness' failure to raise the subject in a meaningful matter was an indication that his information may have been less than accurate.

The short questions regarding the period from October 25 to December 1 closed a possible escape hatch through such answers as "he was out of town," "he was ill" or "he refused to take my phone calls or see me."

Government Witnesses 23

§23.1 WHO IS GOVERNMENT WITNESS

Historically, a government witness in a criminal prosecution was usually a law enforcement agent, some forensic expert or a law abiding witness who had been induced to testify on behalf of the prosecution. However, in recent times, the most prominent government witness is an immunized co-conspirator or prior associate in criminal activity with the defendant.

§23.2 PLEA BARGAINING

It is critical to bring home to the jury that the testimony that they heard from such an immunized witness was the result of a plea bargain, the nature of which could cause the jury to lose faith in the prosecution or, at the very least, demonstrate the witness' overwhelming motive to lie.

Former prosecutors who subsequently undertake defense work have a substantial advantage over persons who are not former prosecutors. That is because the ritual dance of the plea bargain and how it is arrived at is a ballet all its own. If jurors at the outset of cross-examination are not afforded the opportunity to see how the system works, they are liable to be misled by the government's contention and the witness' affirmation that the witness' only vested interest is in telling the truth since otherwise the immunity which they had received for their testimony would be invalidated. An applicable cross-examination at the outset of such testimony is applicable in virtually all situations.

Q: Mr. X, you received immunity from prosecution for any of the crimes which you personally committed that are the subject of this trial, isn't that true [alternatively, the question can be phrased in terms of receiving a plea to a reduced crime with sentencing to be withheld until after the completion of the instant trial]?
A: Yes.
Q: And, in fact, before you agreed to testify your attorney insisted that you get this immunity in writing and both you and the Government signed it, isn't that true?
A: Yes.
Q: Now, let's talk about how you got the immunity. First, you had to tell the Government what you intended to say?
A: I told them what I knew.
Q: Before you got the immunity, didn't you have to make what is known as a "proffer?"
A: They told me they did not want to buy a pig in a poke so I had to tell them what I knew that I could testify about.
Q: And before you told them what you knew, isn't it a fact that they told you what they hoped you would be able to testify to?
A: They told me what they thought I would have information about.
Q: So first they told you what they thought you had information about, right?
A: Yes.
Q: Then you told them whether or not you had that information?
A: Yes.
Q: Now if you didn't have that information that they told you they thought you had, you wouldn't have gotten immunity, isn't that true?
A: Well, they weren't going to give me immunity unless I had valuable testimony.
Q: Isn't it true that they would not tell you if you had immunity until after you told them what you were going to say?

A: Yes.
Q: And you told them what you were going to say after they told you what they thought you had to say?
A: That was the order.
Q: Just so we are clear, first they told you what they thought you had to say, then you said it and then they gave you immunity?
A: Yes.
Q: And you knew that if you did not say that or something they could use against this defendant that you would not get immunity?
A: Yes.
Q: And you would be personally prosecuted?
A: Yes.
Q: And you would be facing the same jail sentence that this defendant is now facing based on your testimony?
A: Yes.
Q: And you're not facing that jail sentence the same as him because of your testimony and your getting immunity, isn't that true?
A: Yes.
Q: And after you got immunity did you meet with the prosecutors to go over your story?
A: Yes.
Q: How many times did you meet with them?
A: Somewhere between six and ten times.
Q: And how long did each session last on the average?
A: Several hours.
Q: And who was present during these sessions?
A: The prosecutor and two agents.
Q: And did they discuss with you the questions that I might ask you on cross-examination?
A: Yes.
Q: And did they work with you on the answers that you would give to questions that I would ask you if they guessed right?
A: Yes.
Q: So that you had a prosecutor and two Federal agents meeting with you for several hours over a number of days working on the answers that you're now going to give me on cross-examination, isn't that true?

A: If you put it that way.
Q: Did they focus on inconsistencies in your testimony?
A: What do you mean inconsistencies?
Q: Well, any trouble spots? Any place where the answer wasn't as good as it could be?
A: We spent a lot of time on that.
Q: And after the meeting with these Government people, lasting several hours, and over a number of days, you tried to figure out answers to the questions you all figured would be troublesome?
A: We spent a lot of time on that.
Q: So now here we are. You're gonna give us the answers to my questions that that team helped you with, isn't that true?
A: Yes.

Anatomy Of Cross-Examination Of An Expert Witness 24

§24.1 INTRODUCTION

Emrolyn White Tail was charged with second degree murder having admittedly killed Robert McKay. However, Ms. White Tail pleaded not guilty by virtue of the fact that she was a victim of ''battered wife syndrome''; and, thus, her homicidal act was excusable under the law. The killing took place on a Native American Reservation; and, as a result, the case came on for trial in the United States District Court for the District of North Dakota located in Fargo.

''Battered wife syndrome,'' like a number of sociological syndromes, is a recent evolution in the concept of justifiable homicide, being a somewhat uneasy marriage between the law regarding self-defense and not guilty by virtue of insanity. Insanity is currently defined as an identifiable psychological condition which is the controlling factor in the allegedly criminal act.

The prosecutor was Lynn Crooks, an Assistant United States Attorney in Fargo, North Dakota. Crooks has been a government prosecutor since 1969 and has tried over twenty major homicide cases. Counted among them are Leonard Pettetier, accused of murdering two agents of the Federal Bureau of Investigation, and Yorie Von Kahl, charged with the murder of two Federal Marshals in a shoot out in Medina, North Dakota. His reputation and professionalism are so widely known that cross-examinations he conducted of experts have caused experts to be unwilling to appear in subsequent cases.

Many of the excerpts used to illustrate the various principles of cross-examination are selected from criminal cases. This is not because cross-examination in civil cases is less complex or less interesting. Rather, it is because, in criminal cases, there is less discovery so that the techniques of cross-examination are more apparent. The cross-examination set forth here is excellent for purposes of illustration and could occur in either a civil or criminal trial. There are not a great deal of documents involved which would break the flow of the narrative as it emerged on cross-examination and which would be known to the jury but not to the reader.

The excerpts are from separate cross-examinations of two doctors. The distinction between them is negligible since the direct simple method and theme are adhered to in both. The cross-examinations selected are excellent examples of the application of the principles of effective evolution of cross-examination of an expert witness. Because of the examinations' lucidity, those principles are recognizable and, with factual modification, easily transferable to a broad range of cases including such intimidating actions as toxic tort, product liability or accounting.

§24.2 THE OPINION TESTIMONY

Q: Doctor, were you able to formulate an opinion concerning whether or not Emrolyn fits the criteria of a person suffering from battered woman syndrome?

A: It would be my opinion that she did fit the criteria. There is no doubt whatsoever. She is a classic case. She would be a perfect case study for any book on battered wife syndrome in its extreme form.

§24.3 EARLY SKIRMISH AND DEMONSTRATION OF PREPARATION ASSERTING CONTROL

Q: The battered wife syndrome is really a phrase that has gotten coined more or less by the works of Lenore Walker, I believe, isn't it, wrote the book ''Battered Women?''

A: Right.
Q: And most of what has been done with battered wife or battered woman syndrome has kind of followed her work, is that correct?
A: A lot of it. She was one of the originators anyway. Other people have picked up on it.
Q: Other people have gone into it and expanded. Actually, the concept should perhaps more appropriately be battered spouse syndrome, isn't that correct?
A: No.
Q: There are males that suffer from similar types of mental syndrome, are there not?
A: If you're asking if there is a percentage of men who are battered, there is about five percent of men are battered and 95 percent women.
Q: Going to get to that.
A: It started with women, not men.
Q: The general concept of a battered person and the concept you talked about percentagewise fits more women than it does men but it actually works both ways?
A: It could be applied, I guess, to men; I don't know. She hadn't done that study. I guess I would have to wait and see if they did a study and came up with the same results.
Q: There is certainly no reason that a man cannot suffer from the same type of psychological and personal damage that a woman could by being battered by the woman?
A: I think psychological damage. Probably not the same on a physical damage given the size.
Q: Depends a little bit on their relative size, obviously?
A: Yes.
Q: The other thing that makes it more recurrent with women obviously is cultural, is it not?
A: In what way?
Q: Of the Indian culture for the last how many thousand years, it is more or less generally accepted that men are supposed to be dominant, they are supposed to be more affirmative et cetera, women are supposed to be more submissive. These are cultural concepts that are perhaps changing but they have been there?
A: I would agree, culturally, it's more acceptable for men to dominate women than the reverse.

Q: One of the problems that women have is basically a belief that the society expects them to take this beating, that is a factor, is it not?
A: That's one of the reasons women stay.
Q: Yes. And that is one of the complicating factors?
A: Right.
Q: Feeling society really expects me to put up with this?
A: Or I shouldn't fit this, I should be able to make this work.
Q: To be a useful concept, the concept of battered wife syndrome is really not intended to be a one size fits all concept, is it? And let me say what I'm getting at. All incidences of domestic violence do not automatically fall into the category of battered wife syndrome, do they?
A: No.

§24.4 DEVELOPMENT OF THE THEME

Crooks' approach in this cross-examination is that some people are simply ''Saturday night brawlers'' and that repeated physical abuse does not always convert to battered wife syndrome.

Q: The obvious example I just gave you, if the wife, in fact, is the aggressor and is beating up on the husband and psychologically and physically abusing him, certainly she would not be deemed a candidate for that syndrome?
A: I would guess not.
Q: All right. Obviously, if you have got a situation where you are simply dealing with two people that fight in marriage, there are couples that fight, are there not?
A: There are couples that fight. I don't know that they batter each other though.

* * *

Q: Well, let me ask you just more specifically. If you have a person who's basically in a relationship which is a combat zone, you have a husband and wife that fight with some frequency; do you not have to make a determination as to who

the principal aggressor is in the marriage before you can determine the criteria of battered wife syndrome?
A: No.
Q: If in fact there is no overbearing, if in fact the husband is not indeed controlling her life, doing anything to prevent her from leaving, things of that nature, isn't that relevant to whether or not you have got a battered wife syndrome?
A: It would be relevant, but that's not the same as determining who's the primary aggressor.
Q: What I'm looking at, are you aware in the records that the last roughly three years Mr. McKay in this case was simply absent, he was in jail?
A: No, I'm not aware of that.

§24.5 GARBAGE IN—GARBAGE OUT

The questions point out that the information on which the opinion was based was incomplete or faulty and that there were steps that could have been taken, facts that should have been checked and that the time spent was insufficient to form a valid opinion.

Q: Well, did you make an independent evaluation or were you provided with any information as to what actually happened when Mr. McKay got out of jail?
A: No. All I did was talk to Emrolyn. I have no—-
Q: My question to you, were you informed by Mr. Becker of incidents occurring after Mr. McKay got out of jail on approximately August 10th, I believe, of 1990 which would be less than a month before his death?
A: No.
Q: Did he give you any kind of factual recitation of what the relationship actually had been like during that month before his death?
A: No.
Q: Did he tell you what the neighbor, for example, the next door neighbor had said, Mr. Joshua I believe, first name Robert?
A: No.
Q: Did he tell you what he had said about whether or not there had been any fights going on next door?

A: No.
Q: Get any information of that?
A: No.
Q: I'd like to just reiterate, your opinion, if I heard you correctly, was based upon an hour and a half conversation with Emrolyn White Tail, is it not?
A: No. It's based on a number of years experience of what I know about it and viewing Emrolyn.
Q: I assumed your expertise and your experience. But essentially the fact is that you had to make an informed judgment in that hour and a half interview with Emrolyn White Tail, is that correct?
A: The facts are what you're talking about?
Q: Yes.
A: Yes. Hour and a half hours interviewed with Emrolyn.
Q: You made no particular attempt to follow this trial or be informed by counsel as to what evidence may or may not have come out at trial?
A: No.
Q: You have made no particular attempts or no attempt at all to independently verify anything that Emrolyn has told you about what happened in the past, have you?
A: No. That's not part of our rule.
Q: Your judgment, therefore, is based essentially on, and dependent upon whether what Emrolyn told you was the truth?
A: No. My judgment is based on working with hundreds of battered women, years of experience and being with them.
Q: If Emrolyn lied to you about being battered by Robert McKay, then your opinion isn't worth much, is it?
A: I think the opinion is still worth—what which are talking about is battered woman syndrome.
Q: If Emrolyn White Tail had simply lied to you about what had happened to her and about how long she's been abused, then there isn't much upon which to base your opinion, is there?
A: If she lied to me about everything?
Q: Yes.
A: I guess it would be hard to base an opinion on her specifically. But it wouldn't change my opinion as far as affects it has on women and battered woman syndrome.

Q: I don't propose to argue at all with your general criteria of battered wife syndrome. The question before this jury is does it apply to Emrolyn, and we are not talking in abstract here. My question then is essentially your evaluation of battered wife is essentially based or dependent upon whether or not what she told you was the truth?
A: I believed her.
Q: When you saw her she had been continuing and recovering, I suppose, from a severe alcohol problem, did she not?
A: When I saw her she had already come out of treatment.
Q: Were you aware or did she inform you that she had a long ongoing history of very severe alcoholism problem?
A: Yes.
Q: And you were aware that she in fact had taken the life of Robert McKay and was facing charges of second degree murder because of that?
A: Yes.
Q: Did she indicate to you that she missed Robert McKay and felt bad that he was gone and had died?
A: Yes.
Q: She felt bad about that?
A: Uh-huh. All battered women do. One of the reasons that they do is they love their batterer.
Q: But my question basically is you're certainly not contending that at the time you saw her she was not subject to great personal stress?
A: I'm not contending that.
Q: Would you acknowledge that at the time you visited with her she was subject to great personal stress?
A: Yes.

* * *

Q: Have you heard Robert McKay's side of the story?
A: No, I haven't.
Q: He's dead, is he not?
A: That's what I have been told, yes.
Q: He didn't have the opportunity to sit down and explain what his feelings and actions or lack of actions were to you, did he?

A: No.
Q: Well, you said that when you saw her there was a feeling of hopelessness. This was after she had been charged with second degree murder, isn't that correct?
A: When I talked to her.
Q: Yes.
A: She often referred to that.
Q: You didn't talk to her before the murder, did you?
A: No.
Q: So you talked to her only after she had been charged with second degree murder?
A: Right.
Q: And at that time she stressed a feeling of hopelessness?
A: Current and past.
Q: Well, I'm talking particularly about her state at the time you talked to her was one of hopelessness?
A: Depression, hopelessness, self-esteem.
Q: Certainly being charged with second degree murder when you had basically admitted the facts of the killing could very well account for feeling fairly hopeless, couldn't it?
A: Can you say that again.
Q: Well, her situation certainly wasn't a very ideal one, was it?
A: No.
Q: Basically—I'm sorry, didn't mean to cut you off.
A: What you're asking me is her feeling of hopelessness was coming entirely from her being charged with murder rather than having—-
Q: I'm simply asking a question, wouldn't that fully explain why she is feeling fairly hopeless when she is talking to you that she's facing some very serious charges concerning having taken someone's life which she has admitted basically to people that she has done?
A: No. It would not fully explain it.
Q: Don't you think that would help explain her feeling of hopelessness?
A: (witness nods head).
Q: And for no other way?
A: From my interview.

Q: You didn't interview friends, family, anyone that could confirm whether that indeed was the case, did you?
A: No.
Q: Did you do anything beyond simply taking her first person account of what had happened in the past?
A: No. No. In talking situations you usually just work with the individual.

§24.6 DEVELOPMENT OF THE THEME (2)

A recurring theme for cross-examination is that battered wife syndrome is not insanity as the law defines it and, therefore, not a defense to homicide. Even if it were generally, it was not in this case since it did not control the defendant's will and is not a license to murder.

Q: My question to you is perhaps again somewhat obvious; but; in situations where basically the battering has ceased and the husband is no longer battering the wife, it's certainly not your contention or the contention of the people you work with that she simply has a free ticket to kill the man at some time of her choosing at random in the future, is it?
A: No. But it doesn't mean that her fear has gone away because he's gone away.
Q: Well, my question is, though, don't you then have to ask the question was there something rationally to cause her fear if you're going to have that battered wife syndrome have anything to do with the now dead body we find on the kitchen floor?
A: It was there previously. What I tried to explain is if she was living in a battering situation, it goes on for a number of years and then, let's say, he's arrested and sent to jail for a year or two, that doesn't mean then that boom, the battered wife syndrome stops and none of those emotional effects are there any more. They are still there and they stay there.
Q: My question comes back to the question I asked earlier though. You're not contending, even though those feelings may be there, you certainly aren't contending that psychologically she has a free ticket to simply kill him at some random occasion in the future, are you?

A: No.
Q: All right. One would then have to make an examination of the facts and see whether or not there was something that happened at the time of death that had some bearing on the battered wife syndrome and to reawaken the fears, wouldn't one?
A: Well, if fears are there, and I don't know if something happened that exacerbated it—-
Q: That's my question, though, you still have to, you have to ask yourself what are the facts of the case at hand, don't you?
A: In what?
Q: In proving that she suffers from battered woman syndrome. Let me back up. You've now got a body lying on the kitchen floor with a stab wound in its back and he's going to die from it within an hour or so bleeding profusely all over the place. You're certainly not contending that all that has to be asked is whether or not he beat her four or five years ago. There are a lot of other questions that have to be asked in between, aren't there?
A: I would guess so, yeah.

§24.7 DEVELOPMENT OF THE THEME (3)

Controlling the witness through his grasp of the subject the interrogator is exploiting an inconsistent symptom, i.e., assertiveness, which the evidence showed was a trait of the defendant.

Q: So the jury understands what we are talking about, the general concept that Mrs. Walker came up with is the idea you start with the tension building phase, then you move to the second phase which is the acute phase of basically the battering itself and then the third phase which is honeymoon phase or the forgiveness phase where the husband professes sorrow, guilt, et cetera, the wife more or less forgives him and takes him back and unfortunately the cycle repeats itself again and again. That was the general concept they described?
A: Right. She spent more studies, more studies that in fact the honeymoon phase gets shorter and shorter to the point where it doesn't even exist anymore.

Q: Well, the point is that the concept still includes a period of relative calm where in many situations, particularly where the beatings have not been relatively recent, are going to include a period where in fact the husband is contrite and the woman probably genuinely forgives him and cares for him. That's very common, is it not?
A: It's been thought to be so. I'm, through the question of studies, what they found the tension is still there. They were saying this is a phase where in fact people really did care about each other and get along well. There is still the underlying tension and psychological, verbal things were happening, maybe even subtle threats flow into the tension phase rather than this is the honeymoon phase. Things up here on the surface appear to be calm.
Q: The concept of the learned helplessness that you described earlier basically includes that feeling of essentially inability to escape the situation, does it not?
A: Fear of being trapped.
Q: Trapped in it, can't get out, nothing they can do about it, is that correct?
A: Right.
Q: Part of the concept of helplessness assumes, does it not, relatively low self-esteem, relatively submissive person who basically is not going to be able to assert and escape?
A: The presumption that the person feels helpless is fact when they started. In fact, our recent theory shows that women who are battered, out of the relationship are very competent, professional, executive type women who have high paying jobs and appear to be very successful people in the community but within their relationship they feel helpless.
Q: If the person in fact, if a woman is in fact a strong-willed, assertive woman both in and outside of the relationship, one would not look for the classification or the labeling of battered wife syndrome?
A: If she was assertive both in and out—-
Q: Both in and out, that's right.
A: Being assertive is not generally one of the criteria.

§24.8 DEVELOPMENT OF THE THEME (4)

Even if the defendant possessed symptoms of battered wife syndrome, the act of homicide could still be an act of volition rather than an act compelled by her condition.

Q: My point is, Doctor, of this little exercise, there have been things that have been read to the jury before. It certainly is very important to the jury what was happening when she stabbed him in this case, is it not?
A: Yes, it is.
Q: If she simply stabbed him out of spite, that's something different than if she stabbed him to save her life. You would acknowledge that, would you not?
A: Yes.
Q: All battered women do not necessarily fit battered wife syndrome, do they?
A: I think that would be fair to say that.
Q: And simply because one has got the label of battered wife syndrome—let me back up before I get to that question. Someone that's suffered from battered wife syndrome is not in a layman's sense crazy, is she?
A: No. But I think a distinction has to be made. There are women who are battered who do not fit the battered wife syndrome. But Emrolyn White Tail—-
Q: You are getting off on a trail I'm not going down right now.
A: I just don't want to have my testimony misinterpreted.
Q: The fact that a woman fits the battered wife syndrome does not mean that she is insane or crazy or mentally ill, it's simply a syndrome which describes a phenomenon which essentially helps explain why she isn't leaving a marriage which anyone else in their right mind would have left, isn't that about the size of it?
A: I don't think that's a very adequate—-
Q: No. I recognize it's simplistic. But it is not that she is crazy, is it?
A: No, it's not.
Q: Because a woman as a victim of the battered wife syndrome, she still has the ability to act with volition, does she not?

A: Yes. At least to a degree.
Q: What you were talking about when you're talking about a battered wife syndrome is essentially the woman that, if you look at the textbooks, depicts that which you have been referring to, a woman with very low self-esteem, that's one of the characteristics, is it not?
A: Yes, it is.
Q: She has a feeling of helplessness which has been caused by several different things, perhaps simply economics, that might be one factor?
A: It's complex factors.
Q: I'm going to go through a few of them. But certainly one would be economics, she didn't have an education, she doesn't have job training?
A: Right.
Q: She may be simply limited by going out on her own?
A: That may be.
Q: It may be part of the condition, correct? It may be she doesn't have a family that will be supportive and help her separate from this?
A: Yes.
Q: It certainly might be that this woman is one that has been abused before and simply is kind of down in her self esteem before she gets to the relationship, isn't that true?
A: Yeah. That would be a feature.
Q: I think you use the example that battered wife may have been battered as children or something like that.
A: Yes.
Q: They generally feel that they are trapped in the situation?
A: Yes.
Q: That's very classical, is it not?
A: Yes.
Q: They feel that, for example, social services or the law enforcement people will not help them probably because they haven't helped them in the past?
A: Yes. Correct.
Q: But with regard to that factor, it makes a good deal of difference whether or not in a situation like New York City where

they don't respond to wife beating cases or when you are in downtown Fargo or elsewhere they did?

A: It makes a difference what the situation, the city.

§24.9 MORE GARBAGE IN—GARBAGE OUT

The questions demonstrate dependency on the work of others. The work may be incomplete and the witness does not have a full grasp of it in any event.

Q: You indicated that there is this well documented history of beatings. Where did you find this history?

A: The history came from all of the reports that I read, the police reports from Fort Totten, Devils Lake area, the hospital medical reports and so on. As you said, some of the times that she was injured in a scrap with somebody else. But the only ones that I was really, the ones I was primarily concerned with was the instances in which she was injured by Mr. McKay.

Q: Essentially what you're talking about is a series of interviews of her sister and I think her mother and that is these series of interviews you're talking about, isn't it?

A: No. There was that interview data, but also looking at police reports of instances where they came to their residence because of altercations between Mr. McKay and Miss White Tail and—-

Q: How many of those were there that actually involved Miss White Tail? Now there was some coming to the residence that involved the assaults on her.

A: I can't give you a number. I think it's, when one looks at the total record, huge thick records, as you know, to imply that there were only, say, one or two beatings by Mr. McKay is not reality.

Q: Well, that's what I'm asking. You're the one that is representing they were documented in the record. There is one involving the hammer. That one I'll concede to you. What other reports are there in those police reports of beatings to her?

A: There will be situations in which—here again by memory I can't separate exactly what medical instances were because of his beatings and what medical things were—but there were a lot of injuries over a lot of times, lot of medical evaluations and treatments and so on. There are certainly more cases other than the beating of the hammer.

Q: Which one other than the hammer involved her?

A: Again, if I give an instance, I can't be sure, I can't remember at this instance exactly which specific injuries happened at the hands of Mr. McKay and which specific injuries happened—-

Q: You aren't asserting that Mr. McKay was responsible for the beating of the sister or the brother or the other individual that apparently she was living with when he was gone?

A: The only beatings I'm concerned about by Mr. McKay were the beatings of White Tail.

§24.10 CONTROL AND KNOWLEDGE NEGATING AN ELEMENT OF THE DEFENSE

Through knowledge, Crooks was able to control the discussion and dissect a concept, i.e., blackouts, so no weight was given to the factual evidence of the defendant's blackouts. The questions spell out the entire subject for the jury in simple fashion and perpetuate the theme that, even if suffering battered wife syndrome, there is enough remaining in the defendant's make up to commit willful deliberate murder.

Q: Let me ask you, you talked about blackouts, is that correct?

A: Yes. We did talk about blackouts.

Q: Blackouts essentially are a phenomenon which essentially involve the mind simply not in-coding by long term memory something that should have been recorded, isn't that correct?

A: That's a rough description of it.

Q: Essentially what happens, the person is not unconscious, he's walking around with short term memory but it just never gets in-coded because the interference of the alcohol?

A: He's walking around, he's not unconscious but he doesn't recall certain events or certain things that happen.

Q: You ask him five minutes after something happened, he would probably be able to give you an answer, just like being able to give you the phone number he looked up?

A: In some instances, in some—-

Q: But his long term memory simply is not fixed because of the chemical interference of the alcohol?

A: I think that doesn't—when you look at blackouts, we are looking at a situation, the classic situations would go, would be the severe alcoholic who intoxicated engages in actions which they cannot recall. It's not an issue whether they can recall it five minutes later but not 10 days later. It's simply breakdowns in memory due to severe alcoholism.

Q: If one is having a genuine blackout, it simply is gone, it doesn't come and go, does it?

A: The person is having a blackout, that means at a given point in time they cannot remember something that they did or said, something that occurred. Maybe some day, maybe at a later time they might remember it. It's an inconsistent kind of thing.

Q: Well, in fact, if the memory comes back, if you have a legitimate blackout which is simply, medically determinable and you then later profess to have a memory of it, normally one considers that they're confabulating, they simply created a memory out of what they thought they should remember, isn't that generally accepted?

A: Yeah. I think in this case when you saw that she had reached a stage of alcoholism such that she was experiencing blackouts, we are saying that there are gaps in her recollection because of that. We gave the example of not recalling the specific action of the stabbing and that to my knowledge that's been entirely consistent in the police reports, in the interview with me and everyone else that she does not recall that specific action.

Q: When one goes out, let's say a relatively normal sober person, one that's certainly not an alcoholic goes out, gets drunk, makes a fool out of themselves, his mind may very well as an escape mechanism fuzzy up the details of what happened the night before?

A: But that would be a very poor description of the term blackout.

Q: That's not a blackout, is it?

A: No, it is not.

Q: That's simply a defense mechanism of selective memory which we all have the ability to do?

A: Or even forgetting.

Q: In fact, in laymen's language we forget on purpose?
A: A blackout only occurs, in the sense we are talking about, it only occurs in the advanced stages of alcoholism.
Q: This blackout we are talking about here has no relationship whatsoever to what I was just describing, it's a chemical thing, your memory is simply gone, there's not a choice involved?
A: I think the experts may be a little uncomfortable in saying it's entirely chemical. It's a phenomenon that occurs in advanced stages of alcoholism which the individual has engaged in actions or has said things, done things, observed things and later has no recollection of it. And that's the term blackouts.
Q: And if in fact someone who has had a blackout starts having a revived memory, you as a psychologist or psychiatrist or anyone else would immediately think of confabulation, wouldn't they?
A: If that were the case, yes.
Q: Confabulation is quite simply that the mind creates a new memory simply out of necessity. I'm not sure of the exact terminology you use, but it creates a memory to take the place of what should be there?
A: Yes. Confabulation—-
Q: Or perhaps wants to be there?
A: That would be a fairly good description of confabulation.
Q: Unconscious by the way, isn't it?
A: Yes. Filling in a gap, so to speak, from something the person really didn't remember very well but fill in the gap.
Q: Confabulation is not the same thing as simply making it up. When you're confabulating, you're not consciously making anything up, your mind is doing it on its own?
A: Yes.

§24.11 WHEN THE WITNESS GETS AWAY

Although prior and subsequent cross-examination mitigated any damage, the following excerpt demonstrates how quickly an expert witness will exploit any opportunity to lecture and explain.

Fortunately, Crooks did not follow the feint and get into an argument or discussion with the witness but merely dismissed it by reiterating his theme that people who suffer battered wife syndrome are still capable of legally accountable murder.

Q: Doctor, if the battered wife syndrome is to have any meaning at all, it has to have some boundaries, does it not?
A: Yes, it has boundaries.
Q: And part of those boundaries by the classic definitions that have been made by Doctor Walker and basically the people that worked on it thereafter has always been a submissive, more or less passive person who is basically dominated, afraid to react, afraid to break the bonds that are keeping her tied up and an aggressive, assaultive behavior is simply not consistent with that, is it?
A: The activity that I have pointed out is that Miss White Tail fits. When we look at any syndrome, whether it's a battered wife syndrome or a posttraumatic stress disorder syndrome or depression syndrome, no matter what syndrome it is, no two people in any syndrome will have every single characteristic of the syndrome. When we look at the diagnostic and statistical manual of the disorders, typical in the manual that the man if he's five of the nine to meet the criteria, sometimes it will be four of these 12. So to one element that's different for her, one or two elements that are not included does not mean that she doesn't fit the syndrome. For example, she does not need to be entirely passive or submissive, even though a majority of women who are in the battered wife syndrome are passive and submissive. She does not have to have every signal characteristic of that syndrome to represent a classic case of that syndrome. She was a person who fits that syndrome extremely well to an extreme degree but she is not a person who is entirely passive, and in her case the complicating factor which we can't ignore is that she was a severe alcoholic in advanced stages of alcoholism and when she is extremely intoxicated, when she was extremely intoxicated, she went through mental changes in the advanced stages of her alcoholism changes, she went through mental changes such that she did become aggressive at times. Obviously she became aggressive on the 4th and 5th of September. And so the fact that one or two elements isn't characteristic of a given individual does not mean they don't fit the syndrome.

Q: What you're saying, then, Doctor, is quite simply that people that have the battered wife syndrome are fully capable of getting mad and stabbing somebody just like you or I or anybody else is, isn't that true?

A: People with that syndrome, if we parcel out the severe alcoholism fact, we could parcel that out, of course, we can't do it in this case, but speaking in general of the syndrome rather than speaking of a person in particular, most people that have that syndrome are passive and submissive and keep taking beatings and don't do anything effective about it. In her case, partly because of the severe alcoholism and the paranoia, the hallucinatory experiences and so on that go with that, there is no question that she eventually regressed and so there is no question about that, but that doesn't at all mean that she is not a case of battered wife syndrome. Be a gross misinterpretation to pick out an element or two and say she didn't fit the syndrome.

§24.12 OVERVIEW

Right from the outset, Mr. Crooks telegraphed to the witness that he was fully prepared. He clearly knew his subject and understood it and made sure the jury understood it even if they had no prior background. His preparation was evident at the outset. Mr. Crooks demonstrated a familiarity with the basic literature from which the concept emanated and, while others may have expanded upon it, the guiding principles basically came down to that seminal work.

There followed a series of questions which, in fact, explained the syndrome in easy understandable terms making sure that the jury had a grasp of what was a complex psychological matter.

Throughout the examination at each step of the way when a complex concept was advanced, Mr. Crooks broke it down to laymen's terms so that at no time was the jury left out of a full appreciation of the subject matter. A juror in that case who had never heard of "battered wife syndrome" or, having heard of it, was unfamiliar with the details, was thoroughly elucidated as the questions unfolded. The jury was given an understanding into which they could digest the opinions offered.

The tone and flow was conversational as if the attorney was simply discussing the subject with the witness for the purposes of arriving at a full understanding. Mr. Crooks was able to make his points without appearing to attack the witness and yet pointed out several weaknesses in the expert's opinion which ultimately eroded his opinion.

The examination evidences the witness being set up. The question of tying the subject matter to the work of Lenore Walker had the effect of creating a parameter from which the witness would have difficulty straying. The witness knows that any straying from the principles in that book would lead to a confrontation with the acknowledged authority on the subject.

This was also the beginning of the attorney exercising control of the witness, having now demonstrated that there had been significant preparation, an understanding of the subject matter and the establishment of an anchor that would hold the witness within manageable bounds.

A significant number of questions ended with the further controlling and narrowing limitation upon the witness' answer such as, "is that correct," "isn't that correct," "are there not," "is it not," "do they," "is it," or "did you" and a number of repetitions of the same technique. The use of the technique of the specific question at the end limits the ability of the witness to roam as evidenced by how often the witness answers "yes" or "no." Even when the specific answer is not limited to yes or no, the witness is almost obliged to keep the answer short and has extreme difficulty in straying. The witness either did or didn't, the proposition contained in the question was either correct or incorrect and something either is or isn't. Time after time, the witnesses are forced to answer within the extremely narrow sphere that they have been permitted by the question.

At the outset of the examination, there is also built in a skirmish which moves the witness away from certainty. Having lost the engagement, the witness becomes much more circumspect and defensive with his choice of words. It also conditions the witness not to tangle with the attorney.

Crooks continually applied common sense while the witness tried to resist. Common sense prevailed, and the witness was forced to acknowledge that he did not know or that the original work had not included that study. When that was followed by the admission that the witness had to wait and see if there was a study that came up with the results that common sense seemed to suggest, the expert was compromised by attempting to resist the questioner. The witness lost credibility because he needed to study matter that seemed to be answerable by common sense. The witness was put on the defensive.

Shortly after the examinations commenced, the emergence of a theme became apparent. Possibly, the better description is variation upon a theme. The first strain of the theme was to indicate that the subject is not so well defined that all of the votes were in or that a clear consensus existed.

Further questioning went into the specific symptoms, whereupon the witnesses were forced to acknowledge that not every person has all of the symptoms. Thus, at one point in the examinations the second witness was forced to acknowledge:

> Q: When we look at any syndrome, whether or not its a battered wife syndrome or a post-traumatic stress disorder syndrome or depression syndrome, no matter what syndrome it is, no two people in any syndrome will have every single characteristic of the syndrome. When we look at the diagnostics and statistical manual of the disorders, typical in the manual that demand at least five of the nine to meet the criteria, sometimes at least four of these twelve.

Every juror knows that headaches and nausea may be a symptom of the most dire disease, but, equally if not more likely, of the flu or a common cold or just a bad day. It may even be something a person ate the night before. It is the rare person who does not read all of the symptoms of any disease without believing he has some of them. However, what the witness was, in fact acknowledging was that, by selecting some of the symptoms while others were absent, destroyed the absolute conclusion that this defendant suffered from this particular syndrome.

The follow-up of the theme continued when the question was asked:

> Q: My question to use is perhaps again somewhat obvious, but in situations where basically the battering has ceased, the husband is no longer battering the wife, its certainly not your contention or the contention of the people you work with that she simply

has a free ticket to kill the man at some time of her choosing at random in the future, is it?

The witness tries to dodge the obvious, but the cross-examiner controls the questioning and takes it right back to the critical essence of the previous question:

Q: My question comes back to the question I asked earlier though. You're not contending, even though those feelings may be there, you certainly aren't contending that psychologically she has a free ticket to simply kill him at some random occasion in the future, are you?
A: No.

Similarly, with the second doctor the question was put:

Q: The fact that a woman fits the battered wife syndrome does not mean that she is insane or crazy or mentally ill, its simply a syndrome which describes a phenomenon which essentially helps explain why she isn't leaving a marriage which anyone else in their right mind would have left, isn't that about the size of it?
A: I don't think that's a very adequate explanation.
Q: No. I recognize its simplistic. But it is not that she is crazy, is it?
A: No, it's not.
Q: Because a woman is a victim of the battered wife syndrome, she still has the ability to act with volition, does she not?
A: Yes. At least to a degree.

Needless to say, those answers strike at the heart of the defense to homicide.

The complex psychological phenomenon, by breaking it into details and measuring it against the legal requirements for a valid defense demonstrates the absence of a defense. The existence of some symptoms does not necessarily amount to battered wife syndrome and, even if such syndrome were present, it may not be so compelling or overpowering that the person cannot control his actions. Thus, the defense under any circumstances is not available given the testimony of this particular case.

The questioning persistently highlighted the steps that were not taken and that an expert's opinion is only as good as the information with which he is provided. The questions included:

Q: Counsel had asked you whether or not you had changed your opinion after the cross-examination or something to that effect. I'd just like to reiterate, your opinion, if I heard you correctly, was based upon an hour and a half conversation with Ms. White Tail, is it not?
A: No. It's based on a number of years of experience and what I know about it and viewing Ms. White Tail.
Q: I assumed your expertise and your experience. That essentially the fact is that you had to make an informed judgment in an hour and a half interview with Ms. White Tail, is that correct?
A: The facts are what you're talking about.
Q: Yes.
A: Yes. Hour and a half I interviewed with Ms. White Tail.
Q: You made no particular attempt to follow this trial or be informed by counsel as to what evidence may or may not have come out at trial?
A: No.
Q: You have made no particular attempts or no attempt at all to independently verify anything that Ms. White Tail has told you about her happened in the past, have you?
A: No. That's not part of our rule.

Follow-up questions brought out the fact that, if, in fact, Ms. White Tail had not necessarily told the truth in that short interview, the opinion that was formed may not be accurate.

After the witness was forced to acknowledge that a number of questions had not been asked or that alleged beatings of the defendant might have occurred at the hands of persons other than the deceased and there was no independent effort made to verify whatever information was provided, there was no part of the direct testimony that essentially survived intact.

Even toward the conclusion of the examination after all the significant points had been made, Mr. Crooks still made sure that the jury understood the meaning of every word used and the concept which it incorporated. Thus, when the discussion of "confabulation" or "black out'' occurred, there was exploration by questioning that clearly defined those concepts and negated the possibility that anything about those concepts would play a significant part in establishing a defense to the charge of homicide.

The defendant was convicted.

The Emperor's New Clothes 25

§25.1 CONDE AND SANTANGELO

Given the volume of litigation and the overload on the courts in the administration of justice, the alleged failsafe to all of the inefficiencies and mistakes liable to occur as a result has been placed upon cross-examination. If the prosecution fails to adequately investigate the circumstances involved in an alleged crime, it will all be straightened out during cross-examination. If a witness lies, that, too, will be cured during cross-examination. Unfortunately, defense counsel rarely have the resources or opportunities to completely fulfill this function and must, therefore, rely on instinct and knowledge of human nature to make full use of any discovery which they are accorded in criminal prosecutions or any cooperation they can secure from persons who may have knowledge of the events. It is an uphill and often exacting task; but, with the proper approach and attentiveness to such details as are provided, the task can be accomplished. The result may well be that the emperor, rather than being regally dressed for his coronation is, in reality, evident to the simplistic mind of a child, "naked."

On February 9, 1993, the United States Attorney for the Southern District of New York issued the following press release:

> Roland Conde and Oscar Santangelo, two New York real estate developers, and Tiffany General Holding Corp., Rosnan Realty Corp. Melnic Realty Corp., Tiffany General Realty Properties,

Inc. and Consant Realty, Ltd., real estate holding corporations controlled by Conde and Santangelo, were indicted today by a Manhattan federal grand jury in connection with a fraud and conspiracy scheme involving multi-million dollar mortgage refinancings guaranteed by the Federal Home Loan Mortgage Corporation ("Freddie Mac"). According to the Indictment, the scheme involved false and fraudulent statements by Conde and Santangelo to Freddie Mac in order to obtain and maintain approximately $12.4 million in mortgage funds. As a result of the false statements, the corporate defendants received approximately $7 million in cash proceeds from the refinancing by Freddie Mac of six apartment buildings in the Bronx. Two of the buildings foreclosed, resulting in an approximately $2.8 million loss to Freddie Mac.

The United States Attorney for the Southern District of New York stated that the Indictment charges that Freddie Mac based its determination of how much mortgage money it would provide to borrowers on, in part, the rental income derived from the properties. The income information assists Freddie Mac in determining the value of the properties and assures Freddie Mac that the borrower is able to repay the mortgage. The Indictment charges that from January 1986 up to and including March 1991, the defendants falsely represented and fraudulently inflated the rental income generated by the six Bronx apartment buildings—1553-55 and 1558 Bryant Avenue, 1765-67 Davidson Avenue, 240 East 175th Street, 735 Walton Avenue, 721 Walton Avenue and 643-47 Cauldwell Avenue—in order to increase the mortgage amounts disbursed to the defendant corporations.

The Indictment charges that the defendants conspired to violate and in fact violated the mail and wire fraud statutes by mailing and telecopying false rent rolls and income and expense statements for the six buildings to Globe Mortgage Corp. ("Globe"), a New Jersey based mortgage broker acting on behalf of Freddie Mac. Globe passed the information on to Freddie Mac, which then approved refinancing mortgages for each building. The false rental information was submitted both

> when the defendants applied for the Freddie Mac mortgages and when annual income updates were required by Freddie Mac.
>
> The Indictment charges that the information provided by the defendants fraudulently inflated the total annual rental income generated by the buildings from a low of 15% to a high of 39%. The average rate of inflation for individual units within the six buildings ranged from 29% to 102%.
>
> * * *
>
> If convicted of the charges, Conde and Santangelo each face a maximum of forty years imprisonment and a $2 million fine. Tiffany General Holding Corp., the owner of 721 and 735 Walton Avenue, Melnic Realty Corp., the owner of 643-47 Cauldwell Avenue, and Tiffany General Realty Properties, Inc., the owner of 240 East 175th Street, each face a $250,000 fine. Rosnan Realty Corp., the owner of 1553-55 and 1558 Bryant Avenue, faces a $500,000 fine. Consant Realty, Ltd., the owner of 1765-67 Davidson Avenue, faces a $750,000 fine.
>
> In announcing the Indictment, the United States Attorney praised the excellent investigative teamwork in this case of the United States General Accounting Office and the United States Postal Inspection Service.

The essence of the Government's case was that the two men who had acquired a number of buildings in the South Bronx had fraudulently inflated rent rolls in order to increase the value of the buildings against which Freddie Mac would ultimately lend money in the form of mortgages secured by the property. The vehicle by which Freddie Mac participated in this area of financing was through organizations known as seller/servicers, which were mortgage banks. Mortgage banks would, in the first instance, grant a mortgage and provide the funds to the borrower. They would take the mortgage in their own name and record it as such, identifying themselves as the secured party. When the transaction was complete, the mortgage bank would then assign the mortgage that it had obtained and all of the security to Freddie Mac who would then reimburse the mortgage bank. Freddie Mac never dealt with the borrower and regarded the mortgage bank exclusively as its client.

Notwithstanding the fact that the borrowers never made any representations directly to Freddie Mac and that there was an intervening significant legal transaction in the middle, it was the government's theory of prosecution that the borrowers had defrauded Freddie Mac by falsely representing the rent rolls for the purpose of inflating the value of the buildings. It was then the policy of Freddie Mac, in reimbursing the mortgage bank, that it would advance 85% of the value of the building. Thus, the government reasoned that, if the value of the building was falsely inflated, the amount of money that would ultimately be advanced by Freddie Mac would be substantially increased.

The transactions took place during the late 1980's when the value of real estate was increasing by geometric margins each year and the lending processes, not only by Freddie Mac but by other real estate lending institutions, functioned in the belief that if the loan to be made was restricted to 85% of the value of the building the lending agency would be protected by escalating values. The entire multi-family loan program of Freddie Mac was premised upon non-recourse loans in which the borrower had no personal liability. The safety was in the escalating values.

With the end of the 1980's came the bursting of the bubble and values declined. When the values declined, Freddie Mac, like all other lending agencies with substantial real estate portfolios, found that it had mortgages in those portfolios in which the value of the property often fell below the amount of the mortgage loan. The fact that the loans were still performing and all payments were made did not play a significant role in alleviating the panic to which Freddie Mac capitulated.

In or about 1990, the General Accounting Office conducted an audit and investigation of Freddie Mac as a result of the savings and loan failures attributable to declines in the value of real estate portfolios and declining rental income leading to defaults. It issued a report repeatedly criticizing Freddie Mac for gross inefficiency, failure to establish any adequate controls, failure to issue clear guidelines to seller/servicers and the exposure to risk faced by Freddie Mac as a result of its own waste and inefficiency. Following the issuance of such report Freddie Mac, in an effort to extricate itself from this criticism and avoid being the next target of savings and loan hysteria, began to point a finger at all other parties to the transactions rather than accepting the responsibility for its own practices which were, in fact, the custom during the late 1980's.

In the course of the fingerpointing, Freddie Mac terminated and accused a number of seller/servicers for failing to verify the income that a borrower reported from which a determination was to be made as to whether or not the mortgage payments could be met. When it became apparent that pursuit against the seller/servicers might be fruitless, in view of the close working relationship with Freddie Mac, the seller/servicers and Freddie Mac then turned their attention to the borrowers. The instant case was one of the initial attempts to place the entire blame upon borrowers to the virtual exclusion of any fault on the part of Freddie Mac or the mortgage bank.

In pursuing this approach, Freddie Mac initiated a criminal complaint against Oscar Santangelo and Roland Conde, the least likely borrowers against whom there should have been any legal proceedings. Santangelo and Conde had become legendary in the South Bronx in that they had taken drug infested, violence riddled buildings which were often shells and restored them to excellence, inhabited by families who took pride in their surroundings even though many were on public assistance and had been referred by shelters for the homeless. Each building in turn became an oasis in an otherwise residential wasteland about which a great deal had been written and for which the men had been honored. As the record showed, Freddie Mac and Congress made repeated tours of these buildings and took great pride in repeatedly proclaiming publicly that the results that Conde and Santangelo had achieved were a vivid demonstration of what could be done by the partnership of government financing and dedicated entrepreneurs who were willing to risk their lives in order to bring about this miracle. For Freddie Mac and the bureaucrats, being seen in the company of Conde and Santangelo was a photo opportunity to use in wooing constituents living in marginal urban areas.

The trial of Conde and Santangelo commenced on July 6, 1993. I and Peter Schlam mounted the defense for the defendants whom we both believed were fine men who had been falsely accused.

The government's theory of prosecution, and virtually the only evidence that it was able to offer in support of the theory, were a series of "rent rolls" which had been submitted at or about the time of the application for the loans. The rent rolls on their face appeared to show virtually full vacancy and a monthly rent assigned to each apartment. The government sought to establish its case through an agent of the General Accounting Office, William Hamel, whose investigation consisted of going to the Department of Housing and Community Renewal and reviewing the registered rents (DHCR) and finding a discrepancy in the numbers appearing on the rent roll submitted to Freddie Mac and the amount of rents which were registered for each of the apartments in the buildings, numbering five, which were the subject of the prosecution.

In finding the paper discrepancy, Agent Hamel did not recognize at the time that the previous owners of these derelict properties had not filed registrations and that the registrations appearing at the city agency were reconstructions which had been subsequently filed by Conde and Santangelo after they took possession of the buildings. Nevertheless, in making the comparison between the two documents, the purported rent roll and the registered rent, and finding that the purported rent roll appeared higher than the registered rents, the ground work was established for contending that Conde and Santangelo had falsely inflated the rent rolls submitted to Freddie Mac for the purpose of obtaining a larger sum of money on the forthcoming mortgages.

Agent Hamel ignored or overlooked the fact that, in a significant number of the cases, the rent for an apartment reported to Freddie Mac was lower than appeared as the registered rent with the DHCR and the amount of mortgage money that could have been obtained was significantly more than Conde and Santangelo requested.

Agent Hamel, who was virtually the only government witness in the grand jury, testified to his findings and, without once enumerating to the contrary, stated that he checked the rent rolls submitted to Freddie Mac against the registered rents and the rent rolls submitted to Freddie Mac were higher.

The position taken by Conde and Santangelo at the trial as well as from the inception of the investigation was that the rent rolls submitted at or about the time of the loan applications were projections. In many of the cases, the buildings were basically gut rehabilitations and everyone associated with the project from Freddie Mac to the mortgage bank to the touring political figures, saw a predominantly vacant building inhabited primarily by drug operations and squatters. In some cases, the previous owner of the building was the City of New York who, under the crisis circumstances of its ownership, maintained few records and certainly did not feel obliged to file annual rent registrations on these properties.

Based upon the anticipated rehabilitation efforts, Conde and Santangelo contended that the rent rolls that they properly submitted with the loan application were, as they were advised and understood, to be a projection of the rent roll as of the time they completed the rehabilitation. Under those circumstances, the apartments could be rented for their market value which was confirmed by a series of appraisals made by themselves, by the mortgage bank and Freddie Mac reviews. In each case, their projected rent roll was lower than the projected rent roll of the mortgage bank and the Freddie Mac forecast of the anticipated rents.

The rent rolls that had been submitted contained a certification by both gentlemen which essentially stated that the rent rolls were true and correct statements to the best of their knowledge. No one in the government questioned what the meaning, use and custom was with regard to the word "statement." It was the defendants' position that the word "statement" as it was used and understood by all concerned meant a true and accurate statement of what they anticipated the rent roll would be at the time that they completed the rehabilitation.

In fact, they completed each rehabilitation. Each of their efforts was applauded; and, they were honored for providing decent, affordable housing where none had existed before. In every case, the actual operating rent roll was higher than their earlier conservative projection.

§25.2 FREDDIE MAC

The case presented by the government was simplistic and, as a result, dangerous. It appeared open and shut that the defendants had reported higher rents to Freddie Mac than they had reported elsewhere. As a result of such inflation, it was charged that they had received millions of dollars of mortgages to which they were not entitled by the current actual rent rolls.

The government fought to limit the issues to this narrow view. The defense was determined to expand the issues and go behind the documents to give true meaning to the certifications. The object was to demonstrate that the entire prosecution approach was nothing more than revisionist ''fly specking'' of documents five years after the fact in order to cover itself and have an available scapegoat in order to avoid further criticism of Freddie Mac.

The danger lay in the simplicity of the government's approach and could not be answered by complicated mathematical computations. Such an approach would appear to be cute and sharp practice looking for loopholes.

It was further necessary that the defense be developed through the cross-examination of the government witnesses so that the defendants, should they choose to testify, not appear to be isolated in contesting what appeared to be plain English. The techniques used on cross-examination were the simple methods repeatedly described throughout this volume.

The first witness for the government was Margaret Schmidt who testified to the Freddie Mac system described above and acknowledged that, in fact, she had personally inspected two of the properties and had certified that based upon her inspection and the appraisal submitted by the mortgage bank the rent rolls were adequate representations of the rent and vacancy levels of the building. She quickly ignored that fact and went on to say that her own inspections and the inspections and appraisals of the mortgage bank notwithstanding, total reliance was upon the statements made by the borrowers with regard to the rent rolls which they had presented to the mortgage bank.

On cross-examination, she acknowledged that she had visited the properties and had seen vacancies where rent had appeared on the rent rolls submitted to the mortgage banks but that she was easily satisfied as to that discrepancy by asking the borrowers to explain that apparent discrepancy. She testified that, when the borrowers said that they anticipated finishing the renovation of those apartments and anticipated having them rented at the number appearing on the rent roll, she was satisfied and took no action. It did not occur to Ms. Schmidt that this was precisely what the defendants were contending with regard to the figures that appeared with respect to some of the apartments on the rent rolls.

As cross-examination of Ms. Schmidt went on, she became defensive and contentious. Having been trapped once, she would not agree to anything and would attempt to dispute each point or become evasively non-responsive. It reached the point that, in discussing a particular mortgage, in an attempt to show that she had an opportunity to discover any discrepancy in the defendants' rent rolls, or if projections were improper, she was asked:

> Q: Will you agree with me that $2 million is a significant amount of money?
> A: How are you using the word significant?

With that single answer, Ms. Schmidt thoroughly discredited her earlier testimony. It was clear that she was disagreeing for the sake of disagreeing and that the rest of her testimony was not straightforward but rather the result of a determination to slant her testimony.

Further, she had questioned the plain meaning of a word that was understood by every member of the jury in the context in which it was used. The suggestion from a Freddie Mac witness that plain words are not always clear but have to be considered as possibly having a variable meaning was not lost on the jury in terms of the defense's position.

The question to Ms. Schmidt was instinctive using a common technique at the right time. It is often productive when an attorney recognizes that a witness is fighting and is reflexively disagreeing with any question about which there can be no disagreement, to ask an obvious question. Should the witness, as here, disagree, the result is a gift.

In this case, had the witness agreed to the obvious, nothing would have been lost and it would have established the predicate for a series of questions that hopefully would have led to the indication that she had thoroughly inspected the matter, recognized the significance of the amount of money involved, learned that the rent rolls were, in fact, a projection and did nothing because that was the custom and understanding at the time in buildings of this type.

§25.3 THE MORTGAGE BANK

Ms. Schmidt was followed by Judith Hillas, the first Vice President of the Globe Mortgage Bank who had in fact advanced the monies to the borrowers on each of the buildings at issue.

The purpose on cross-examination of Ms. Hillas was to demonstrate that everybody knew that the documents submitted by the borrowers at the time that they submitted such documents had to be projections and were known to be such. In fact, cross-examination sought to demonstrate that the projections were not those of the borrowers at all but, rather, the projections of the mortgage bank who were sophisticated professionals and who had their own staff and independent appraisers who established the projected rent roll even before the borrowers put in a loan application.

The cross-examination proceeded by establishing that the mortgage bank was not fair with persons with which it had extensive dealings for many years and from which it had made a great deal of money in commissions and servicing fees:

Q: Good morning, Ms. Hillas. Have we ever met before, Ms. Hillas?
A: No, we have not.
Q: Have we ever spoken before?
A: Not that I am aware of.
Q: In fact, did there come a time when I asked if I could speak to you?
A: Yes.
Q: And you refused?
A: No. I said I would contact Globe's attorney and have him call you.
Q: And subsequent to that time, you have never spoken to me, that is correct?
A: That is correct.

Note that the witness was not given the chance to explain what took place in the gap between the referring me to her attorney and her failure to speak to me afterward.

§25.4 THE GENESIS OF THE "FRAUDULENT" RENT ROLL

Q: Let me show you what's been marked defendants' Exhibit AB for identification. Do you recognize the handwriting on that document?

A: I believe it's Lisa's, but I couldn't be positive.
Q: That is Lisa Dauphine, the person that works for you?
A: Worked for us.
Q: In fact that was in the files of Globe?
A: That is correct.
Q: Ms. Hillas, is this document in Lisa Dauphine's handwriting not an apartment by apartment with the rents listed?
A: Yes, it is.
Q: And does it not contain in Lisa Dauphine's handwriting a column called surcharge?
A: Yes.
Q: Would you tell us what that is?
A: A surcharge as I understand it is if a rent is below a certain amount, under $250 or $300, I'm not sure of the amount, at the time of lease renewal this $15 surcharge can be added.
Q: So that isn't something that existed, that is something that Ms. Dauphine said could be added later, correct?
A: Correct. This is what goes to the appraiser when we asked that he correct the economic rents.
Q: Surcharge is something different than 6 or 9 percent increase, isn't it?
A: Yes, it is.
Q: So here we have, just to be clear, in Ms. Dauphine's handwriting a surcharge based upon something that might occur later or could have occurred later, right?
A: It is our understanding it will occur.
Q: But it hasn't happened yet?
A: No, it hasn't.
Q: Didn't Ms. Dauphine compute that surcharge number in the final number she put down on the apartment rent, apartment by apartment?
A: Yes, she did.
Q: Is it a fact, Ms. Hillas, after adding that surcharge that is going to come later apartment by apartment, isn't that included in the total of Five Hundred Fifty-Four Thousand Eight Hundred and Eighty Nine ($554,889) Dollars?
A: Yes, it is.

* * *

Q: My question, Ms. Hillas, is specifically, isn't it a fact that the highest rent coming on a rent roll from Mr. Conde and Mr. Santangelo was 525,000?
A: Without having it in front of me, I would have to accept that you are telling me what's on there.
THE COURT: There is no dispute about that, isn't there?
MR. GOLDMAN: The January 27, 1987 rent roll, does it not say $525,000 on it
MR. HALPERN: I believe it's 525,000.
MR. GOLDMAN: 525,540.272 with respect to 175th Street. 300 A 2 was the specific exhibit.
Q: Specifically, right?
A: That's right.
Q: That was approximately 29,000 or $30,000 lower than 554,000, is it not?
A: That's correct.

* * *

Q: Isn't it a fact, Ms. Hillas, that with regard to this reclamation area, everybody knew you could only function with projections?
A: No, sir.
Q: Well, let's take 175th Street, for example. What was the date that these gentlemen acquired that building?
A: 11-12-86.
Q: Do you know when was the first day they actually got the keys to that building?
A: No, sir.
Q: Can we assume November 12th or some time subsequent?
A: That's what I would assume.
Q: Okay. And when did they submit that rent roll?
A: Which one?
Q: The one for 240 East 175th Street. Let me show you, to refresh your recollection. What is the date on it?
A: This thing right here? December 1st, 1986.
Q: That's some 18 days after they might have gotten the keys to that building; is that correct?

A: That's correct.
Q: Is it your testimony that anybody in this world wouldn't know that any rent roll 18 days later had to be a projection?
A: No, sir.
Q: Who owned that building before these gentlemen acquired it?
A: I don't know.
Q: What was the state of that building before these gentlemen acquired it?
A: I don't know.
Q: For all you know, it was a burned out shell, for all you know?
A: For all I know.
Q: Right? But you do know it was only 18 days prior that that building was acquired, correct?
A: Yes.
Q: And you are telling this jury that 18 days later when it might have been a burnt out shell, nobody raised a question as to whether a rent roll showing full occupancy was a projection, is that your statement?
A: Yes, sir.

* * *

Q: And I think you were asked that at the time of this meeting, it is stated on behalf of Globe that Globe would then contract with and pay an independent appraiser to perform a Freddie Mac appraisal for the building, do you recall that statement being made in that meeting?
A: Yes.
Q: So now you have indicated Globe interviews tenants, Globe sends out an independent appraiser—right?
A: Right.
Q: —Globe also makes several inspections before a loan is closed?
A: One or two. I don't think several.
Q: In addition to that, Globe makes one or two inspections of the property before the loan is closed, correct?
A: Correct.
Q: Freddie Mac makes inspections?
A: Yes, they do.

Q: How many buildings did these gentlemen do with Freddie Mac loans?
A: I think there were 7, but I'm not sure.
Q: Somewhere between 7 and 10, but more than 7 at least, okay. So that on 7 occasions they submitted rent rolls?
A: Yes.
Q: And loan applications?
A: Yes.
Q: And on 7 occasions Globe interviewed tenants?
A: Yes.

* * *

Q: Ms. Hillas, I asked you, there are at least 7 buildings, each one has a rent roll, each one has a number of inspections by Globe, each one has tenant interviews, each one has appraisals, each one has an additional inspection by Freddie Mac and on all those 7 plus occasions, nobody picked up that these gentlemen were using projections in their rent rolls.
A: I don't know what you mean by projections.
Q: Did anybody marching across the situation say wait a second, you fellows have projections instead of having actual rents in your records, did that ever happen?
A: No.
Q: From all these people who visited the property inspecting and checking the tenants, right?
A: That is correct.

After generally setting up the predicate points with the witness, she was questioned with regard to a specific example to further spell out the point attempted to be made on cross-examination:

MR. GOLDMAN: May we have this marked for identification (defendants' Exhibit AG marked for identification).
Q: Let me show you what's been marked AG for identification. Is it not the multifamily loan application on Bryant Avenue?
A: Yes, it appears to be.
Q: What is the date on that document?
A: There is something attached to it that isn't part of the application a letter of certification—the date on this is 6/20/88.

Q: And that is the date on which Mr. Conde and Mr. Santangelo signed this document, is that correct?
A: That is correct.
Q: And in signing this document they are signing a certification that says they understand about a crime punishable if they knowingly make any false statement, isn't that true?
A: That is correct.
Q: On the first page of the document it says gross rental income from apartments; does it not?
A: The way you hold it, it's very difficult for me to see.
Q: I apologize. Gross rental from apartments?
A: Yes.

* * *

Q: Ms. Hillas, this is the multifamily loan application in this particular case?
A: Yes, it is.
Q: Where I point my finger, the form says gross rental income from apartments. And it says $449,028, do I read that correctly?
A: Yes, you do.
Q: Right above that number, are there 2 boxes to be checked?
A: Yes, there are.
Q: And 2 boxes, do I correctly read the first box is annualized estimate based on present levels of income and expenses?
A: Yes, you do.
Q: The next box is pro forma statements, do I read that correctly?
A: Yes.
Q: Which box is checked?
A: Pro forma statement.
Q: The date is June 20, 1988, just so I read it correctly?
A: That's correct.
MR. GOLDMAN: May we have this document marked for identification, please (defendants' Exhibit AH marked for identification).

* * *

Q: Ms. Hillas, I direct your attention to the last page of the document. Does a signature appear there?
A: Yes.
Q: Whose signature?
A: My signature.
Q: What is the date of this document?
A: June 3, 1988.
Q: June 3, 1988, some 17 days before June 20, is that correct?
A: That is correct.
Q: On this document, Ms. Hillas; does it have an entry for operating statement?
A: Yes, it does.
Q: The number is 439,594?
A: Yes, it is.
Q: And this is 2 weeks before the defendants signed the previous sheet, correct?
A: If that is the final sheet, it would be different. As we have stated before, there were around three or four prior to it.
Q: This particular sheet which you have identified as a document in the possession of Freddie Mac, which they get from you—
A: Yes.
Q: —Dated June 3, 1988, contains an operating rental income number of $42,494, is that correct?
A: That is correct.
Q: And the date on this sheet is 2 weeks earlier than the document signed by these gentlemen as a certified loan application isn't that true?
A: That is true.
Q: In fact, on this document signed 2 weeks earlier, is there not a column in addition that says seller's forecast?
A: Yes, there is.
Q: That number is it 449,028?
A: That is correct.
Q: That number is the number that appears on the application 2 weeks later, is that the correct number?
A: That is correct.
Q: Thank you. Let me show you again what's been marked defendants Exhibit AF, now in evidence, Ms. Hillas. That is the apartment analysis and rental overview?

A: Yes, it is.
Q: And signed by you?
A: Yes, it is.
Q: With the certification signed by you that we read before?
A: That is correct.
Q: What's the date on that?
A: June 6, 1988.
Q: That is 14 days before June 20, the date these gentlemen signed the application, right?
A: That is correct.
Q: And 2 weeks earlier you certify to the adequacy and vacancy levels of the rent roll?
A: That is correct.

* * *

BY MR. SCHLAM
Q: Would you take a look at Exhibit X, please, Ms. Hillas. This is in connection with the property known as 240 East 175th Street?
A: Yes, they are.
Q: Were these submitted in connection with the application for the loan on this property?
A: Were all of them submitted?
Q: Were all of them submitted?
A: No. I would assume the final one was submitted.
Q: Isn't it the fact, just to move this along, that the interest rate was going down during this period of time and that the amount of the loan changed, which required new applications, do you recall that?
A: That would make sense.
Q: I offer Exhibit X into evidence (defendants' Exhibit X was received in evidence). Is it your testimony again that this document, the application which is dated November 28, 1986, was filled out as of the time that it's dated?
A: Yes.
Q: There is a number which appears on that document, which shows gross rental income from apartments, 570,190, is that correct?

A: That is correct.
Q: That is the number that's designed to indicate what the gross rental income from apartments is on that property, am I correct?
A: Yes, it is.
Q: Where did that number come from?
A: It normally comes from the appraisal.
Q: Normally comes from the appraisal. But the appraisal hadn't yet been done, am I correct?
A: As I stated previously, the borrower provides these numbers to the appraiser. He is aware of what that number is.
Q: But isn't it a fact that this document, Exhibit X, is submitted to Globe before the appraisal is even begun?
A: Roland and Oscar started working with the appraiser prior to these loan documents being filled out.
Q: The appraisal is dated December fifth, am I correct?
A: That is correct.
Q: You are saying that Roland and Oscar somehow got together with the appraiser and came up with numbers that were going to come down—were going to be written down on the multifamily loan application?
A: That is not what I said. It took approximately 6 to 8 weeks to get an appraisal. All of this had to be done months in advance.
Q: In other words, you are saying then that there are certain items on this application form as well that were blank when they were submitted and were later filled in after the appraisal had been completed? Is that your testimony?
A: No, I don't know that to be a fact.
Q: And you don't know it not to be a fact?
A: No, I don't know it not to be a fact. But I know they had those numbers at the time of submission.
Q: Where would the multifamily loan application be after it was submitted? Would it be in Globe's offices?
A: Yes, it would.
Q: If there were blanks on this document that had to be filled in, who would fill them in?
A: We would.
Q: We, being Globe?
A: Yes, that is correct.

Q: Isn't it true that for 240 East 175th Street Mr. Conde and Mr. Santangelo submitted a rent roll dated December first, 1986?
A: I assume they did.
Q: Would you care to look at this document to eliminate any doubt you might have.
A: It's dated December first, 1986.
Q: And it's signed by both of them, am I correct?
A: You are correct.
Q: Does it—just a second—doesn't it say that the rent total yearly is 515,700.17?
A: Yes, it does.
Q: According to you that was the gross rental income that they were saying this building was actually generating in or about the beginning of December of 1986?
A: Yes.
Q: This form was later submitted to Globe, was it not?
A: Yes.
Q: And it was ultimately determined that the gross rental income from apartments was not going to be 515,700, but rather 570,190, am I correct?
A: You are correct.
Q: Is it your understanding that somebody at Globe filled that number in on the application form?
A: No, that is not my understanding.
Q: Did you ever ask anybody why it was, Mr. Conde or Mr. Santangelo, why it was that the number next to gross rental income on a document that is dated 11/29/86 wasn't the number that he had certified on a rent roll that was dated 3 days later and which was approximately 55,000 less than the number that appears on this loan application form?
A: I would have to see the appraisal to see the numbers (pause).
Q: Are those the numbers?
A: They appear to be.

* * *

Q: Does the rent roll indicate a super's apartment?
A: I don't know.

Q: Isn't it a fact that the rent roll does not indicate a superintendent's apartment, Ms. Hillas?
A: I don't know. I haven't looked at it.
Q: Is it also a fact that in the 240 East 175th Street property, there happens to be another letter from Mr. Axelrod, is that correct?
A: That is correct.
Q: And this is after you claim that you allegedly told Mr. Conde and Mr. Santangelo that they were not to use any information or calculations based on the MCI [major capital improvements], because Freddie Mac had told you that they weren't going to be going along with that, after Walton, am I correct?
A: Correct.
Q: Did you notice when you saw this appraisal, which is marked Exhibit W, that the appraiser had enclosed a letter from David Axelrod regarding 240 East 175th dated December 4, 1986?
A: I don't recall whether I did or didn't.
Q: Did you call up the appraiser after you receive this appraisal and ask him how it was that he included a letter from David Axelrod when it was now Freddie Mac and Globe policy not to have any calculations based upon the MCI increases?
A: As long as the appraiser didn't include them, I don't know why it would be a problem.
Q: What did you understand the purpose of this Axelrod letter to be in the appraisal?
A: To show that he had done the improvements and he expected to gain further income on the property.
Q: Isn't it a fact, Ms. Hillas, that the appraisal for 175th Street included a component based on the MCI increase?
A: Not that I am aware of.
Q: I am looking now at the rent roll submitted by Mr. Conde and Mr. Santangelo December 1st, 1986, correct?
A: Yes.
Q: The monthly total according to this document is $42,975.06, am I correct?
A: Yes.
Q: If you analyze that you come up to 515,700, am I correct?
A: You are correct.
Q: If you add to that an item for $525 for the super's apartment, which does not appear on the rent roll, and add to it another

$750 per month for a day care center, which appears on the rent roll at the monthly rate of $750, you come to a monthly rent roll of $43,684, do you not?

A: Yes, you do.

Q: And if you analyze that, you come to the number of $524,208, is that correct?

A: That is correct.

Q: How do you understand that the appraiser got from $524,208 to $570,190?

A: I don't know if that is the final number. That was sent down to Freddie Mac.

Q: You just got done telling us, if I understand, you tracked the 570,190 number which appears on Exhibit X, came from the appraiser?

A: No, that isn't what I said. I said that is what's normally filled in in that spot. We have 3 different applications here.

Q: Where did this number, 570,190—

A: It says here pro forma statement from the sellers.

Q: From the sellers or for the sellers?

A: I assume from the sellers.

Q: Does the word F O R read "from" or "for?"

A: It reads for.

Q: When you say pro forma estimate for the sellers, this is on a document entitled multi-family loan application that had been filled out by the borrowers, am I correct?

A: You are correct.

Q: Is it normal practice at Globe for borrowers to make pro forma estimates for Globe on the multifamily loan application?

A: Yes.

Q: Is it your testimony now that this statement, pro forma estimate, is a pro forma estimate for the borrower or is it a pro forma estimate from the borrower?

A: My understanding is that this form was filled out by Oscar and Roland and that that is their pro forma.

Q: Where did this pro forma come from?

A: I don't know.

Q: Did you ask them?

A: As I said, I don't know that this went to Freddie Mac. Somebody can fill out anything, that doesn't mean it's going to stand, that we are going to say that is fine, you can do that. There must be accuracy.

Q: I understand that. Can you tell us as you sit here right now, where the number 571,090 comes from?

A: I don't know.

Q: Did you have occasion in your review of the document in your preparation to testify here to attempt to determine where that number came from?

A: No, I didn't.

Q: Isn't it the fact, Ms. Hillas, that in all of the applications that were filled in for the 240 East 175th Street loan that on each of them the same number appears as being the gross rental income from apartments, 570,190?

A: I have to look at it.

Q: Sure. (pause)

A: Yes, it does.

MR. SCHLAM: Your Honor, may I offer this document marked, please (defendants' Exhibit Y marked for identification). Would you take a look at what has been marked defendants' Exhibit Y and tell us if you recognize it?

A: Yes. It's the Freddie Mac multifamily property underwriting analysis form.

Q: That is for 175th Street?

A: Yes, it is.

MR. SCHLAM: We offer this into evidence. (Pause) (Defendants' Exhibit Y was received in evidence). Incidentally, you signed this document, did you not?

A: Yes, I did.

Q: That was February third, 1987?

A: That is correct.

Q: Looks under the item, part of the second page of this document—

A: That income analysis?

Q: Income analysis, and I ask you, is there a column which is headed seller's forecast?

A: Yes, there is.

Q: And is that where the number 570,190 appears?

A: Yes, it is.

Q: Isn't it a fact that the number 570,190 came from Globe?
A: Yes.
Q: And isn't it a fact that when it appears on the multifamily loan application next to the statement gross rental income from apartments, that that number was a number that was generated by Globe?
A: We had been informed by Oscar and Roland that if you get a 9 percent increase, I believe, and that is where this difference is, the appraiser had used the increases for one year, and Oscar and Roland said they had 2 year leases in which they were using this higher number.
Q: Is it your testimony that the number 570,190, which is a Globe number, came to be put on this form because Globe asked that it be put on the form, isn't that correct?
A: That is correct.
Q: That is correct?
A: That is correct.
Q: So to the extent that gross rental income is on the form as 570,190, that is Globe's number as opposed to Mr. Conde and Mr. Santangelo's number?
A: No, it's based on, as I recall now, the rent stabilization. But what the increases were that year.
Q: It's Globe's number?
A: It's Globe's number.
Q: You understood when that number was placed on the form, that there was the same certification, which I won't read again, that appears on this form marked X is as well; you understood that, did you not.
A: Yes, I did.

In the course of the trial, what is always to be faced upon cross-examination is the unfortunate intervention of the court at a critical moment. This is not to suggest that such intervention is deliberate or willful or an attempt to protect the witness, although in many cases it is. Rather, the judge does not know all of the details of the defense's position and can oftentimes misperceive the significance of interrupting cross-examination at a critical moment. Such an event took place in the course of the cross-examination of Ms. Hillas and the following excerpt from the transcript demonstrates how it should be handled:

Q: The rent roll we just looked at, it said as of April, 1988, correct?
A: Right.
Q: And at the certification it says as of June, 1988?
A: Correct.
Q: Now, the application was filed June 20, was it not—
THE COURT: Do you know when the original application was filed?
THE WITNESS: I believe it went back to Freddie Mac in the beginning of June.
THE COURT: There were some documents on June third, 1988 that you saw?
THE WITNESS: I believe that was my inspection report.
THE COURT: Would that have been filed before any other application was made?
THE WITNESS: Possibly the whole thing came together. It sometimes comes back to us before we submitted a full application in front of them, where they found there was something wrong they would ask one of the companies, and it would be re-filled out and re-executed and sent to them.
Q: This is dated June 20, 1988, is that correct?
A: That is correct.
Q: Are you suggesting that this was sent in unsigned and came back and signed later?
A: No sir, I'm not suggesting that.
THE COURT: There may have been a prior application signed and submitted—
MR. GOLDMAN: Objection, your Honor, there is no evidence to that effect at all.
THE COURT: I am clarifying that
MR. GOLDMAN: There is no evidence that that happened.
THE COURT: Did that happen?
THE WITNESS: I don't now that that happened, but it has happened in the past.
THE COURT: So there might be times when a loan application would be submitted signed as of one date, and in a second application signed there is one date and the other date.
THE WITNESS: Absolutely.

THE COURT: Would there be anything on the second application to indicate it was an amended or second application?
THE WITNESS: No.
BY MR. GOLDMAN.
Q: Do you have any information whatsoever, however slight, however nominal, written or otherwise, that that is what happened in this particular case?
A: Not without going to the file.
Q: As you sit there now, do you have in any manner, shape or form the mildest recollection whatsoever that that's what happened in this particular case regarding this particular application?
A: No, sir.

It was later reiterated by one of the jurors that, when the court assisted the witness who was in a difficult position by suggesting a scenario that the witness never testified to, it was resented and benefitted the defense.

As is the custom in the Federal Courts pursuant to Rule 3500 of the Federal Rules of Criminal Procedure, any statements made by a witness which are incorporated into a report by a case agent are furnished to the defense. In this instance, the defense had the report of William Hamel's interview with Mrs. Hillas and determined that in several significant areas the statements that she had made to him in the course of his investigation were materially different than the statements which she made on the stand. In the subsequent cross-examination of William Hamel, these differences would be focused upon and exploited.

In anticipation of the forthcoming testimony of William Hamel, Mrs. Hillas was questioned to set up a negative impression of Agent Hamel, also by utilizing Hamel's report furnished pursuant to Rule 3500, as well as eliciting answers that would be flatly contradicted by Agent Hamel, further impugning Ms. Hillas. To that end, cross-examination brought out that Agent Hamel tried to slant the witness' testimony.

Q: During the course of the interview that you had with the Government, did you find at any time that they were attempting to put words in your mouth?
A: No, I don't.

Q: Do you recall a discussion about whether or not Davidson was a gut rehabilitation or not?
A: Yes, I recall that.
Q: And do you recall basically that everything you knew about it, it was in fact a gut rehabilitation?
A: Yes, I do recall that.
Q: Do you recall Mr. Hamel trying to convince you it wasn't?
A: I remember Mr. Hamel telling me it wasn't.
Q: In other words, your company had dealt with that property, correct?
A: Yes.
Q: Right?
A: Yes.
Q: Your company had inspected the property?
A: Yes.
Q: Freddie Mac had inspected the property?
A: Yes.
Q: You were living in the belief that was a gut rehabilitation?
A: Yes, I was.
Q: And he was telling you it wasn't?
A: That is correct.
Q: By the way, Ms. Hillas, in the course of that interview also, did you tell Mr. Hamel that from your viewpoint, back in the late 80's, it was "anything goes"?
A: No, sir.
Q: You never recall making that statement to Mr. Hamel?
A: No, sir, I do I do not.
Q: As you sit there today, you have no recollection of making that statement to Mr. Hamel?
A: Absolutely not.

The cross-examination of Ms. Hillas concluded by turning her into a character witness for the defendants, despite the fact that that was the last thing she wished to do at that juncture:

Q: Earlier you had identified a letter for identification and I'd like to offer it into evidence. (Pause)
"MR. HALPERN: No objection."

[Defendants' Exhibit AI was received in evidence]

MR. GOLDMAN: It's on the letterhead of Globe Mortgage Company, Re: Roland Conde, Oscar Santangelo. Dated January 27, 1989. "Dear Mr. Conde and Mr. Santangelo: as I previously informed you, the Bryant Avenue inspection tour of December 25, 1988 was a huge success. Freddie Mac president Leland Brenzell and the full executive committee were so impressed with the report they received regarding your property that they were eager to see the building for themselves. We were all extremely grateful for your taking out time again on December 29, 1988 to lead this group on a permanent inspection. This follow up visit to New York was very enjoyable to the Freddie Mac committee. The positive feedback which they had gotten from the House and Senate Subcommittees was proven to be well founded. The group expressed great appreciation for your hospitality and look forward to continuing their association with Tiffany Construction. Once again, on behalf of this committee, may I express my personal gratitude for your involvement with this project. I look forward to working with you again on future ventures. If I may be able to provide any personal assistance to you, please do not hesitate to contact me at 201-469-6120. Sincerely Globe Mortgage Company, Judith Hillas."

Q: You wrote that letter?
A: Yes.
Q: You signed it?
A: Yes.
Q: It was true when you wrote it?
A: Yes.
Q: That was in 1989?
A: Yes.
Q: After five or six years of dealing with these men?
A: That is correct.

§25.5 THE "SPECIAL" AGENT

William Hamel, Special Agent of the General Accounting Office, followed shortly after Ms. Hillas finished her testimony. The object of the cross-examination of Agent Hamel was to demonstrate all of the flaws in his investigation.

The cross-examination was designed to demonstrate that he was totally biased, both in his testimony before the grand jury and the trial jury in that he wilfully and deliberately excluded any fact that he came across which was inconsistent with his theory of the defendants' guilt. There was a concerted effort to show that he had overlooked simple fairness in failing to check a number of available facts and details which might have either mitigated or contradicted the impressions which he sought to convey and which might be an indication of a lack of intent on the part of the defendants. The cross-examination was also designed to demonstrate, of which the excerpts herein are only a part, that a case such as this cannot be made by simply comparing two pieces of paper, neither of which can be established as to which one is inaccurate or that to the extent that there are any discrepancies between the two, that the discrepancy is attributable to a guilty intent on the part of the defendants. Thus, after a short series of questions designed to take away the aura of infallibility on the part of William Hamel or, conversely, demonstrate pretentiousness on his part, the cross-examination commenced as follows:

BY MR. GOLDMAN:
Q: Agent Hamel, how do people normally call you, Bill, Agent Hamel—
A: Whatever suits you.
Q: Do you mind if I call you Bill?
A: That is fine.
THE COURT: I do.
MR. GOLDMAN: Yes, your Honor.
THE COURT: "Agent Hamel."

The first matter addressed upon cross-examination of Agent Hamel was the testimony of Judith Hillas, while her testimony was still fresh in the minds of the jury:

Q: Let me clear up some matters, Special Agent Hamel. You have been sitting in on this trial since the beginning, have you not?
A: Yes, I have.
Q: You were present in the courtroom, I believe, when Mrs. Hillas was testifying?

A: Yes, I was.
Q: Do you recall Mrs. Hillas denying on a few occasions that she ever made the statement telling you that in the late 80's, "anything goes"? Do you recall that?
A: Do I recall her testimony in this courtroom to that effect?
Q: Do you recall her saying that in this courtroom in response to my questions on—
A: I don't recall that exact testimony, but if you showed me a transcript—
Q: Let me ask you. Special Agent Hamel, did Mrs. Hillas tell you that in the late 80's anything goes?
A: I recall a conversation, not those exact words.
Q: Let me show you what has been marked Government's Exhibit 3508W. I direct your attention to the highlighted portion in the middle of the page. Does that refresh your recollection that she specifically said to you that in the late 80's "anything goes?"
A: That refreshes my recollection, yes.
Q: Now that your recollection is refreshed, she in fact did say that to you, did she not?
A: If it's in my report, the likelihood is that she said that to me.
Q: You wouldn't put anything in your report she didn't say, is that correct?
A: No, that is correct.
Q: Thank you. Additionally, did Mrs. Hillas tell you that Globe would contact and pay an independent appraiser to perform a Freddie Mac appraisal for a building?
A: Did she tell me that?
Q: Yes.
A: Back at that time?
Q: In that very interview?
A: I don't recall. That interview was over a year and a half year and a half ago. If you show me that exhibit—
Q: By all means. Agent Hamel, if you take a look at the highlighted paragraph here. Does that refresh your recollection that she told you that Globe would contract and pay an independent appraiser to perform a Freddie Mac appraisal for the building?
A: Yes, it refreshes my recollection.

Q: And Special Agent Hamel, were you told in the course of that meeting that vacant apartments or vacant buildings were a more desirable lending situation than an occupied one?
A: Yes, I recall that.
Q: And do you recall, Agent Hamel, that you were also told in the course of that interview, that each building was inspected two or three times before a loan closed?
A: I was told that they were inspected. I can't recall at this time whether she said it was two or three times.
Q: Let me show you the same exhibit, Special Agent Hamel. I direct your attention to the highlighted paragraph. Does that refresh your recollection that she said the buildings were inspected two or three times before closing?
A: Yes, it does.

The effect on cross-examination was enhanced by Agent Hamel being fuzzy about his report, which he had obviously read just before testifying, knowing how such reports are used by defense counsel on cross-examination.

After dealing with the matter of Mrs. Hillas, the cross-examination then turned to demonstrating the bias of Agent Hamel:

Q: Agent Hamel, in the course of your grand jury testimony you testified as you did here today, that without being specific that these gentlemen submitted higher rent rolls to Freddie Mac than they submitted to, let's say, the State of New York, is that correct?
A: That is correct.
Q: And you weren't specific, you just said that, as you did to this jury on direct examination, that they submitted higher rent rolls to Freddie Mac, correct? In other words, you didn't give any number of instances, you just characterized it as higher, is that correct?
A: I don't believe that I gave—I believe I testified in the grand jury that there were some buildings had more than others and I think I had gave percentages of the number, the total percentage of units that were being inflated from the hundred percent total of units in the building.

Q: But you didn't give any number of times specifically that they reported higher——higher numbers to Freddie Mac than they reported to the City of New York, is that true?
A: Didn't have to, because I gave the percentages. If it was 20 percent, that was 20 percent of the units.
Q: Let me ask you, Special Agent Hamel, I believe you said that you created—by that you meant you assembled these charts that you are talking about, is that correct?
A: I assembled them, yes.

§25.6 THE CASE BUILT ON QUICKSAND

Q: Let me ask about these DHCR rent rolls for a moment. Can you tell me, Agent Hamel, within your knowledge if in the years '85, '86, '84, was it possible to track the rental history of a building in New York through the DHCRs?
A: I suppose one could.
Q: You suppose. Do you know?
A: You should be able to, yes.
Q: On what do you base that assumption?
A: That the submissions have to be submitted on a yearly basis.
Q: Suppose the landlords don't?
A: Then there would be no record.
Q: In fact, Agent Hamel—Special Agent Hamel—in fact, were the records even computerized in those days? Were the records even computerized in those days?
A: I don't know if they were computerized. The summaries I received in '91, 92 and 93 were a computerized summary of those records.
Q: In fact, Agent Hamel, those records were not kept on computer until after 1988, is that true?
A: I wouldn't know.
Q: So that, Agent Hamel, just so we are clear, there is nothing that you know of your own knowledge that a landlord entering a new building in the year 1985, 6 or 7, would be able to track the rental history of an apartment through DHCR records?
A: I don't know.

Q: Special Agent Hamel, you have indicated you testified before the grand jury to situations in which the DHCR rent rolls were lower, in other words, a lower amount was reported to the State than was to Freddie Mac?
A: Correct.
Q: On any single occasion, just once, did you ever tell the grand jury that in fact these gentlemen had reported lower numbers to Freddie Mac than were registered with DHCR?
A: I was answering questions—
Q: Did you even once?
A: I didn't give that testimony, but I wasn't asked that question.
Q: Were you aware that that had ever occurred?
A: Yes.

At this juncture, the witness gave the most disastrous answer that a government agent can give and which answer discredits his entire testimony. In the minds of any juror, and properly so, justice should not be withheld simply because a question was not asked. It is the belief of the public that the testimony of such agents is to be evenhanded, and exculpatory as well as damaging evidence should be furnished without being prompted and without depending on the luck of the proper question being asked. In these circumstances, the jury immediately wonders what other evidence they are not hearing because the prosecution has simply not asked the question and the defense may not know enough to ask.

Additionally, it contaminates the prosecutors themselves because it sets up the following no win series of questions:

Q: Upon becoming aware of such instances did you bring them to the attention of the prosecutor?

If the witness answers "yes," the next question is:

Q: And after bringing those instances to the attention of the prosecutor, he did not ask you those questions to bring the information to the attention of the Grand Jury or this jury, is that what you are saying?

The jury focuses on wondering what other exculpatory evidence the prosecution is deliberately hiding from them and it is clear that the prosecutor and the witness are acting together to deny the defendants a fair trial.

If the witness answers "no," then the witness is discredited and the prosecutor, albeit well meaning, simply does not have all the facts and should not ask a jury to convict.

The cross-examination continued:

Q: All right, Agent Hamel. Let's go to the chart on 175th Street.
A: Which one?
Q: 240 East—
A: Which chart. There are 2 charts.
Q: The chart listing all the apartments and registered rents for 240 East 175th Street. Do you have it before you?
A: Yes, I do.
Q: Do you need any other reports, charts or records before you at this time in order to have the full picture?
A: I'm not sure quite what you mean by that.
Q: I mean, are there any charts or figures or documents you might need to review the amounts on that sheet at this time?
A: At this time, no.
Q: Take a look at apartment 103.
A: Yes.
Q: How much was reported to Freddie Mac?
A: $408.99.
Q: How much to the DHCR?
A: $433.53.
Q: In that instance, the amount they reported to Freddie Mac was lower than the registered rents, correct?
A: Yes. By $24.25.
Q: Go to apartment 104. How much was reported to Freddie Mac?
A: $435.
Q: And how much to DHCR?
A: $450. A $15 difference.
Q: Again, lower to Freddie Mac than to DHCR, right?
A: Correct.
Q: Go to apartment 105. How much reported to Freddie Mac?
A: $454.86.
Q: And the registered rent to DHCR?
A: $495.80.
Q: Once again less to Freddie Mac than the DHCR, correct?

A: Correct.
Q: On none of these occasions so far did you offer any testimony previously either to the grand jury or to this jury, is that right?
A: I wasn't asked any questions about those units.
Q: Go to apartment 108. How much to Freddie Mac?
A: $393.26.
Q: How much to DHCR?
A: $428.65.
Q: Once again, lower to Freddie Mac than DHCR, correct?
A: Yes.
Q: Go to apartment 112.
A: $460.82 to Freddie Mac.
Q: And registered with the City?
A: $502.29.
Q: Once again lower, correct?
A: Correct.
Q: How about apartment 119.
A: It was reported $390 to Freddie Mac and $575 to the DHCR.
Q: In other words, they short changed themselves by $185 on that one, didn't they?
A: That is correct.
Q: How about apartment 205?
A: $472.97 to Freddie Mac and $514.45 to the State.
Q: Short changed themselves again, right?
A: Correct.
Q: How about apartment 303?
A: $404.39 to Freddie Mac and $440.78 to the State.
Q: Short changed again, correct?
A: Correct.
Q: How about apartment 304?
A: $303.46 to Freddie Mac and $345.77 to the State.
Q: On the short end once again, correct?
A: Correct.
Q: How about apartment 318?
A: $250 to Freddie Mac, $287.50 to the State.
Q: Short again, correct?
A: It's lower, yes.
Q: How about apartment 320?

A: $295.25 to Freddie Mac and $327.70 to the State.
Q: Short again?
A: Correct.
Q: How about apartment 405?
A: $306.80 to Freddie Mac, $340.20 to the State.
Q: Same story?
A: Correct.
Q: How about apartment 406?
A: $248.41 to Freddie Mac and $310 to the State.
Q: How about apartment 408?
A: $420.57 to Freddie Mac and $458.42 to the State.
Q: How about apartment 409?
A: $323.39 to Freddie Mac and $381.50 to the State.
Q: How about 402?
A: $276.90 to Freddie Mac and $308.51 to the State.
Q: Short changed again, correct?
A: It's lower, yes.
Q: How about apartment 608?
A: 608?
Q: That's right.
A: $323.13 to Freddie Mac, $326.72 to the State. A $3.59 difference.
Q: How about 610?
A: $285 to Freddie Mac, $310.43 to the State.
Q: How about 615?
A: $264.38 to Freddie Mac, $317.86 to the State.
Q: All short changed again?
A: They are lower, yes.
Q: How about 621?
A: $435 to Freddie Mac and $450 to the State.
Q: In fact, Agent Hamel, there were more instances where they short changed themselves and reported a lower number to Freddie Mac than was registered then there was instances where they reported higher numbers to Freddie Mac with lower DHCR's, isn't that true?
A: I don't know. I will have to count.
Q: Do you mean that prior to your testimony in this case, prior to your testimony in this courtroom, you never counted up the

times whey they reported a lower figure to Freddie Mac than was registered with the City of New York while you were on those occasions testifying to occasions when they reported higher numbers to Freddie Mac?

A: Could you repeat that question?

Q: The question is, did you ever before count up the number of instances in which higher rental was reported to the State.

A: I did count them up. But it was a long time ago. I could redo it for you right now if you like.

Q: Do you have any recollection in any of the counts that you claim to have made that the instances where they short changed themselves were more in number than the instances when they reported a higher number to Freddie Mac than to the DHCR?

A: I don't have any recollection of there being instances where there was more reported that was higher to the State than Freddie Mac. However—

Q: Let's go it again. Do you recall each of the apartments I just asked you about?

A: Yes.

Q: Is it not true that on each of those occasions with regard to those apartments they reported a lower number to Freddie Mac than they did to the City of New York? That is my question.

A: Could you repeat it again?

Q: Yes. With regard to the instances that I just went through with you, as to each apartment, was there not in each apartment a lower number reported to Freddie Mac on these rent rolls than appeared on the rent registrations filed with the City of New York?

A: In the instances we just went through, yes.

Q: My questions to you have been, aren't there more of those instances than there are of instances where they reported a higher apartment rent than was registered with the City of New York?

A: I don't think so.

Q: Have you ever added them up?

A: I did, a long time ago.

Q: Do you have any recollection of what your totals came to?

A: Not offhand, no.

Q: Incidentally, if I ask you the same questions about other buildings, your testimony would be the same? You never testified before the grand jury as to instances when lower rents were reported to Freddie Mac than to—registered with the DHCRs, is that correct?
A: I was never asked the question.
Q: The question is, did you testify? The answer is no, correct.
A: Correct.

By bringing out the entire picture and carrying out the witness' approach to its conclusion, it became clear that the government's position regarding fraudulent intent could never be proven by this method. Their explanation simply did not cover instances where the defendants had submitted lower rent figures to Freddie Mac than the amount of the registered rents.

Conversely, it absolutely supported the defense's position that the defendants were projecting their honest belief and calling it like they saw it, whichever way it turned out.

The key in preparation was to take the government's theory and run it to its logical end and see of the theory held up to fit all of the circumstances that were known to exist at that time. When certain facts did not fit the theory, the cross-examination was obvious. Questioning every instance only reinforced the point so that no one could miss it.

Q: Now, Mr.Hamel, let's go—I'm sorry, Special Agent Hamel—when are the DHCRs supposed to be filed?
A: My understanding is they are supposed to be filed as of April 1st each year. But they have until the end of July to get them in.
Q: Mr. Hamel, we were talking about when the DHCRs are supposed to be filed? I think you said your recollection is—
A: As of April 1st each year, but they have I think until some time in July to get them in.
Q: But basically April first, is that correct?
A: That is correct.
Q: What happens, Agent Hamel, if a DHCR is filed April 1st or July 2nd or whatever the date it's actually filed, and the next day an apartment renovation is completed and the rent goes up? What happens to the DHCR?

A: I don't know.
Q: Do you think it goes up?
THE COURT: He doesn't know. Next question.
Q: Isn't it a fact, Agent Hamel, that the rent would be higher but the DHCR would be lower?
THE COURT: Move on. He said he doesn't know. Let's proceed.
MR. GOLDMAN: Your Honor, I'd like to bring out the fact that he should know.
THE COURT: Please proceed. The jury will disregard counsel's last comments.
Q: Agent Hamel, if in fact there is a higher number on the rent roll and a lower DHCR, you wouldn't know what period of the year it applied to, would you?
A: No.
Q: In fact, Agent Hamel, there could be any number of circumstances where the rent actually could be higher at a time when the DHCR was lower?
A: I wouldn't know.
Q: In fact, Agent Hamel, on the instances where you took note of the DHCR being lower, did you ever go forward to the DHCR that was filed in the following year?
A: In some instances, yes.
Q: In all instances?
A: I don't think I did in all instances, no.
Q: In fact, Agent Hamel, for example, let's take apartment 107 at 175th Street. Is that not one of the instances that you were referring to when you said that these gentlemen had filed a higher rent with Freddie Mac, that was higher than the DHCRs?
A: That is correct.
Q: That is correct. And I believe the number there is that Freddie Mac was reported on the rent roll as $314, and the DHCR was $246.82, correct?
A: Correct.
Q: Now, I ask you: did you ever check the DHCR for the following year?
A: You mean for 1988?
Q: Correct.
A: No, I don't think so.

Q: If I were to tell you that it was registered for $314, than you could not quarrel with that statement, could you?
A: I'd have to see the registration.
MR. GOLDMAN: Well, as a matter of fact it's here. Can I have it please, those were those computer sheets that you had (pause).
Q: Let me show you what's been briefly marked as Government's Exhibit 300 H2 and I ask you what that is?
A: This is a yearly summary from the DHCR.
Q: Just so we are clear, we have been talking about that on the rent roll submitted to Freddie Mac the rent was forwarded at $314, and the DHCR for the year 1987 was $246.82, correct?
A: Which unit was this again?
Q: That was apartment 107.
A: Okay, yes.
Q: I just asked you if you have ever gone to the DHCRs for the following year, and you now have before you the DHCRs for the following year on East 175th Street, correct?
A: Correct.
Q: Would you tell us the number reported to the City as the rent on apartment 107.
A: $314 as of 4/88.
Q: If I were to ask you if you ever went to the following year's DHCR to see if there was a revision, your answer would be the same, would it not?
A: No, that was not my answer. I said I did in some instances.
Q: But not all?
A: Not all.
Q: Did you ever find any instances in going forward to the DHCRs that the rent was lower than reported to Freddie Mac, but that the rent reported on the subsequent year's DHCR was higher than reported to Freddie Mac?
A: Did I ever look for that, or did I ever find an occasion for that?
Q: Did you ever specifically look for it?
A: No.
Q: If I asked you that question with regard to each and every building your answer would be the same, would it not?
A: That answer would be the same, yes.
Q: Just to reiterate, Agent Hamel, did you testify in the grand jury about reviewing subsequent DHCRs to see if in the course of

the year a change had taken place as a result of renovation or change in tenants?

A: No, I did not.

Q: Let me ask you another question, Agent Hamel. Did you ever check that subsequent to the filing of the rent rolls with Freddie Mac, did you ever check the actual operating statements of the buildings to see what rent was being collected?

A: The operating statements from where?

Q: These buildings had an independent management company, didn't they, most of them?

A: Yes.

Q: And that management company kept computerized records on a month by month basis of what the rent roll was, didn't they have that?

A: I don't know if they did or didn't.

Q: Did you ever check?

A: I don't believe so, no.

Q: So that you never checked how much rent was actually being collected in these buildings, did you?

A: No.

Q: Well Agent Hamel, you have these rent rolls that you as the case agent, that you are claiming are fraudulent, correct?

A: I didn't claim they are fraudulent. I said there is a difference.

Q: You have been working on this case since its inception, am I correct?

A: Not since its inception but for a long period of time.

Q: During that period of time you were aware that the thrust of the investigation was to attempt to establish that these documents were false, incorrect and fraudulent, isn't that true?

A: It's true.

Q: Okay. And you are telling us now that in the entire course of that investigation you never checked the actual operating rent collections in the buildings that we have been talking about?

A: Actually I'd like to correct myself. When we subpoenaed the records from the defendants, which I testified to earlier, with one building, 1765-67 Davidson, which I believe is managed by the defendants themselves or Consant Realty, we did obtain some of those records from them.

Q: Okay. Did you check to see what the actual rent roll was?
A: Yes, I did.
Q: And?
A: In most cases the amounts of the units that I found that were overstated to Freddie Mac—
Q: No, no. The bottom line, Mr. Hamel.
A: When I looked at the units which I believed were inflated to Freddie Mac as opposed to the State, those individual units, I found there to be continually less on their own internal documents than what was reported to Freddie Mac.
Q: Let's talk about Davidson, Mr. Hamel. You say individual units you found some discrepancies, correct?
A: Yes.
Q: How about the bottom line. Did you find the bottom line less than reported to Freddie Mac?
A: I didn't look at the bottom line, sir.
Q: You know that people come and go in apartments, don't you?
A: I don't know.
Q: You are aware that there is turnover in these apartments?
A: I'm aware that there is turnover in apartments.
Q: You are aware sometimes there are certain communication difficulties?
A: I am not sure what you are talking about.
Q: Did you find some people have a different mother tongue than yours?
A: I still don't follow.
Q: Do you speak Spanish?
A: Do I speak Spanish? No.
Q: Possibly some communication difficulties?
A: Between whom and whom?
Q: Between yourself and whoever it was that you interviewed.
A: In some instances there were, yes.
Q: Okay. So let's go to the bottom line. Did you ever check if the rents actually being collected were higher or the rent roll that was actually being used in daily operations was higher than the rent rolls that were submitted to Freddie Mac?
A: The bottom line yearly figure or monthly figure?
Q: How about the yearly figure?

A: No, I did not.
Q: So that in fact, Agent Hamel, notwithstanding a rent roll reported to Freddie Mac, let's say $500,000, the actual operating rent roll in the building, for all you know, was higher, correct?
A: I wouldn't know.
Q: In fact, Agent Hamel, is it not a fact that in every building except Davidson, in every building the actual operating computer run rent roll maintained by an independent organization showed higher rents as total than submitted to Freddie Mac?
A: I wouldn't know.
Q: In fact, Agent Hamel, are you aware that the rent roll reported for Walton Avenue, the 2 properties, was $1.1 million.
A: The bottom line on the Freddie Mac rent roll?
Q: For Walton Avenue. Do you know what it was?
A: For which year?
Q: The ones that were submitted as part of the case.
A: For '86, '87, '88?
Q: For the ones in this case, that these gentlemen are charged with being wrong.
A: Yes, I looked at those.
Q: What was the total rent roll reported to Freddie Mac?
A: I don't know without looking at them, but I recall in excess of $600,000 on each one, 597, 624—I'd have to look at them.
Q: Approximately 1.1 million dollars?
A: For the combination of the 2?
Q: Yes.
A: I would imagine 1.1, maybe.
Q: In fact, the annual rent roll as we speak is so far 1.6 million, isn't it?
A: I don't know.
Q: With regard to Davidson, do you recall the bottom line number that was reported to Freddie Mac on the rent roll with regard to Davidson Avenue?
A: Not off the top of my head.
Q: Are there any documents here with which you can refresh your recollection?
A: Yes.

Q: Let me show you Government's Exhibit 500 A-1 for identification.
A: I am familiar with this.
Q: What's the amount reported per month for Davidson?
A: For that period of time, $27,985.
Q: Are you familiar with any reports submitted to Freddie Mac subsequent to that time?
A: Yes.
Q: In fact, let's take a look at Government's Exhibit 500 A-2. Is that a subsequent rent roll submitted to Globe and Freddie Mac on Davidson Avenue?
A: Yes, it is.
Q: What's that number?
A: $27,990.75.
Q: In fact, Mr. Hamel, do you recall testifying about Davidson in the grand jury?
A: Yes, I do.
Q: And you testified there was very little deviation between what was reported to Freddie Mac and what was registered—
A: I don't recall that testimony.
Q: Did you find, Agent Hamel, that after a period of time—this is your findings now—did you find that after a period of time as time went by, they were accurate as compared with what was reported to you by the tenants?
MR. BRUDNER: Objection.
THE COURT: Are you asking him was he asked the question—
MR. GOLDMAN: I am asking him if he found in the course of his investigation that as later rent rolls were submitted as the renovation continued, he found them to be accurate or more accurate in terms of what was reported to him by the tenants.
A: If I could see my Grand Jury testimony which you have—
Q: Surely.

[Pause]

A: I see what I testified to.
Q: And you did so find, did you not, Agent Hamel?
A: Excuse me?

Q: And you did so find that accuracy got better with the updates as the job continued?

A: That is not the substance of the testimony.

THE WITNESS: May I be permitted to read my testimony, your Honor?

THE COURT: You can read it to yourself.

THE WITNESS: Okay.

[Pause]

A: That period, yes, I see.

Q: Okay? My question to you is a simple one: that after a period of time the submitted rent rolls were accurate as compared to what was stated to you by the tenants, isn't that what you found?

A: Yes, after several years.

Q: Thank you. And with regard to those accurate statements after years, those were statements that were sent in to Globe and Freddie Mac, right?

A: I wouldn't know. I don't know if they were. I would imagine they were.

Q: Weren't you working from the statements that were sent in to Globe and Freddie Mac?

A: That is correct.

Q: Just so we are clear, Agent Hamel, if I were to ask you, and I believe I did, just for clarification, you did not check the DHCRs going forward over a period of years with regard to these buildings, is that correct?

A: No in every case, no.

Earlier, at the conclusion of his testimony upon direct examination, Agent Hamel testified to his findings with regard to his review of the American Express bills of the defendants. In an effort to further prejudice the defendants, he offered the bills to suggest that the defendants had used the proceeds of their "crimes" to maintain a lavish lifestyle. Strenuous objection had been made earlier to the introduction of such testimony on the grounds that it was only inflammatory and in no way probative. Over such objection, the testimony was introduced.

In response to such testimony, Agent Hamel was cross-examined as follows:

BY MR. GOLDMAN

Q: Agent Hamel, let's go to the American Express bills that you had in front of you. Could I have the ones that you used that you were reading from in your testimony? Are they segregated in any way?

A: These are what I read from.

Q: To your knowledge are there any restrictions on how these men spend their money?

A: How they spend their money generally?

Q: Yes.

A: I hope not.

Q: Are there any restrictions on how they spend the money they get from Freddie Mac?

A: At the time these loans were given, no.

Q: None whatsoever, isn't that true?

A: Yes.

Q: They were free to spend it any way they wanted, is that correct?

A: At that time, yes.

Q: In fact, Agent Hamel, did you feel something was strange because they took a vacation?

A: I'm not sure—

Q: You made a point of telling us that somebody went down to Puerto Rico.

A: I was reading from the bills.

Q: Nothing wrong with taking a vacation, is there?

A: No.

Q: And I think you said there was a hundred some odd dollars spent in a kiddie shop?

A: Some kind of children's clothing store, I believe it was.

Q: That would suggest they were there with their family?

A: I don't know if they were on vacation or what the purpose of this trip was.

Q: You read they got some gym equipment?

A: Yes.

Q: Do you know where that equipment went?

A: No.
Q: Anything wrong with buying gym equipment?
A: No.
Q: I think you said they ate out in restaurants?
A: That is correct.
Q: Anything wrong with that?
A: Not per se, no.
Q: Any restriction on eating out in a restaurant because of their dealings with Freddie Mac?
A: Not that I am aware of.
Q: Let me ask you a further question, Agent Hamel. With regard to any trips that these people took that you observed, do you know the purpose of those trips?
A: No, I don't.
Q: And expenditures at Great Dane, do you know what that's for?
A: No.
Q: Thank you for sharing these dramatic findings from your investigation with us. Withdrawn.

* * *

Q: Mr. Hamel, in the course of your investigation, did you have occasion to review the documents of Freddie Mac?
A: Some of them, yes.
Q: The documents of Globe?
A: Some of them, yes.
Q: Have you had the opportunity to speak to people from both of those places?
A: Yes.
Q: Did you ever find any instances where they were offered more in mortgage money than they took?
A: Who was offering more to who?
Q: Freddie Mac was offering a larger mortgage than Mr. Santangelo and Mr. Conde took.
A: Yes.
Q: Which one was that?
A: The only one I can think of is Davidson Avenue.
Q: How about Walton in addition to that?

A: I don't have a recollection of that.
Q: In other words, they were offered more money than they actually took, right?
A: I don't believe it was an offer.
Q: The building qualified for higher amounts of money than they took?
A: The building qualified for a higher mortgage than the defendants were asking for.
Q: And that was true on Walton also, wasn't it?
A: I don't know.
Q: And once again, Special Agent Hamel, are you aware that in each case the rent roll ultimately achieved was higher than reported to Freddie Mac?
A: No, I am not aware of that.
Q: But you are not aware to the contrary either, are you?
A: That the amount that was reported—I am trying to think how that question would be.
Q: The question is did they ultimately always achieve a rent roll higher than it was reported to Freddie Mac?
A: I am not aware of that situation.
Q: One way or the other, right?
A: That's correct.
Q: And you didn't check that, did you?
A: I didn't have records to check it against.
Q: There was an operating independent company managing the properties, they kept computer runs, month by month?
A: I don't know if they did or they didn't. I didn't see the records.
Q: Did you run out of subpoenas? Did you run out of subpoenas that you couldn't serve them with a subpoena if you wanted their records.
A: Serving a subpoena wasn't my decision.

As can be seen, the cross-examination concluded by further demonstrating that the effort by Agent Hamel was a desperate effort to attempt to prejudice the jury and again reiterating the bias that had been shown throughout the investigation and during the course of his testimony.

This was an investigation that was praised by the United States Attorney in its initial press release.

The jury took less than an hour to find both defendants and the corporations not guilty of all charges. In conversation with the jury following the verdict, I was informed that, their not being sure of who was to be the foreperson, most of the time was spent in drawing straws for who would have the privilege of delivering the verdict of acquittal.